Using Folktales

Eric K. Taylor

CAMBRIDGE
UNIVERSITY PRESS

CAMBRIDGE UNIVERSITY PRESS
Cambridge, New York, Melbourne, Madrid, Cape Town, Singapore, São Paulo

Cambridge University Press
The Edinburgh Building, Cambridge CB2 2RU, UK

www.cambridge.org
Information on this title: www.cambridge.org/9780521637497

First published 2000

A catalogue record for this publication is available from the British Library

Library of Congress Cataloguing in Publication data

Taylor, Eric K. (Eric Kenneth)
Using folktales / Eric K. Taylor.
p. cm. – (Cambridge handbooks for language teachers)
Includes bibliographical references and index.
ISBN 0-521-63749-X (pbk.)
1. Language arts (Elementary) 2. English language – Study and teaching – Foreign speakers. 3. Tales – Study and teaching. 4. Tales – Study and teaching – Activity programs.
I. Title. II. Series.

LB1576.T34 2000
428'.0071 – dc21   00-028901

ISBN-13 978-0-521-63749-7 paperback
ISBN-10 0-521-63749-X paperback

Transferred to digital printing 2006

Using folktales

CAMBRIDGE HANDBOOKS FOR LANGUAGE TEACHERS

This is a series of practical guides for teachers of English and other languages. Illustrative examples are usually drawn from the field of English as a foreign or second language, but the ideas and techniques described can equally well be used in the teaching of any language.

In this series:

Drama Techniques in Language Learning – A resource book of communication activities for language teachers *by Alan Maley and Alan Duff*

Games for Language Learning *by Andrew Wright, David Betteridge, and Michael Buckby*

Discussions That Work – Task-centered fluency practice *by Penny Ur*

Once Upon a Time – Using stories in the language classroom *by John Morgan and Mario Rinvolucri*

Teaching Listening Comprehension *by Penny Ur*

Keep Talking – Communicative fluency activities for language teaching *by Friederike Klippel*

Working with Words – A guide to teaching and learning vocabulary *by Ruth Gairns and Stuart Redman*

Learner English – A teacher's guide to interference and other problems *edited by Michael Swan and Bernard Smith*

Testing Spoken Language – A handbook of oral testing techniques *by Nic Underhill*

Literature in the Language Classroom – A resource book of ideas and activities *by Joanne Collie and Stephen Slater*

Dictation – New methods, new possibilities *by Paul Davis and Mario Rinvolucri*

Grammar Practice Activities – A practical guide for teachers *by Penny Ur*

Testing for Language Teachers *by Arthur Hughes*

Pictures for Language Learning *by Andrew Wright*

Five-Minute Activities – A resource book of short activities *by Penny Ur and Andrew Wright*

The Standby Book – Activities for the language classroom *edited by Seth Lindstromberg*

Lessons from Nothing – Activities for language teaching with limited time and resources *by Bruce Marsland*

Beginning to Write – Writing Activities for Elementary and Intermediate Learners *by Arthur Brookes and Peter Gundy*

Ways of Doing – Students Explore Their Everyday and Classroom Processes *by Paul Davis, Barbara Garside, and Mario Rinvolucri*

Using Newspapers in the Classroom *by Paul Sanderson*

Teaching Adult Second Language Learners *by Heather McKay and Abigail Tom*

Using Folktales *by Eric K. Taylor*

Contents

Contents

List of folktales

The following stories appear in this book. For references to other stories and for activities based on these and other stories, see the *General Index*.

Preface

In school I had been told that materials real people use for real reasons were better for teaching than materials contrived to teach grammar or vocabulary. Sounded good, but it left me with a question: What do you use with low-level adults? Soup cans, clothing labels, and bus schedules can be used for only so long, and they don't go much beyond survival-level skills. Was there any real language that fit somewhere between soup cans and the newspaper, or was I stuck teaching grammar and vocabulary with artificial texts until students reached a higher level?

I thought about children's and adolescents' literature. Although I think both have useful features, neither seemed right for adult beginners. Most early children's books aren't interesting or challenging enough for adults. And literature for older children and adolescents quite quickly becomes fairly sophisticated: The vocabulary, idiom, and style make them impossible for beginners.

As I continued my search, I began to consider folktales. These stories contain a striking mix of the typical characteristics of children's and adult literature, a mix that might be ideal for the audience I was trying to reach. I began to experiment with folktales with a group of Asian immigrant students I was teaching (some of whom were completely illiterate and most of whom had not made it beyond survival skills). I found that folktales effectively addressed my lowest and highest students at the same time and helped me work on a variety of important language items. Equally important, the folktales generated considerable interest and enthusiasm from my students; at the end of the course, they indicated that the folktales were their favorite part of the program.

As I continued to explore the possibilities folktales offered, I found that I had stumbled on much more than I was looking for. Folktales turned out to be well suited to the development of language and cognitive skills at nearly any level. I have since used folktales in other beginning immigrant classes, in advanced writing classes, and for various intermediate levels. In addition, although folktales have often been used successfully with children, in classes in which there were both children and adults, I found that folktales could simultaneously capture the attention of both.

This book grew out of that exploration. It offers some reflections on why folktales are good for language teaching. It also provides a collection of activities that have worked well in addressing a variety of language needs. And it provides a number of useful stories to get you started and some sources to help you begin to find stories of your own.

Eric K. Taylor

I Theoretical background

1 What makes folktales so good for language teaching?

Introduction

Although they are certainly valuable in their own right – as good stories, as literature, as social and cultural expressions, and as moral teaching – folktales have many special characteristics that make them exceptionally good for language teaching. Their frequent repetitions make them excellent for reinforcing new vocabulary and grammar. Many have natural rhythmic qualities that are useful for working on stress, rhythm, and intonation in pronunciation. And the cultural elements of folktales help both bridge common ground between cultures and bring out cultural differences – developing cultural awareness that is essential if we are to learn to think in another language and understand the people who speak it.

Because folktales began as oral stories, they also have many characteristics that make them easier to understand than other types of literature. Since folktales are often published as children's books with easy language and context-providing illustrations, many are accessible to students with limited language abilities. Yet there are also many more difficult, literary retellings of folktales. This means that folktales provide material for all levels from beginner to advanced, with natural bridges from each level to the next. The varying levels of difficulty also make folktales very useful in the multilevel classroom.

In addition, folktales are especially useful for developing cognitive and academic skills. For example, academic tasks often require students to compare, contrast, and evaluate. You can require students to use these skills at nearly any language level by having them read or listen to different versions of folktales (for example, the French, Japanese, and Native American versions of Cinderella), identify how they are similar and different, and then consider how important the similarities and differences are. Folktales are similarly well suited for academic skills like analyzing, drawing inferences, synthesizing, summarizing, and noticing underlying text structures.

Folktales also fit well with the growing emphasis on content-based instruction and with communicative approaches that focus on teaching language while communicating meaning. Folktales fit in not only with literature but also with sociology, history, religion, and anthropology.

And folktales, because of their moral nature, fit in with values education, an aspect that a growing number of educators feel has been critically lacking in mainstream language teaching.

Finally, as we will see, folktales are excellent for addressing listening, speaking, reading, and writing – either separately or in integration with each other. Because of the many different versions and the varieties of potential activities, they are especially suitable for use in the multilevel classroom. Because of their flexibility, folktales can also be easily integrated with a variety of approaches to language teaching.

Just what is a folktale?

The term "folktale" is used for several related kinds of stories. Most narrowly, a folktale is a traditional story that has been passed on by word of mouth – told from parent to child over many generations or passed on by countless storytellers sitting around countless evening fires. No one knows who the original author was, and there are usually different versions of the same story. *The Stonecutter* (see page 5) is an example of this.

In addition to referring to these directly oral stories themselves, the term "folktale" has also been used to refer to literary retellings of these tales. Thus, even though *Little Red Riding Hood* began as an oral tale, Perrault's retelling begins like this:

There was once upon a time a little village girl, the prettiest ever seen or known, of whom her mother was dotingly fond. Her grandmother was even fonder of her still, and had a little red hood made for the child, which suited her so well that wherever she went she was known by the name of Little Red Riding Hood. . . .

These literary folktales use the same basic stories and themes, and they keep some of their oral characteristics, but they are often longer, and their language is often both more ornate and more difficult.

Some more recent stories with identifiable authors include many or all of the traditional characteristics of oral folktales. For example, I wrote *The Princess's Suitors* myself (see page 122), intentionally incorporating both the style and the themes that are common in oral folktales. Using the term more loosely, these stories are also called folktales.

The Stonecutter

Once there was a poor stonecutter. Each day he went to the mountain and cut blocks of stone, and then took them to the market to sell.

He was quite happy, until one day he looked through the gate of a rich man's house. He saw the rich man sitting in the shade with servants bringing him food to eat.

"Surely the rich man is greater than I am," sighed the poor stonecutter. "If only I were a rich man, then I would be truly happy."

The spirit of the mountain heard the stonecutter and gave him what he wanted. At once the stonecutter found himself sitting in the garden of a nice house with servants bringing him food.

"Now I will be truly happy," thought the stonecutter. But a few days later the rich man looked out the window. He saw the king's palace. He saw many servants hurrying to obey the king, and he saw how great the king's palace was.

"Surely the king is greater than I am," he sighed. "If only I were a king, then I would be truly happy."

The spirit of the mountain heard the stonecutter and gave him what he wanted. At once the stonecutter found himself sitting on a throne in a great palace, with servants hurrying to do whatever he wanted.

"Now I will be truly happy," thought the stonecutter. But a few days later he was standing outside. The sun was beating down on his head. It was so hot that he had to go inside.

"Surely the sun is greater than I am," he sighed. "If only I were the sun, then I would be truly happy."

The spirit of the mountain heard the stonecutter and gave him what he wanted. At once the stonecutter became the sun, burning in the sky. He shone down on the earth, and people cowered under the heat.

"Now I will be truly happy," thought the stonecutter. But soon a cloud came between him and the earth so that no one could see him.

"Surely the cloud is greater than I am," he sighed. "If only I were the cloud, then I would be truly happy."

The spirit of the mountain heard the stonecutter and gave him what he wanted. At once the stonecutter became a cloud,

continued

raining upon the earth. Where the rain came, people ran for their houses.

"Now I will be truly happy," thought the stonecutter. But he noticed that when the rain beat down on the mountain, the mountain was not affected.

"Surely the mountain is greater than I am," he sighed. "If only I were the mountain, then I would be truly happy."

The spirit of the mountain heard the stonecutter and gave him what he wanted. At once the stonecutter became the mountain, strong and firm.

"Now I will be truly happy," thought the stonecutter. But soon he noticed a small stonecutter coming up the side of the mountain. The stonecutter cut blocks of stone from the mountain and took them away.

"Surely the stonecutter is greater than I am," he sighed. "If only I were a stonecutter, then I would be truly happy."

The spirit of the mountain heard and gave him what he wanted. At once he was a poor stonecutter once again. At this he was thankful, and never wished again to be something that he was not.

Notes on the Story

This telling was mostly based on Japanese variants of this story. One published version with pictures that provide good support for the text is *The Two Stonecutters* by Eve Titus (1967).

Note that this story provides repeated occurrences of comparatives (here only *greater* was used, but others could be substituted) and conditionals (*if . . . then*).

Finally, stories known as "urban myths" or "urban legends" have appeared in recent years. They have many modern elements, but they are becoming (or perhaps have become) modern folktales. They generally have no known authors, and they have developed (and continue to develop) recognizable variant versions. Because they are passed from person to person, they are often oral in quality (though they are now often distributed over the Internet). Some of them are rooted in a real event; others – perhaps most – appear to be completely fictitious. In urban myths (unlike traditional folktales) the teller often believes the story is true. They are often told as having happened to a relative or acquaintance of a relative or acquaintance. For example, the teller might begin with, "Well, my boss said his wife knows this woman who told her about something that happened to her cousin. . . ." (The relationship of the teller to the person the story happened to is always too remote to verify the story.) They often have horrific or sexual themes. As such, they will not be suitable for many classrooms, but in the right contexts, they may be useful for raising questions about the values and direction of the society in which we live. As in traditional folktales, the element of horror is often tied to behavior that is not moral or that does not conform to social standards, though not all urban myths have an obvious moral.

There are several subtypes of folktales. Fables are very short folktales with animals as the main characters and with a very obvious moral lesson, often summed up in a single line at the end. Fairy tales are folktales that include some magical element (not necessarily fairies); the German word *märchen* is sometimes used for these. There are hero stories (like those about Johnny Appleseed or Paul Bunyan), some of which have some real historical parts and others of which may not. And there are myths, legends, parables, and Sufi stories. (Sufi stories are stories from a mystical Islamic tradition; the Nasrudin story on page 12 might be considered part of this tradition.) The point is not that we have to figure out which group any particular story belongs in; these groups often overlap and many stories fit into several categories. It is just helpful to realize that a wide variety of folktales are out there, all of which are potentially useful for language teaching. This variety not only adds interest but also helps ensure that there are ample materials for all levels and for a variety of approaches.

Intermediate

Cakes and Cider – An Urban Legend

This is a true story that happened at Cambridge University. During an exam one day, a bright young student stood up and asked the professor to bring him cakes and cider.

"I beg your pardon?" asked the professor.

"I request that you bring me cakes and cider," repeated the student.

"Certainly not," replied the professor.

"Sir," said the student, "I really must insist. I request and require that you bring me cakes and cider."

continued

7

"Excuse me, young man," said the professor, "but you are distracting the other students. Please quietly continue your work."

At this point, the student produced a copy of the 400-year-old Laws of Cambridge, written in Latin, which were still – theoretically – in effect. He pointed to one section and announced, "It says here in the rules of our university, 'Gentlemen taking examinations may request and require cakes and cider.'"

The professor examined the sheet, spoke quietly with the student, and then excused himself briefly. A short time later an assistant arrived with a soda and a hamburger. (Apparently they had agreed that this was an acceptable modern equivalent.) The student then wrote his exam, happily chewing and slurping away.

Three weeks later the student was fined five pounds for not wearing a sword to the examination.

Notes on the Story
Like traditional folktales, this urban legend has a number of variants. It always takes place at either Cambridge or Oxford in England, but the items the student may ask for vary. The student's infraction also varies; for example, in one it is for not wearing a ceremonial sword, in another it is for not wearing shoes with silver buckles while on university premises. Another interesting variation involves when the student is fined for his violation of the rules; in some cases it happens immediately (showing the professor outsmarting the student by knowing the ancient rules better than the student did); in others, it takes the professor or university several weeks to find the item for which to fine the student. One variant presents a student who calls for a pint of cider during class but is reprimanded by the lecturer for not wearing a tabard, or tunic. The student later arrives for the final examination so dressed and receives his pint.

Note the beginning of the story: It is not unusual for an urban legend to begin by announcing that it is a true story.

Characteristics that contribute to easy reading and listening

Although there is a lot of variation between one folktale and the next, and even between two tellings of the same tale, certain characteristics typical in folktales contribute to relatively easy reading. These include:

- Time-ordered story structure
- Repetition and redundancy
- Predictability
- Relatively simple grammar
- Concrete vocabulary
- Concrete ideas
- Illustrations that provide support and context for the text
- A unique reader–writer relationship

These are explained more fully in the following pages.

Time-ordered story structure

When presenting an argument or conveying information, different cultures have very different ways of arranging material, or even of deciding what material to include. But when it comes to telling stories, all cultures appear to do the same thing: tell about events in the order they happened. *First . . . then . . . after this . . . finally. . . .* Time provides a structure for the story. One culture may speak in terms of passing hours, another of the position of the sun, still another of the waxing and waning of the moon, but the idea is the same: Material is arranged in time order.

A familiar discourse structure makes a text easier to understand and remember. Since folktales use a structure that is familiar to everyone, they are more readily understandable than many other types of literature.

Repetition and redundancy

When you are listening, you can't slow down or go back and reread if you miss something. Because of this, stories that have come from an oral tradition tend to have much more repetition and redundancy than those that haven't. One type of repetition is the repetition of main themes. For example, in *The Three Little Pigs* (*The Three Little Goats* in Middle Eastern cultures), each pig's encounter with the wolf follows the same pattern: The pig builds a house, the wolf comes and asks to be let in, the pig says "No," and the wolf then tries to blow the house down. (Note: This story is commonly known and so not included in this book.) Another example of the repetition of main ideas is seen in both *The Stonecutter* (Japanese; see page 5) and *The Fisherman's Wife*

(European; page 232). In both of these stories, the main characters begin in a very humble place in life; they wish for more and more powerful stations in life, thinking that this will make them happy; in the end, they end up back where they started.

In addition to repetition of key themes, sometimes sections are repeated word for word many times in the story. The repetition may consist of short phrases like the "Not by the hair of my chinny-chin-chin" and "I'll huff and I'll puff and I'll blow your house down" in *The Three Little Pigs* and the "Fee-Fi-Fo-Fum, I smell the blood of an Englishman" in *Jack and the Beanstalk* (see page 246), or it may be longer refrains, such as the "*Cow (sheep, horse, mill) of mine, cow of mine, Have you ever seen a maid o'mine, With a wig and a wag and a long leather bag, Who stole all the money I ever had?*" that occurs nine times in *Gold in the Chimney* (see page 269).

Sometimes there are also building refrains – portions that repeat and get longer each time. This can be especially useful for language learning, since a great deal of material is repeated, but students only need to deal with one new piece at a time. *Stone Soup* (see page 83) provides a good example of this. Near the beginning of the story we find:

So the man stirred the pot with the salt and the pepper and the round, gray stone.
And the woman said, "Imagine that – soup from a stone."

One ingredient at a time, the refrain builds until we find near the end of the story:

. . . So the man stirred the pot with the creamy, yellow butter; the round yellow onion; the fine, white flour; the long, red bone; the leafy, purple cabbage; the long, orange carrots; the salt and the pepper; and the round, gray stone.
And the woman said, "Imagine that – soup from a stone."

In addition to broad repetitions of theme and repeated refrains, numerous local redundancies also occur in folktales. The wolf is not merely going to blow; he is going to huff and puff and blow. The man in *It Could Always Be Worse* (page 88) is not just a man with difficulties; he is always a "poor unfortunate man" with difficulties. Saying the same thing more than once or in more than one way helps students get the idea even if they missed it the first time.

The repetitions help language learners in several ways. Repetition is important in helping new vocabulary stick in the mind. Repetition also gives students many examples of a particular grammatical form in context. For example, some tellings of *Stone Soup* have more than half a dozen examples of negative conditionals with *if . . . then. . . , but not so. . . :* "If only you had some (carrots, onions, barley, etc.), then this soup would be (perfect, fit for a king, etc.), but you don't, so we'll just make do with what we have." Repetitions also help students become more automatic in their recognition of language – an important part of becoming fluent. Finally, repetitions make a story easier to understand for at least two reasons: They make the story more predictable (this is discussed below), and they give students less new language to process. For example, even though *The Stonecutter* (page 5) is about 570 words long, it isn't 570 words of new material; there is a brief introduction, a single-line conclusion, and one basic event that is repeated six times. Reading this story is no more difficult than reading a 200-word story without any repetition.

Predictability

When we can predict or guess well at what is coming, it easier to deal with difficulties and gaps in understanding; when we have no idea what is coming, the text is potentially much more difficult to understand. Two aspects of folktales make them predictable: the repetitions of main events and ideas, and the moral or ethical quality that lies behind many folktales.

Aside from reviewing vocabulary and grammar, repetitions in folktales help the listener or reader guess what is coming. After the wolf has blown the first little pig's house down, we can guess what will happen when the wolf knocks at the second pig's door. After the rabbi has told the poor, unfortunate man to bring his chickens and goose into his house, we can guess what will happen when the rabbi asks the man if he has a goat (see page 88). When the old woman claims she has nothing and the beggar gets her to bring out carrots and cabbage for the soup, we know what will happen when the beggar expresses his wish for flour, onion, and butter (see page 83). Similarly, when the little boy cries wolf and the townsmen come running twice for nothing, we can predict what will happen when the wolf actually appears (see page 139).

The moral nature of folktales also makes them predictable. Folktales have been used to teach about values in many societies, and we often find characters in folktales that clearly demonstrate particular moral qualities. We find lazy and hardworking sons, the wicked stepmother, the miserly man, the wise woman, and the like. There is no subtle character development and no subtle working with moods and feelings. Although in real life, life doesn't always seem fair, in folktales it usually is: The hardworking girl who is badly mistreated will marry the prince in the end, and the wicked, lazy stepsisters will miss out; the proud sons who fail to help the old beggar by the road will fail in their task, while the

The Perfect Wife

Mulla Nasrudin was sitting in a tea shop when a friend excitedly came in. "I'm so happy, Mulla," his friend blurted out, "I'm about to get married. Mulla, have you ever thought of getting married?"

Nasrudin answered, "I did think of getting married. When I was young, I very much wanted to. I set out in search of the perfect wife. I traveled far and wide to find her. I went first to Damascus. There I met a beautiful woman who was gracious, kind, and deeply spiritual, but she had no worldly knowledge, so I decided she was not the perfect wife. I traveled further and went to Isphahan. There I met a woman who was both spiritual and wise in the ways of the world . . . she was beautiful in many ways. But we did not communicate well. Finally, after much searching, in Cairo I found her. She was spiritually deep, graceful, and beautiful in every way, at home in the world and at home in the realms beyond it. I knew I had found the perfect wife."

His friend stared at him, "Then why did you not marry her, Mulla?"

"Alas," said Nasrudin, shaking his head, "She, unfortunately, was waiting for the perfect husband."

Notes on the Story
Nasrudin is a traditional character in Middle Eastern tales. (In Turkish tales, he is Nesreddin Hodja.) Sometimes a trickster, sometimes a fool, sometimes possessing a spiritual wisdom, stories about him are generally entertaining and yet often have some underlying moral.

young simpleton who helps the needy will himself in turn be helped. In *Mother Holly* (see page 149), a pretty, hardworking girl and her ugly and lazy sister fall through a well into another world. There, bread cries out to be taken from the oven, an apple tree calls out to be shaken, and old Mother Holly asks for help with the housework. The first girl does all these tasks well and is richly rewarded with gold. The second has no interest in helping anyone but herself, so she leaves the bread in the oven to burn, the apple tree heavy with fruit, and Mother Holly's tasks poorly done. In the end she is covered with pitch. While my students rarely know the word "pitch," they nearly always correctly guess that it must be something very bad or dirty. One can usually guess from the nature of the characters what kinds of things will happen to them. This moral quality helps students expect what is coming, and so makes stories easier to understand.

Characters in folktales often have standard physical characteristics: the good princess is beautiful (usually with long, flowing, golden hair in Western tales), the wicked stepsister is ugly, and the miserly man is thin and pinched looking. There are exceptions – a wicked stepsister is sometimes outwardly beautiful – but physical characteristics still often provide a clue that helps students predict what is coming.

This predictability is useful in helping students develop strategies to figure out unknown words from context. It also helps students understand a story's main idea more clearly when they are struggling with some of the language in it. This greater understanding of the whole helps them grapple more effectively with the pieces that make it up.

Simple grammar

Folktales, especially those closest to the oral tradition, tend to have simple grammar. Sentences tend to be short. Simple past and present tenses are common. Subordinate clauses are not very common. The connectors between the sentences and the relationships between the ideas tend to be simple; sentences are connected with "and" and "but," not with phrases like "not withstanding the fact that." The more literary forms of folktales have somewhat more complex grammar, but are still less complex than the language of essays or academic writings.

The simple grammar of oral tales makes folktales easier for low-level students to understand; the various levels of grammatical difficulty provide natural links to more difficult materials.

Concrete vocabulary

Concrete language is much easier to grasp than abstract language. (Contrast trying to explain concrete words like "table" or "lamp" with trying to explain abstract ones like "insight" or "hope" and you see the difference at once.) The vocabulary in folktales tends to be very concrete; most of the words are things you can see, feel, taste, touch, and smell. This doesn't mean that all the vocabulary is common. Nouns like "treasure," "princess," and "wolf" aren't commonly used in everyday conversation. Nor are verbs like "haul" and "trudge." But this type of vocabulary is concrete and fairly easy to understand: A picture, a simple sketch, or some simple acting out conveys the idea instantly. The concreteness of the vocabulary helps students understand new language more easily, which in turn helps them understand the story as a whole more easily. Folktales are very good for general vocabulary building.

What makes folktales so good for language teaching?

Concrete ideas

Apart from the language used, the difficulty and abstractness of the ideas affect how hard a text is to understand. Even in your native language, simple, concrete ideas are easier to talk about than complex, abstract ones. Talking about how to cook potatoes and talking about Einstein's theory of relativity are very different in how much mental effort they require. When the idea is easy to understand, the learner has more attention to focus on the language used to communicate that idea. (This is part of the reason why some students who seem very fluent in social contexts can still have extreme difficulty doing academic tasks.)

In folktales, the goals are plain and concrete. To get some soup for supper, to marry the princess, to get rid of the monster in the forest, to find three people more foolish than one's wife – the ideas are plain and easy to understand.

The concreteness of folktales helps students understand them more easily, while at the same time leaving more mental energy available for noticing the language and how it is used to convey meaning. The concreteness of folktales helps students in another way. Even though folktales are very concrete, the characters often embody abstract qualities like greed, patience, humility, arrogance, foolishness, sneakiness, and benevolence. Such abstract ideas are not in themselves simple to explain, but when they are represented in such concrete images as folktales provide, they become much easier to explain. This representation of abstract ideas in very concrete images makes folktales excellent for teaching abstract vocabulary. Whenever students ask me something like "What does 'greedy' mean?" I only have to say, "Remember Spider?" (see page 75), and they remember the meaning at once.

Illustrations

Many folktales are now published as richly illustrated children's books. While good illustrations may make a story more fun (which is also helpful for language learning), pictures are useful for much more than this. Illustrations provide information to help the reader figure out parts of the text that are difficult. When the text mentions seven dwarves, the reader who has never encountered "dwarf" before can figure out what it means from the seven little men in the picture. Most other adult reading doesn't have much to provide context and support for the words on the page, but the illustrations with many folktales provide valuable help in figuring out parts of the text that are a little beyond the reader's grasp. Note, though, that the illustrations in some books are much more helpful to the reader than in others. Some illustrations correspond very closely with the text on the page; other books have illustrations that contribute only a very general idea of what is happening, without any direct correspondence to the text.

A unique reader–writer relationship

The relationship between the reader and the writer is different with folktales than with most other kinds of writing. With many texts, especially academic ones, students regard the authors as experts who know "the facts" and regard themselves as novices who may receive these facts. For many students this puts the text in an unquestionable position: It has authority and must be accepted. But folktales put the reader and writer on different terms; the relationship of storyteller to audience is much more of a peer relationship – the author, even if a great storyteller, is not necessarily an authority on morality or the problems addressed in the story. Furthermore, since the reader has heard many stories, he or she is not a novice. Finally, stories are subjective rather than factual. All this helps students interact with stories as one should interact with all writing: questioning whether they agree with the author's perspective and conclusions, whether they like the style and content, whether the ideas are logical and supported, and whether any confusion is the fault of the reader or the writer. Students still may need to be encouraged to question whether they agree with the author's perspective, but the unique reader–writer relationship in folktales makes this easier.

Characteristics that contribute to interest and relevance for both adults and children

Folktales are typically considered children's stories in the modern Western world, and they certainly often appeal to children. But despite their outwardly simple appearance, folktales address themes and issues that are profound and significant for all ages. Folktales raise important social questions: What is our duty toward the elderly? Toward the poor? Toward our parents? Folktales touch on many social problems and concerns: mistreatment by a stepsibling, the death of a parent, finding a wife, leaving home and finding your way in the world, isolation, poverty, and failure. They are filled with hopes and dreams and sorrows and pains that all of us share. They include many psychologically significant themes: betrayal, revenge, jealousy, arrogance, greed, generosity, forgiveness. Tied in with the above are morally significant issues as well: what is right, what is wrong, and the consequences of both. All of these factors, combined with the fact that people of all ages like good stories, make folktales interesting and relevant to children and mature readers alike.

Language teaching and the cultural elements of folktales

In addition to fitting in with the current educational interest in multicultural issues, the cultural aspects of folktales also contribute to their usefulness for language teaching. Some common elements in folktales help build bridges between cultures, helping us relate to speakers of other languages. Other elements in folktales draw attention to our differences, showing us things we need to learn to understand the thoughts behind the language we are learning.

Folktales are also important from a cultural perspective because native speakers assume that their listeners have certain background knowledge, and a fair amount of this knowledge is rooted in folk literature. *Crying wolf, the sky falling, sour grapes, wolves in sheep's clothing, the lost sheep,* and *the good Samaritan* . . . the stories behind these and many similar common expressions – the stories that give them meaning – are folktales, fables, and parables. Exposing students to folk literature, aside from the direct language practice, helps fill important gaps in nonnative background knowledge and improve understanding of various idioms and figures of speech.

Common elements across cultures – a cultural bridge

While folktales from different cultures display many differences, some elements are common to many or all cultures. Aside from the common time-ordered story structure discussed earlier, the social, moral, and relational themes that lie behind the stories tend to rise above local cultures. Even when different cultures offer different solutions, many of the problems and the underlying struggle to find what is right are the same. Finding a spouse, coming of age, dealing with death and loss and unexpected bad fortune – such concerns are issues in any culture. The attitudes characters reflect – pride and humility, greed and generosity – are common to all humanity. Food and family and music appear in tales from all cultures. So do weddings and celebrations and the births of children. The general struggles and joys common to humanity occupy an important place in folktales. Similar types of characters also seem to appear in folktales from many lands. The trickster, the noodlehead, the diligent son, and the wise old woman appear in the tales of many cultures. The struggles, joys, and hopes common to humanity addressed in folktales provide a bridge between cultures, a feature useful in teaching in cross-cultural contexts.

In addition to these elements, folktales from students' own cultures can improve their attitudes toward language learning, which appears to help them learn more effectively. Kristen Oscarsson (1992) reported extremely positive responses when she used Haitian folktales with Haitian immigrant children. They were surprised and impressed that she knew stories from their culture. This sparked a great deal of interest, which resulted in measurable increases in both the quality and the quantity of language they produced. Although she worked with children, I have seen similarly positive responses from adults in both academic and refugee contexts when they discovered that I knew and valued stories from their own culture(s). It is a fair expectation for people of any age: Using tales from their own culture is likely to increase interest, motivation, and positive attitudes toward the learning. Because folktales are fairly short, you can easily include tales from each of the nationalities in your class. Having students share tales from their own culture, either in writing or orally, lets all the students have their own culture and their own favorite tales represented.

Culturally distinctive elements – an opportunity to introduce and discuss cultural differences

Although some elements in folktales are common to all cultures, other elements are culturally distinctive. You can use these elements to draw attention to cultural differences. While characters in European tales are likely to eat potatoes and cabbage and bread, in Asian tales they are more likely to eat rice. The houses in European tales are markedly different from the houses in African and Asian tales. Countless differences of this sort exist in the tales of different cultures; you can use these elements to show how different other cultures can be and to generate discussion about cultural issues. What are typical foods? How does one settle a disagreement? How does one dress for different occasions? What are the differences between the rich and poor? How are weddings celebrated? Folktales provide a natural context for discussing cultural similarities and cultural differences, which, as mentioned above, is essential for understanding the thoughts and people that lie behind any language.

Integrating folktales with any language skill

Folktales are useful for working on listening, speaking (including pronunciation), reading, and writing. They can be used to work on these skills separately, but folktales make it easy to integrate any or all of these skills. Some activities with folktales that develop key language skills are listed briefly below.

Listening
– Stories read aloud by the teacher
– Stories told orally without a book by the teacher

- Tapes of stories
- Folktales from other cultures as told by other students
- Dramatic presentations of folktales
- Jigsaw and information-gap activities

Speaking
- Students telling tales from their own cultures
- Discussion activities
- Negotiating with other students to create new variations for existing stories or to create completely new stories
- Jigsaw and information-gap activities
- Creating and presenting stories dramatically

Reading
- Individual, extensive reading
- Jigsaw reading
- Analytical reading involving comparison/contrast, analysis, and so on

Writing
- Recording stories from the student's own culture
- Writing new endings to existing stories
- Composing original tales
- Writing papers comparing, analyzing, evaluating, and criticizing stories
- Writing summaries of stories
- Responding to stories on a personal level

Pronunciation
- Chanting rhymed portions of tales and repeated refrains to practice aspects of pronunciation like stress, rhythm, and intonation that go beyond the individual sounds
- Using *Jazz Chant Fairy Tales* by Carolyn Graham (1988), also for practice of stress, rhythm, and intonation

In addition, folktales are exceptional for expanding and reviewing vocabulary – an element needed for all of the basic skills. Folktales can also be used in countless ways to teach and reinforce grammatical points. And they can be used to develop various cognitive strategies that are useful in a variety of contexts. Part II, *The activities*, develops these and other activities in detail.

2 Some tips for the classroom

This chapter contains a miscellaneous collection of ideas that I have found helpful but that are not connected to any specific activity.

Copying the activities in this book

A number of the activities in this book include materials that can be photocopied and distributed to students. If you want to save paper, copy the activities at their current size so that each fills half a page; by putting two copies side by side and copying that, you can get two handouts on one page.

If you prefer to use full-page ($8\frac{1}{2} \times 11''$) handouts, enlarge the activities to about 140%; each should then fill a full page.

On the levels of the stories in the book

Most of the stories in this book are labeled at a particular level. These labels are intended as a rough guide only; stories can be adjusted up or down with just slight changes in the telling. More difficult vocabulary and a fast pace can make them suitable for higher levels; slightly easier vocabulary combined with extra sketches, mime, and verbal explanation can make them suitable for lower levels.

Building a collection of materials over time

As you begin to work with folktales in the classroom, it will take time to find material that you like and that suits the needs of your classroom. When I first started using folktales, I sometimes spent several hours searching for the right books and right themes for the classes I was working with. As I continued reading and looking for folktales, this became much easier.

This book includes a collection of stories that I have used in the language classroom; these should give you a good start. The easiest way to accumulate additional material is to regularly get a few folktales or a different ethnic collection from the library. Whenever you find a story that you like, make a note of it (or even make a quick summary), also noting specific themes and language purposes that the book might fit. For a while, I made notes like those shown in the box on page 21. (If you keep all these notes in one document on the computer, you can search the document to find particular themes.) If you just keep reading folktales and noting ones that you like, you will fairly quickly accumulate a lot of material you can use.

Differences between reading and telling

Reading a story from a book to your students and telling the same story from memory are both useful, but reading and oral telling are usually very different in the language used (both vocabulary and syntax) and in the feeling of the interaction between the teller and the listeners. It helps to understand the differences so you can choose what technique is best suited to your aims with a particular activity, and to your abilities as a storyteller.

Oral telling tends to use much simpler language. Sentences are generally shorter. You usually use coordinating conjunctions. If you suspect that any listeners might not understand a particular word or idea, there is a subconscious tendency to substitute an easier word or paraphrase. With oral telling, you usually repeat things more often and include more redundancy, especially if you suspect that any students are having difficulty following. Since there is no text to read, continuous direct eye contact makes the presentation more personal and brings communication breakdowns to your attention more immediately, allowing spontaneous adjustments to your telling. Although there are no pictures to support the meaning, there is much more freedom to support the communication with gestures, facial expressions, actions, and simple sketches on the board. Oral telling can be done with no materials at all, but you must know the basic story fairly well.

In contrast, when you read a story aloud to students, you use the vocabulary and language structures that are written on the page, which are almost always much more varied and complex than those you would use in an oral telling. Because you must look at the page, you have much less eye contact with students. With an illustrated book, you have the advantage of the illustrations; when you come across new vocabulary items, you can often just point to the picture. But this also presents a problem: With stories that have a fair amount of text on the page, it is hard to read the text and show the pictures at the same time. Reading also has the advantage of not requiring you to know the story very well.

It is possible to use some combination of reading and oral telling. You can read some text from the book and then set the book down (or hold

---

Sample note format for collecting story information

By keeping notes like these when you read stories, you can quickly locate the book you need when you want something on a particular theme. Such notes also let you orally retell the story without the book if you need to.

The Empty Pot (Demi, 1990)

Summary: The emperor decides to choose his successor by seeing who can grow the best flowering plant from the seeds he provides. A boy who can usually make any plant grow and thrive is unable to get the seed to sprout. His father tells him that if he did his best, that is good enough, so the boy returns to the emperor with an empty pot. All the other children return with beautiful flowers. The emperor reveals that the seeds had been cooked and could not grow, so he chooses the boy with the empty pot as the next emperor.

Origin: Chinese (?)

Themes: honesty; success; gardening; selection of rulers

Illustrations: Nicely done but provide limited support for the text. Provide a nice Asian flavor.

Discussion topics: Were the children who used other seeds really dishonest? Is honesty really that important? What makes a good leader? Is a trick like this a valid way to choose a leader?

Hands-on activities: Give the children each a seed and have them plant it to see what will grow.

Comments: The amount of text per page was quite brief but the vocabulary is too difficult for beginners to read without help.

---

up the picture) and paraphrase what the page said. You can interrupt the reading to mime the actions or to draw sketches on the board. But this still has a different feel from true oral telling.

When I first started using folktales, I preferred reading stories from illustrated books. I liked the support of the pictures, and I liked having a specific text that I didn't have to generate. While I still occasionally find reading aloud useful, I tend to do much more oral telling. I like the more direct interaction with the students. What is more, I have found that students generally seem to prefer oral telling to reading as well. Other teachers with whom I have spoken have reported a similar preference in their students (both children and adults) for oral telling.

Recommendations

Read the story if you don't know it well enough to orally tell it. Read the story if you want to focus on specific vocabulary or specific language structures in the text. Read the story if students need the exact words to complete the activity. (For example, it can be awkward for students to do a cloze exercise if the story you told is different from the version they have.) Read the story if you especially love the way a particular writer tells it. But if your goal is just general listening practice, try oral telling. Use oral telling whenever students don't need the exact words, just the ideas of the text.

Tips on telling stories orally

Choosing stories for oral telling

The best stories for oral telling are those that most strongly reflect the oral tradition, that is, stories that contain a lot of repetition and that are not too complex. Stories like *The Three Little Pigs* are good because the same basic event – the wolf asking to be admitted, being refused, and his attempting to blow the house down – happens three times: this type of redundancy is extremely helpful when one has only oral input to rely on. More local repetitions and redundancies (like repeatedly referring to the "big, bad, wolf" rather than just "the wolf," or the wolf "huffing, and puffing and blowing" rather than just "blowing") are also especially helpful in oral tellings.

For beginning students, choosing stories from the students' culture(s) can help students understand the story more easily and promote positive attitudes toward English.

Intermediate

The Riddle

A king once lost his way, and happened to come to the house of a poor charcoal maker. The man, though obviously poor, welcomed the king graciously and offered him what little food there was in the house.

Seeing the poor charcoal maker's humble condition, the king was filled with curiosity and said to the man, "Tell me, my good man, how much money do you get from making and selling charcoal?"

"Ten cents a day, Your Majesty," the man answered.

"Ten cents a day! And you manage to survive?" asked the king in amazement.

"Oh yes," said the man cheerfully. "It is enough to live on. And with that ten cents a day, I also manage to pay a debt, save for my old age, and have something left to throw out the window."

"This I cannot believe," said the king. "How is this possible?"

"Well," said the man, "my aging mother lives with us, and caring for her pays the debt that I owe to my parents. And I care for my son whom I hope will care for me in my old age; thus, I save for the future. And every so often I set aside another penny for my daughter's dowry, which is certainly like throwing money out the window."

The king chuckled. "That is good. Very good. Now, you must do me a favor and promise not to tell that riddle again until you have seen my face 100 times." To this the poor charcoal maker agreed.

The king's party soon came along. The king reminded the man of his promise, and then he left.

Soon after, the king posed this same riddle to his court. "How is it possible that a man who makes only ten cents a day can have enough to live, to pay a debt, to save for the future, and to throw some out the window? The first man who can answer this within the next month will be freed from paying taxes for the rest of his life."

Everyone was baffled by this riddle, but after thought, one of the members of the court concluded, "The king asked this riddle right after he got lost and went to that poor man's hut. He must have learned it there." So he jumped on his horse and rode back to the place where the charcoal maker lived.

"You know," said the man, "how a man can live on ten cents a day and still pay a debt, save for the future, and throw some out the window.

"Yes," said the charcoal maker, "I know, but I may not tell you."

"I will pay you ten silver pieces," said the man.

"No, I cannot tell you," said the charcoal maker.

"Very well, I will give you fifty silver pieces," said the man.

"No, I cannot tell you," said the charcoal maker.

continued

"What if I give you one hundred silver pieces?" said the man.

"Let me see the coins," said the charcoal maker. After examining and counting them carefully, he said, "Very well, I will tell you the answer." And he told the man the answer to the riddle.

The man smiled, thanked the charcoal maker, and then rode back to the court at once. There he told the answer to the court, much to the astonishment of the king.

The king became furious. "Summon the charcoal maker at once," he cried.

The charcoal maker was brought into the court and made to stand before the king's throne. "Did you tell the answer to the riddle?" asked the king.

"Yes, Your Majesty."

"Why? You broke your word to me!" shouted the king. "You will be beaten and thrown into prison for a year."

"I did not break my word to you, Your Majesty," answered the man humbly. "You said that I could tell the answer once I had seen your face one hundred times."

"But you have not seen my face again even once since the day I left your house."

"But Your Majesty," replied the charcoal maker, "I have. Your face is stamped on each of the silver coins I was given, and since there are one hundred of them, I have seen your face one hundred times."

At this the king was greatly impressed. He set the poor charcoal maker free, and gave him a gift of three bags of gold.

Notes on the Story

This particular telling is based mostly on a Catalan tale, though many versions of the tale exist. For example, in a Jewish variant of the tale, the riddle has to do with why a man's beard was black and the hair on his head was gray, but the rest of the story, including the 100 coins, is fundamentally the same. (The answer, by the way, is that the beard didn't start growing till the man was grown, so it was 20 years younger. The reward is also different; the man is appointed to be one of the king's councilors.) For an illustrated version of the Catalan tale, see *The Riddle* by Adele Vernon (1987).

Before you go into the classroom

Do *not* try to memorize the story. Memorization takes too long and requires too much mental energy. Even if you succeed, you will probably sound very awkward, and you can get really stuck if you forget what comes next.

If you have never told the story before, make a brief outline. Doing the activity in the *Introductions, Episodes, and Conclusions* activity yourself (see page 225) can be really helpful for this. You don't have to use the notes when you do the telling, but making them will help you prepare for the telling and give you something to refresh your mind if you get stuck.

Write down your opening sentence and your final sentence. Getting into the story and getting out are often the most difficult part.

If there is a repeated refrain or short segment where exact wording is critical, write these words down. Again, the hope is that you won't need to look at this, but if you need exact words, it's better to have them written down just in case.

Think about how the different characters are feeling at different points in the story. Are they sad? Disappointed? Angry? If angry, are they just annoyed or are they furious? Being conscious of feelings will help you convey the right emotions when you speak.

Think about ways to get students involved. Depending on the story and the ages and backgrounds of your students, there are a variety of options. If there is a repeated refrain, have students chant it with you. [This provides a good opportunity for students to practice stress, rhythm, and intonation – aspects of pronunciation (called *suprasegmentals*) that usually result in great gains in intelligibility.] With *The Greedy Old Spider* (see page 75), you can divide the class into two villages and have each group mime pulling the ropes at the appropriate points. Or ask a few students to act out what you are saying as you are doing the telling. In a story like *The Three Little Pigs,* you might have students knock on their desks whenever the wolf comes to the door. By involving as many of the students' senses as possible and increasing general participation, you increase involvement with the language in the material and accommodate students with different learning styles.

The Riddle: Sample notes for oral telling

Your notes might look quite different from these; there are as many ways to make notes as there are people to make them. However, good notes should be quite brief, listing only the story's key points.

Opening: Once there was a king who lost his way.

Outline: King asks about earnings
Man tells riddle
Promise: Don't tell until you see face 100 times
King tells court
Bribe: 10 coins – refused; 50 coins – refused;
100 coins – riddle revealed
King angry
Man saw face 100 times

Riddle: enough to live on
to pay a debt   (care for mother)
save for the future   (care for son)
throw out the window   (daughter's dowry)

Closing: And the king was impressed with the man's wisdom, and sent him home with a gift of three bags of gold.

Preteaching key vocabulary or concepts

The critical word here is "key." Much of the new vocabulary that students will encounter in a story can be dealt with as it comes up. Context may make it clear with no explanation at all, or quick paraphrase, explanation, miming, gestures, or sketches may explain it in a moment. There is no need to bog down the preteaching time for such vocabulary. However, for many stories there are a few key words that you really should teach in advance. Words like "dowry" in *The Riddle* (see page 22) or "suitors" in *The Princess's Suitors* (see page 122) are examples; they're important for understanding some part of the story, and they aren't easy to explain in passing; to deal with them during the telling would generally lose some of the momentum of the story. Recurring parts of the story, especially those you want students to join you in saying, are also often worth preteaching. For example, "not by the hair of my chinnny-chin-chin" in *The Three Little Pigs* and "Imagine that!" in *Stone Soup* (see page 83), keep recurring and aren't obvious from context, so they warrant some advance comment. Finally, if the story has a punch line or a humorous twist at the end, make sure students have the vocabulary they need to understand it when it comes. A punch line is generally ruined if you have to explain it.

During the telling

If possible, sit or stand without obstructions between you and your students. Don't sit behind your desk if you can help it.

Maintain continual eye contact. Sometimes scan your eyes across the class; at other times look directly at specific students.

If you want more guidance on oral story telling, *The Story Teller's Start-up Book* by Margaret Read MacDonald (1993) offers a number of useful suggestions.

Reinforcing your telling with mime, gestures, and simple sketches

Clarify meaning through mime, gesture, facial expression, and tone of voice. Simple sketches on the board also help. For example, you might tell *The Greedy Old Spider* (see page 75) as something like this:

There was once a great [arms stretched wide], big [arms reaching high], fat [arms reached around an imaginary enormous belly], greedy [hands bent like claws and arms reaching out and pretending to pulling things toward yourself] old [walk like an old person] spider [either make a spider with hand and fingers, or use your whole body to imitate a great spider, and/or draw a sketch on the board] who lived in the middle of the jungle. He lived in the middle of the jungle – with tall, tall [arms reached high] trees [sketch on board] and great big vines [sketch and/or mime moving hand from high to low as if hand was around thick rope] – he lived in the middle of the jungle, halfway between two villages [if trees are sketched on board, sketch a few huts on either side]. Here is one village [point to one side of the room, or to houses in the sketch] or town. Here is the other village [point to the other side of the room] or town. The spider lived here [point to spot in the middle], right in the middle between them. . . .

If you act out parts of the story, the greatest danger is being afraid of looking silly. You may in fact look silly at times – that's part of the fun – but if you are afraid of looking silly, it leads to half-doing the actions, which looks far sillier than doing them wholeheartedly.

If you really feel uncomfortable and unnatural gesturing, don't force it; if it just doesn't fit with your personality, it may be better to leave this out than to be distracted or feel awkward. Gesturing is a very good way to reinforce meaning, so it is at least worth periodically experimenting with; many of us (including myself!) felt awkward at first but learned to feel comfortable with a little practice.

27

Rewriting stories

Sometimes it is necessary to retell or rewrite a story in simpler language to make it intelligible to students. Teachers sometimes wonder how far to go, since they don't want to lose culturally important parts of the tale or simplify too much. I suggest the following.

Get rid of language that isn't standard native speaker knowledge. For example, in Jewish tales one occasionally finds a *rebbitzen*. Without the context of the story to help them guess, most native speakers couldn't tell you what a *rebbitzen* is, so don't give your students the chance to be distracted by it or add it to their vocabulary lists; replace this with standard vocabulary (in this case, a rabbi's wife). Similarly, in Japanese tales one sometimes encounters an *oni* (a being like an ogre, I think, though I'm not quite sure). Since virtually no native speaker knows what an *oni* is, replace this with ogre or some other creature known to native speakers (unless, of course, you're teaching Japanese students and want to leave a culturally familiar element for them). Even if your substitution is not perfectly accurate, it will help build English knowledge without doing a real injustice to the story.

Keep nonstandard language that is standard native speaker knowledge. For example, the "not by the hair of my chinny-chin-chin," in *The Three Little Pigs* is not a phrase that occurs in most daily conversations, but it is language that nearly all native speakers know, so leave it in. Depending on the level of the students, I might also leave words like "kimono" in a Japanese story; even though this is a Japanese word, it is one an educated native speaker would be expected to know.

Keep cultural elements in stories that are fairly readily explainable. For example, many Korean tales begin, "Once upon a time when the tiger smoked. . . ." While I would take this out for beginning students, for intermediate or advanced students I would leave it in. Students might not know what to make of it, but if they ask, the explanation of what the phrase is about can provide some really good language practice. ("When the tiger smoked" conveys the idea that the story took place in the very distant past, back when animals talked and smoked and did other things that people do.)

As a story teller, feel free to adjust stories to your liking (unless you are using a story to show something particular about a culture). We are not folklorists who are committed to preserving a particular culture's tales; we are language teachers who happen to think that story telling is a good way to practice and develop language. As story tellers, we can feel free to adapt or combine tales as we like. For example, in the first version of *Salem and the Nail* (see page 104) that I heard, Salem got his house back for nothing. To me this didn't make sense: If he got nothing, Abraham could as easily have burned the house to the ground or left it vacant rather than giving it back to Salem. So I adjusted the story and had Salem offer to buy the house back for half-price. Crafty Salem still pulls off his deal, but Abraham has some reasonable incentive for his action.

Using real objects

It perhaps goes without saying that bringing in real objects is a great way to reinforce meaning, especially for beginners. The many concrete nouns in folktales make them especially good for this. For *Salem and the Nail,* you might bring in a nail and a bag and a coat (but skip the dead donkey); with *Stone Soup* you could bring in a stone and a pot and various vegetables; for *The Greedy Old Spider,* you could bring in a spider in a jar and a rope; and so on. Folktales provide a great way to connect language with the things of real life.

Preparing students for folktales in the classroom

Before using folktales with some students (especially adults), you may need to let them know what you are doing and why you are doing it. In reflecting on the use of folktales, DeBarros (1991, p. 12) comments:

. . . students were more concerned about practicing English than telling their stories. In cases where there was not enough pre- and post-language practice, the students were dissatisfied. They did not view the telling of the story or the writing of it as a goal in itself.

The problem was not that story telling did not provide good language practice, but that students were not aware of the language practice they were getting.

Because folktales are often fun, and because they are "just stories," some students may not feel they are studying language. (This is occasionally the case with adults in intensive English program settings – I have never had a negative reaction from immigrant students.) If your students are concerned, it is worth taking the time to show them what types of language the various folktales and activities are exposing them to. Point out the various grammatical points that you have covered and the various cognitive strategies they are learning. Make it clear to them that you are teaching language, not just stories. If your students have confidence in your approach, they will learn more effectively.

Although most students I have worked with have shown positive attitudes toward folktales, some adults and adolescents regard them as childish. They may feel the tales are beneath them, that you are condescending to them by using them. Again, the problem is not the material but the students' perceptions. If students perceive folktales as childish, talk about the fact that most folktales were not originally children's stories (and in many cultures still aren't). Point out the important social and moral issues folktales deal with – issues many children are not conscious of. If you can reassure your students that the tales are worth their serious attention, your use of them will be more profitable.

Sources for material

In the United States and Britain, public libraries are usually good sources for finding folktales. The children's section of the library usually has both individual illustrated tales and collections of tales told in relatively easy language. The adult section of the library usually also includes collections of tales. In the United States, interlibrary loan enables you to get virtually any book from any library.

The Internet also has a large number of folktales from many cultures that you can download (copy to your computer) for free.

In this book, in addition to traditional folktales, I have included a few stories from the Bible, a historical story, an urban myth, and a story from personal experience to illustrate other possible sources for stories. Religious writing, history, and daily life are all full of stories that can be adapted to the language classroom. Once you start to look, you will discover many fascinating stories in a variety of places. You can use these stories as you find them or retell them to suit your own purposes.

The *Bibliography* at the end of this book suggests a number of books if you need further help getting started. It also lists a number of Internet sources that have good collections of material.

Building a bridge from folktales to other types of literature

Some fantasy literature for children and adolescents is useful in making a transition from folk and fairy tales to a broader genre. These books have elements in common with fairy tales: a struggle between good and evil, chronological narrative structure, concrete imagery, a certain amount of predictability, and highly motivating stories. Yet they are also more demanding: They are much longer, have more complex plots, and lack the support of illustrations, and their language is more embellished. The familiar qualities, combined with new elements to stretch the students, make them potentially useful as a transition. Another helpful element in children's and adolescent fantasy is that these books are often published as series. This means that while the first book in the series may be difficult because, as well as including new language, the characters and places are unfamiliar, subsequent books in the series become easier because the students have some background knowledge: They know the main character and the types of things to expect. This also means that prereading preparation before the first book prepares the students for a number of books rather than just one. (The *Bibliography* suggests a few possibilities; a children's librarian may be able to suggest others.)

For those using folktales to introduce academic skills and higher thinking processes to more advanced students, one can move from folktales to adult short stories, and then to longer literature.

3   Folktales in the multilevel classroom

The problem of the multilevel classroom

Language classrooms often include students at different levels of proficiency, and the challenges for the teacher are great.

Partly because of the limitations of time, and partly because we just aren't sure what else to do, teachers often just shoot for the middle and hope the students at the upper and lower levels will get something out of the lesson. Although in the real world, this is sometimes unavoidable, most teachers would agree it isn't the best way to meet all of the students' needs.

The first idea that comes to many teachers when they think of multilevel teaching is to prepare two sets of materials, for the higher and lower levels. The teacher gets one group working independently and teaches the other group, and then switches the roles and gets the second group doing individual or group work while teaching the first group. While occasionally this approach is useful, it more often than not creates more problems than it solves. The already overbusy teacher is now burdened with creating two or more independent lessons for one class; this is impractical and, given our human limitations, often impossible. There may also be difficulties with the length of the activities, since there is a potential problem if one group finishes before the other. The biggest problem is that the teacher is not available to answer questions or provide much feedback to students doing independent work, since the teacher is always teaching the other group.

Fortunately, there are other options.

Alternative approaches to multilevel teaching

Two basic alternatives work especially well with folktales and other stories: Students respond to the same story with different but related tasks, or they read (or listen to) different stories and then respond with the same task. These two approaches translate into five options:

1. Students respond to the same story with different versions of the same type of activity.
2. Students respond to the same story with the same activity, but lower levels get extra support to help them complete it.

3. Students respond to the same story with the same task, but higher levels get an extra task.
4. Different levels get different stories but do the same type of activity, working with other students at the same level.
5. Different levels get different stories (or parts of stories) and work in mixed-level groups to complete a cooperative activity.

Each of these options is further explained and illustrated in the following sections.

Each of these options requires a little extra preparation, but since the same material is being adapted and since the easier set is often a subset of the harder material, the extra preparation is much less than creating completely separate lessons. In addition, these activities have all the students doing their individual or group work at the same time, leaving you free to provide feedback to students who need it.

Self-access materials are another option for the multilevel class; that is, you set up a number of activities that students can do fairly independently, and then let each student do whichever activities he or she wants. Since everyone is doing something different, each student can choose a task at an appropriate level.

Responding to the same story with different versions of the same type of activity

In this approach to multilevel teaching, present one story orally to the entire class, being sure to direct some language at the highest-level students and some at the lowest students (making sure they follow what is going on). Then ask students to do something like a strip story (see page 34), but create two or three sets of strips at different levels and give different sets to different groups.

Activities that can be used in this way
Strip story: Create different numbers of strips for different levels. You can also make slightly more complex strips with more subtle differences for higher levels. See page 102.
Concentration matching cards: Low-level students get pictures of concrete nouns; mid-level students get single-word synonyms; high-level students get sentence halves. See page 182.
Crossword puzzles: Create several puzzles at different levels. This does require a fair amount of extra work on your part, but they can be used repeatedly with subsequent classes. See page 196.
Cloze passages: For the easier version, leave fewer gaps and/or edit some sentences out for lower levels. See page 148.

For example, for *It Could Always Be Worse* (see page 88) . . .

Notice that the strips on the right are basically a subset of those on the left, so once the longer set is created, it takes only an extra minute to eliminate or simplify some of them. The set on the right also has three strips that are identical, making the set easier without reducing the number of strips too much.

you might give these strips to intermediate students . . .	while you give these to low-intermediate students . . .
The man was unhappy.	The man was unhappy.
His house was too noisy.	The man went to the rabbi for help.
The man went to the rabbi for help.	The rabbi told the man to take his chickens into the house.
The rabbi told the man to take his chickens into the house.	The man went to the rabbi for help again.
The house was noisier than before.	The rabbi told the man to take his goat into the house.
The man went to the rabbi for help a second time.	The man went to the rabbi for help again.
The rabbi told the man to take his goat into the house.	The rabbi told the man to take his cow into the house.
The goat pushed everyone, and the house was noisier than before.	The man went to the rabbi for help again.
The man went to the rabbi for help a third time.	The rabbi told the man to take his animals out of the house.
The rabbi told the man to take his cow into the house.	The house was very quiet and peaceful.
The cow trampled everything, and the house was noisier than before.	The man went to thank the rabbi.
The man went to the rabbi for help a fourth time.	
The rabbi told the man to take his animals out of the house.	
The house was very quiet and peaceful.	
The man went to thank the rabbi.	

Responding to the same story with extra support for lower-level students

In this approach, all students listen to the same story (or other oral presentation). Again, a key element of the presentation is that comments be directed at all levels – there should be enough simple explanation for the lowest levels to follow what is going on, with enough more difficult language to challenge more advanced students. All students then participate in the same activity (e.g., creating a timeline, writing a summary, analyzing the text structure), but with different levels of assistance to help them complete the task.

Activities that can be used in this way

Problem/solution analysis: Give lowest-level students a list of problems and a list of solutions; all they have to do is match the right problem with the corresponding solution. Give mid-level students a list of problems; they must write in the solutions. Give highest-level students nothing; they must identify the problems as well as find solutions for them. See page 236.

Cause/effect analysis: Same as *Problem/solution analysis.* See page 242.

Timeline: See the sample graphic organizers on page 74.

Analysis of story structure: See page 225.

Compare/contrast variants: See the sample graphic organizers shown on page 255.

Cloze: Give the highest level just the cloze exercise; give mid-level students a word list as well; give lowest-level students a multiple-choice version. See page 148.

Crossword puzzles: Give higher-level students only the crossword puzzle. Give lower-level students a word list with the puzzle, so that when they don't know an answer, they can search the list to find one that fits. See pages 199–201.

Providing different levels of support for the same activity

Here the task is for students to identify various cause-and-effect relationships in the story *The Princess's Suitors* (see pages 122–125). You might give a handout like the upper one to the lowest-level students and the lower one to mid-level students. The highest-level students might get no external support.

Instructions: Connect the cause on the left with the effect on the right. The first one is done for you.

Cause	Effect
The princess was kind and beautiful.	The princess did not choose the first two princes.
The princess did not know who to choose.	She decided to test the princes secretly.
The king loved the princess.	The princess chose him for a husband.
The princess didn't want to be recognized.	He gave her more time to choose.
The princess asked for a job in the stable.	Many princes wanted to marry her.
The princess dumped water on the first prince and scared his horse.	She was given a job.
The first two princes were rude and angry.	He got angry and told her to go away.
The princess spilled both water and soup on the third prince.	These things did not make him angry.
The third prince was kind and polite.	She put on a disguise.

Cause	Effect
The princess was kind and beautiful.	
The princess did not know who to choose.	
The king loved the princess.	
The princess didn't want to be recognized.	
The princess asked for a job in the stable.	
The princess dumped water on the first prince and scared his horse.	
The first two princes were rude and angry.	
The princess spilled both water and soup on the third prince.	
The third prince was kind and polite.	

Responding to the same story with an extra task for higher-level students

In this approach to the multilevel class, all the students begin doing the same activity. Since higher-level students will finish it before the lower-level students will, create an additional, more difficult activity based on the same story for the higher-level students to do once they finish the first part of the activity. For example, while the lower-level students complete a strip story (see page 102), higher-level students might complete the strip story and then evaluate the relative importance of each of the strips (see page 251). Students who are between these levels would be able to start the evaluation part of the activity but not complete this part. Similarly, lower-level students might match concentration matching cards with sentence halves; higher levels would do this and then also order the sentences as a strip story.

Different levels get different stories but do the same type of activity with other students at their level

For this option, students work together with students at the same level, doing the same activity as students at a higher level but using either a different story or a different telling of the same story. The multiple story scramble (see the example on pages 40–41) has the advantage of making it look as if all of the students are working on the same activity, when for most of it they are actually working at different levels.

Activities that can be used in this way
Multiple story scramble: Each story can be at a different level; see pages 40–41 for examples.
Independent writing activities: Students can write stories at different levels; see page 153.
Drama: Give each group a story to convert to a skit and then have the group present the skit to the rest of the class; see page 212. Every group can have a story at a different level. You could also create a skit for the lowest level so they would just have to focus on understanding and presenting it, but higher levels would convert a story to a skit and prepare to present it; see pages 206 and 212.
Multipart story drama: Divide one story into several parts, but tell each part at a different level; see page 217.

Different levels get different stories (or parts of stories) and work in mixed-level groups to complete a cooperative activity

For this approach, each student receives a different text or part of a text that is needed for a common goal; the student needs to understand and communicate the information to the rest of the group. (This is called an *information gap*.) For the multilevel classroom, create these different parts so they are written at different levels but still leave students with a similar amount of information to share. This creates a good opportunity for peer assistance between students of different levels. An example is shown on page 42.

Activities that can be used in this way

Compare/contrast: Give shorter and more simply written variants to lower-level students and longer, more difficult variants to higher-level students. See pages 262–263.

Jigsaw activity with different levels of material: Give different lengths and/or different levels of materials to different group members, so that each is reading and presenting material at his or her own level while still working with students of other levels. See pages 42 and 117.

Creating self-access materials for the multilevel class

Self-access materials are materials that students can do and evaluate independently. Students have a fixed amount of time (perhaps 30 minutes to an hour) during which they can choose from any of half a dozen or more activities. For example, they might have the choice of listening to a tape and doing a strip story, doing concentration matching cards based on a story, reading a story and doing a crossword puzzle, doing a grammar exercise, or creating an original story. For each, answer keys should be provided so students can evaluate their own work. For example, if a student chooses a strip story, the answer key would show the strips in the right order so that he or she can check his or her own work. This gives students immediate feedback and also saves the teacher from having a pile of extra work to correct.

Note that doing the activities independently does not necessarily mean that students will work individually; while some activities might be set up for students to do singly (like reading a story or doing a crossword puzzle), others might be set up for pairs or small groups (for example, a strip story or concentration matching cards). Since students are in control of what they choose, if an activity requires pairs, the student who wants to do it must find someone to do it with him.

Note also that "independent" does not mean free from teacher supervision and input. You might ask students to keep a log of which activities they did and what problems they encountered. You might also have a folder for each student to keep his or her work in, and then quickly review it every few weeks. You might even recommend to students that they choose a particular type of activity if they need work in a particular area. And, of course, you should be circulating while students work on the activities to provide help as needed.

In the multilevel classroom, the key is to create activities at a variety of levels so that all students have a few choices at their level. For example, with concentration matching cards (see page 182), you might have a beginning set where students match concrete vocabulary to pictures, a low-intermediate set where students match synonyms or antonyms, and an intermediate set where students match sentence halves. If students wanted to do this activity, they would choose the set at the appropriate level. (Find some way of marking how difficult the activities are to help students identify appropriate materials.) Many of the activities in this book can be set up as self-access materials on a variety of levels. For example:

Listening: Record various stories on tape and provide a tape player. (Try to get different readers if possible so students can practice listening to people other than you.) Have students listen to a tape and complete a picture sorting activity (see page 54), a strip story (see page 102), a timeline (see page 72), or an outline of the text's structure (see page 225). They could also mark the story's events on a map (see page 63), use concentration matching cards, or do other activities.

Reading: Have stories available for students to read. Students can then complete comprehension questions, do crossword puzzles (see page 196), create timelines (see page 72), mark events on a map (see page 63), create outlines of text structure (see page 225), complete problem/solution (see page 236) or cause/effect charts (see page 242), or write summaries (see page 251). You can also have variants of stories available and have students do comparison/contrast activities (see page 255).

Speaking: Create jigsaw stories with three or four parts; see page 117. Put the parts in an envelope and have students who want to work together each take a part, read it, and then work together to re-create it. You might have students make an outline while re-creating the story and then compare it to an outline that you have prepared to check their work.

A multilevel multiple-story scramble
(see page 126)

The stories here are *The Man and His Two Wives* (adapted from Aesop), *Poor Fish* [a Jewish tale, loosely retold based on a version in *A Treasury of Jewish Folklore* (Crown, 1948)], and *The Woodcutter's Axe* (a common Asian tale which also occurs in Aesop as *Mercury and the Woodman*).

Once a man had two wives. One wife was older than the man, and the other was younger.

The man's hair was starting to turn gray. His younger wife did not like this. It made him look too old. So every morning she combed his hair and pulled out all the white ones.

A fish dealer once put out a sign that read, "Fresh Fish Sold Here."

A customer came in and said, "Why did you put the word 'fresh' on your sign? It is understood that your fish are fresh – or are yours rotten?"

"Of course not!" answered the fish dealer, and quickly he painted out the word 'Fresh' from his sign.

A little while later another customer came in. "Why do you need the word 'here' on your sign? How could you be selling them somewhere else?"

Once a kind woodcutter went to the mountains every day to cut firewood. One day, while cutting wood, his axe slipped and fell into a pond.

He began to weep because it was his only axe and he needed it to support his family. Just then a spirit rose out of the pond. "Why are you weeping?" it asked.

He answered, "I lost my axe in the pond."

The spirit went down and returned with a golden axe. "Is this yours?" it asked.

"No," answered the man. " Mine was an old iron one."

The spirit went down again and returned with a silver axe. "Is this yours?" it asked.

"No," answered the man. So the spirit went down again and returned with the woodcutter's old iron axe.

"Yes," answered the woodcutter, his face brightening. "That one is mine."

Then the spirit said, "The golden and silver axes are now also yours. I give them to you as a gift for your honesty."

Without communicating to students how you are passing the squares out, give each of the lowest-level students one of the squares on the top. Give intermediate students one of the squares in the middle. Give the highest-level students one of the squares from the bottom. This lets all of the students participate in the same activity while each works at his or her own level.

The older wife liked the man's gray hair. She wanted him to look old. She didn't want people to think she was his mother. So every night she pulled out some of his black hairs.

Soon the man found that he had no hair at all; he was completely bald.

"You're right," agreed the fish dealer, and quickly he painted out the word 'Here.'

Soon another customer came in. "Why," he asked, "do you have the word 'sold' on your sign? Only a fool would think you were giving them away."

"That's true," agreed the fish dealer, and so he painted out the word 'sold'.

Not long after, an old woman came in. "Why do you have the word 'Fish' on your sign? Do you think we cannot smell? Everyone can tell that it is fish that you have."

So the fish dealer sighed, and picked up his brush, and painted out the word 'Fish.'

Soon a rich man heard the rumor of how the woodcutter had gotten the gold and silver axes. He was wicked and greedy, so he bought a cheap old axe and headed off to the pond. He started to cut some wood and then threw his axe in the pond and began to weep loudly.

The spirit appeared from the water and asked, "Why are you weeping?"

He answered, "I lost my axe in the pond."

The spirit went down and returned with the iron axe. "Is this one yours?"

"No," said the man. "Mine was golden."

The spirit returned with a silver axe. "Is this one yours?"

"No," answered the man again. "Mine was golden."

The spirit appeared again holding a golden axe. "Yes," cried the greedy man. "That is my axe."

"You are a liar," said the spirit. "I will not give you any of them."

The man leapt into the water and snatched the golden axe from the spirit, but the weight of it pulled him to the bottom. Since he would not let go, he drowned.

Cooperative activity with texts
of different levels for *Hungbu and Nolbu*

Notice the different levels of difficulty of the four parts of this jigsaw story. Notice also that the first part is the easiest; this is an extra help for the lower-level student, since it is easier to start at the beginning than to pick up in the middle.

1 Once there were two brothers, Hungbu and Nolbu. Nolbu was older; Hungbu was younger. Nolbu was often mean, but Hungbu was very kind.

When their father died, Nolbu took all of their father's money and land. He didn't give Hungbu anything. Instead, he sent Hungbu and his family away.

So Hungbu and his wife and their children left. They had only their clothes and a few other things they could carry. They found an empty house, and they stayed there. But it was winter and they had no food. So Hungbu went back and begged for some food from Nolbu. But Nolbu and his wife would not give him anything. Hungbu went back home. His family was very hungry all winter.

2 In the springtime, Hungbu found a swallow with a broken leg. He brought it home and cared for the bird carefully until it had healed. Soon the swallow flew off, but it returned shortly after with a few seeds in its beak. Hungbu took the seeds and thanked the bird. Then he planted them in his garden.

Over the next few months the seeds grew. By the end of the summer, several large gourds had grown and ripened. When Hungbu went to pick them, they burst open on their own. Gold and jewels and fine clothes spilled out of one of them. From another came a horse and carriage. Soon Hungbu and his family had everything they ever could have wanted.

3 Rumor of Hungbu's great fortune spread, and soon Nolbu heard about it as well. Nolbu scowled, furious that this good fortune had come to his brother instead of to him. Nolbu went and demanded that Hungbu tell him how he came by all this wealth. Hungbu revealed everything that had happened to his brother. Then Nolbu went home, and since he was very greedy, he kept thinking about how he too could get greater riches.

Nolbu looked for an injured swallow, but he could not find one. So he hunted for a swallow and at last caught one. Then he broke its leg and dropped it in a box. After this, he cared for it, though rather poorly. Still, the swallow managed to heal itself, and once better, it too flew away. After a few days, the swallow returned, bearing a few seeds in its beak.

**Cooperative activity with texts
of different levels (continued)**

---

4 Nolbu took the seeds without a word of thanks, and planted them in this garden. Gourds began to grow, and Nolbu hungered for the riches he would gain. He could not sleep at night as thoughts of great wealth burned in his mind. At last, though they were not quite ripe, Nolbu impatiently took a knife and went out to cut them. As his knife pierced the gourds, they exploded. Filth and slime flooded out of the first, covering Nolbu and his wife and all their property. Evil spirits rushed shrieking out of another; they began beating Nolbu and his wife. The spirits also shattered their treasures and destroyed their house and uprooted their crops, leaving them with nothing.

Nolbu went begging in the village for something to eat, but everyone knew of his stinginess and cruelty, so no one would give even the smallest scrap of food. Finally Nolbu went to his brother Hungbu's house and begged for a bite to eat. Hungbu and his wife welcomed Nolbu and shared generously with them. Nolbu saw how evil he had been and begged Hungbu for forgiveness, which Hungbu granted. And so, from that day on, Nolbu's heart was changed, and their families lived happily together for many years.

Writing: Let students choose to write individually or in parts using any of the writing activities in Chapter 8 starting on page 153. (Students can't really self-correct their writing, but you can have students work in pairs or small groups if they choose a writing activity, so they can do peer review.)

Creating self-access materials typically requires a fair amount of work initially, but once they are created, they can be reused with other classes. Further discussion of the creation and use of self-access materials is beyond the scope of this book; see *Self-Access* (Sheering, 1989) or *Self-Instruction in Language Learning* (Dickinson, 1987) for suggestions and ideas.

Conclusion

The approaches to the multilevel classroom presented in this chapter do require some extra work on the teacher's part, but they keep it to a manageable level. They also leave the teacher free to interact with all of the students during the individual or group work activities, and they keep the class feeling like a unified unit – without creating strong segregation between students at different levels – while still providing appropriately challenging work for all students. The multilevel classroom remains a challenge, but a much more exciting and workable challenge – one that we have a reasonable hope of meeting.

II The activities

4   Focus on listening

Calling this chapter *Focus on Listening* is in one sense misleading, since most of the activities in this book involve listening. But in another sense, it is helpful because these activities can be done basically with only listening; they provide a way for students to actively respond to the listening, but with little or no speaking, reading, or writing. This can be helpful for beginners, since students may understand before they are able to produce, and many students seem to prefer a silent period during the early stages of language learning.

Discussion of story pictures

Class level: Low-beginner to low-intermediate
Group size(s): Whole class
Objective(s): To build vocabulary and to prepare students to listen to
    or read a story (i.e., a prereading or prelistening activity) or to give
    them material so they can tell a story
Approximate class time: 15 to 30 minutes

The activity

1. **Pick an illustrated folktale with pictures that are suitable for your students.**
2. **Show each picture and talk about it – the various objects in it and what appears to be going on.** The goal is not to tell the story but to introduce students to the language needed to tell it. Target comments to the highest and lowest students as well as to those in the middle. Also invite students to talk about the pictures; this is a good way to find out what they know and to let them learn from each other. In a multilevel class, use different levels of questions to involve each student at an appropriate level. For example, look at the picture below.

Does he look happy? (Yes/no; very easy; almost no production required.)
Is the mountain beautiful or ugly? (Multiple choice; fairly easy; can be answered with a single word from the question.)
What is this? What is he doing? (Short factual answer; moderately easy; requires productive knowledge of vocabulary.)
Why is he here? (Opinion question; more difficult; probably requires at least several words.)
What do you think will happen? (Opinion with conjecture; more difficult; requires more thought and probably more language.)

Follow-up

After using this activity to introduce students to the language needed for the story, read or tell the story or have students read it themselves. (When discussing the pictures, you might want to skip the last few pictures so that some surprise remains when students get to the end.)

Another option is to have students tell what they think the story is, based on the pictures. Some sets of pictures are more obvious than others. Again, if you leave out the last few pictures, there is more room for creativity and guessing for the students.

Stories to use with this activity

Any story with interesting pictures is great. Since you are not actually reading it, as long as the basic story line is accessible, it doesn't matter if the text is appropriate for the students (unless you plan to have them read it themselves afterward). Some published folktales that have pictures that are particularly good for talking about are included in the *Bibliography* under *Illustrated picture books and folktales that are good for beginning students*.

Oral reading with comments on the pictures

Class level: Beginner to low-intermediate
Group size(s): Whole class
Objective(s): To provide input students can understand, expand
    vocabulary, and also help students see that English can be fun. One
    can also work in some grammar review or begin to relate stories to
    real life.
Approximate class time: 15 to 30 minutes (depending on length of
    story and amount of elaboration)

The activity

CREATING THE ACTIVITY

1. **Select a story with a limited amount of text and good pictures.** (If you
   try to elaborate much on the pictures in a story with a lot of text, the
   activity tends to drag and students lose interest.)
2. **Review the text and pictures, looking for ideas on which you can
   provide additional comments and/or from which you can develop
   tangents to provide extra language input that students can understand.** The vocabulary and ideas on which you provide additional
   comments should be based on your students' needs. Make sure you
   plan elaborations directed at all levels of students in your class. For
   example, for the picture on page 51, very low-level students might just
   need to connect "fish" and "boat" with the objects they represent,
   but to get new language, higher-level students might need some talk
   about the nets, oars, and anchor; the boat rocking and drifting; and
   so on.
3. **Look for examples of grammatical points that you have been working
   on or that your students have trouble with and plan ways by which
   you can briefly draw attention to these points.** I stress *briefly:* You
   want students to notice the structures but without disrupting the flow
   of the story.

USING THE ACTIVITY

1. **Read the text aloud, elaborating on appropriate items and repeating
   and rephrasing the text as you go along.** For example, using the
   picture on page 51, you might say something like:

   . . . and they fished together from the same boat. See the fish . . . [point to
   fish] . . . and the boat [point]. . . . They fished together from the same
   boat. . . . Look. Fished. [point to word] -ed ending. Why? . . . Right, past
   tense. . . . It happened before now. . . . They fish*ed* together in the same

boat. So, there they are fishing together in one boat . . . a rowboat [mime action of rowing]. . . . Do you see the oars? And it looks like the waves are rocking [rock yourself from side to side] the boat a little . . . and they're pulling [mime action] in their fishnets and putting the fish on the bottom of the boat. . . . And there's a rope and anchor here on this end; the anchor is to keep the boat from drifting while they are fishing. . . . Anyway, they fished together from the same boat. . . .

This includes the text on the page and also repeats and rewords it. Combined with pointing to the pictures and gestures, this helps the lowest-level students understand the story more clearly, while at the same time it gives more advanced students more difficult vocabulary and other grammatical forms (here, a number of -*ing* forms, etc.), and gives all of the students much more language input than if you just read the text. Notice also that attention was briefly drawn to a grammatical point (regular past) without disrupting the flow of the story.

2. **As appropriate, include questions to get students to talk about the picture themselves, to relate the story to life, and to predict what is coming.** (This reviews what they already know, provides opportunity to learn from peers, maintains a focus on meaning, and helps students relate the language to what they know.)

And they fished together from the same boat.

What do you see in this picture? Yes, a boat. . . . And what are they doing in the boat? Right, fishing! And what do they have in the boat?

Nam, do you like fishing? . . . Shin, have you ever been in a boat? . . . A big boat or a small boat? . . . How do people fish in Vietnam? . . .

What will they do with the fish? . . . Sell it or eat it? What do you think they will find in the net? [after a guess or two, you may want to remind them of the title: *Hidden Treasure*].

Comments on choosing the right questions for students at different levels are included on page 49.

Note that I have provided rather too much expansion here for a single picture; if you talk this much about one picture, you risk losing the momentum of the story. I provided an excessive amount of elaboration to illustrate the variety of ways that you could expand on and take off from the text; you would focus your extra input based on your goals and your students' needs.

Stories to use with this activity

Any story with limited text (so beginners can understand it and so it doesn't take too long to make it through the story) and that has interesting pictures is great. A few that I have used successfully are included in the *Bibliography* under *Illustrated picture books and folktales that are good for beginning students.*

Drawing pictures based on a story

Class level: Beginner to low-intermediate
Group size(s):   Whole class
Objective(s): To provide input students can understand and provide a
   nonverbal way to respond
Approximate class time: 15 minutes plus the time to tell the story
Notes: This activity is primarily suitable for children

The activity

1. **Pick any story with lots of concrete action and orally tell it.**
2. **After you have told the story, ask students to illustrate their favorite scene.** If you are working on writing, also ask them to write a caption for the picture or a summary of the scene in the story.
3. **While the students are drawing, walk around the class and get students to talk to you about what they are drawing.** This provides an opportunity for them to use some of the language they just heard in a nonthreatening, one-on-one context.
4. **When students are done, have them show their pictures to the rest of the class.** You can have them say a brief sentence about the scene they chose to illustrate.

Variation

After students have drawn their pictures but before they have shown them to the rest of the class, have the class order themselves based on where their picture fits in the story. For example, they might form a semicircular line; students who illustrated scenes from the beginning of the story would be at one end of the line, and students who illustrated scenes from the end of the story would be at the other end of the line, with others lined up appropriately ordered in between. This generates some language output and requires students to review the sequence of events from the story.

Picture-sorting listening activity

Class level: Beginner to low-intermediate
Group size(s): Small groups, pairs, individuals
Objective(s): To provide a context for students to be able to
  demonstrate listening comprehension without being required to
  speak
Approximate class time: 15 to 30 minutes
Notes: Good activity to introduce or review sequential connectors like
  first, second, next, then, after that, and *finally*

The activity

Ordering pictures demonstrates understanding without requiring students to read, speak, or write. This helps beginning students who still can't produce much.

CREATING THE ACTIVITY

1. **After picking an appropriate story, draw five to seven pictures based on the story.** Make sure they have enough distinctive elements so that listeners can put them in the right order after listening to the story. Put them in scrambled order on a single page. Stick pictures are OK; the pictures don't need to be beautiful, only recognizable.

   If you can't draw, photocopy pictures from an illustrated book (reducing them so they will all fit on one page), or use the variation below that involves students in the drawing process.

   For high-beginners and up, you can also create a caption for each picture. Scramble these as well.
2. **Make copies of the pictures for each individual or group.** If resources are limited, put the pictures on an overhead, or draw them on the board.

   Variation: dictate instructions for simple pictures so students draw their own. This provides an excellent context for preteaching vocabulary and other language needed for the story. See page 63 for an example of this variation used with another activity.

USING THE ACTIVITY

1. **Give out the pictures, have students look at them, and ask if there are any questions.** If needed, talk about the items and actions in the pictures, providing prelistening preparation for the language in the story.

2. (*Optional*) In small groups, have students predict what the story will be about and what order the pictures should go in. This helps further prepare them for what they are about to hear.
3. Read or tell the story.
4. After the reading is done, have students put the pictures in the right order.
5. If you provided captions for the pictures, have students associate each caption with the corresponding picture. For slightly more advanced students, instead of giving them captions, have them write their own captions for the pictures.
6. **Review if needed.** Summarize the story, pointing to the appropriate pictures at the right time, or get students to tell the story back to you and the rest of the class, showing the pictures in the right order.

Variations

VARIATION I: HAVING STUDENTS CREATE THE MATERIALS
FOR OTHER GROUPS

This is more advanced than the basic activity presented above.

1. **Divide students into groups and give each group a different story.** For a listening focus, have students listen to a tape of the story. For a reading focus, have them read the story.
2. **After reading or listening to the story, have each group plan and create five to seven pictures based on their story.** Each group member would draw one or two of the pictures. This can be done on the board if desired.
3. **Copy the pictures if needed, and then give the pictures to one or more other groups.** If copying is needed, you may want to split the activity over two days, having students create the pictures one day and doing the sorting part the next.
4. **Have students in the other groups listen to the story and try to put the pictures in the right order as in the main activity.** Listening to the stories on tape lets all groups continue to work simultaneously. You could also read each story to all of the groups, or have a reader from the group that created the pictures read to the group sorting the pictures.

VARIATION 2: CREATING STORIES BASED ON THE PICTURES

Either individually or in groups, give out the pictures without telling the story or indicating the correct order. Have students create stories (either oral or written) to go with the pictures. Then have them share their stories with the rest of the class. Then tell the real story. Students would then listen to see which story(s) were closest to the "real" story.

VARIATION 3: CREATING SELF-ACCESS MATERIALS

Record the story on tape so students can do the activity on their own. Students can listen to the tape, order the pictures, and then check their own answers. If the pictures are taken from a relatively easy book, students can check their answers by looking through the book; this gets them to review the language in the story and helps connect spoken and written forms. If the book is unavailable or if students don't have the skills to deal with that much written text yet, provide an answer page. If students made mistakes, they can be encouraged to listen to the tape again.

In the multilevel classroom

Give different levels different sets of pictures. For beginners, use pictures that are very different from each other; this makes the activity easier, because students can order them even if they understand only part of what you say. For higher levels, choose pictures that have more similarities to each other or that could almost fit with a few parts of the story, so students must understand more to be sure they have the right order.

You can also generate nine or ten pictures for the story and give five of the pictures with the most obvious differences to the lowest-level students, seven or eight to the middle level, and all of them to the highest level. (For example, for *The Lost Son,* on page 60, give all the pictures to the intermediate students, give only A–G to low-intermediate students, and give only A–E to the high-beginners. Note that the last three pictures have the greatest number of similarities; to sequence them requires the most accurate listening.) Put the harder pictures at the bottom of the page; this lets you create one set of materials and then just cut off the bottom of the page for the beginners. This way the beginners are still working with sequential numbers or letters, and it is easy to keep track of which set is for which group.

Another option for the highest level is to throw in a few pictures that don't fit with the story; it requires much more complete understanding to be sure that something wasn't mentioned.

Still another option is for the lower group to just order the pictures, while the higher group orders the pictures and writes captions for them.

Stories to use with this activity

Any story at the right level that you can draw or find pictures for works well for this activity. Many fables are good, because they are quite short and fairly simple, and the animals and scenes in them are not too hard to represent with simple pictures. In addition to the stories discussed here, some other stories to use in this book include:

Salem and the Nail	see page 104
The Greedy Old Spider	see page 75
The Boy and the North Wind	see page 238
Mother Holly	see page 149
The Fourth Question	see page 68
Goldilocks and the Three Bears	see page 185
The King and the Baby	see page 113
The Man Who Kept House	see page 244
The Wise Judge	see page 221
Amin and the Eggs	see page 147

Resources

Frank Schaffer Publications (1028 Via Mirabel, Palos Verdes Estates, CA 90274, 1-800-421-5565) offers a set of reproducible black-line drawings for sequencing fairy tales. These pictures are most suitable for children.

High-beginner

The Dog and the Meat

Once a dog got a piece of meat. He was carrying it home in his mouth so he could eat it there. On the way home he came to a bridge over a river. As he crossed the bridge, he looked down into the water. In the river, he saw another dog with a piece of meat. He wanted that meat too, so he tried to bite the other dog. But when he opened his mouth, his meat fell into the water with a splash and was gone. And so he went home with nothing.

Notes on the Story
This story is adapted from a tale by Aesop.

**A beginning-level picture-sorting activity
for *The Dog and the Meat* (see page 57)**

The dog went home with nothing.	The meat fell in the water.
The dog came to a bridge.	The dog tried to take the other dog's meat.
Once a dog had some meat.	The dog saw another dog in the water.

A high-beginner/low-intermediate picture-sorting activity for
The Man, the Boy, and the Donkey
(see page 66)

An intermediate (potentially multilevel) picture-sorting activity for *The Lost Son* (see page 61)

The Lost Son

Once a father had two sons. The younger son came to his father and said, "Father, give me my half of your money. So the father gave half to the older son, and half to the younger son.

The younger son took his money and went far away. He wasted his money on wild parties. When the money was all gone, all his friends left him. He had no food. He had no shoes. He was alone in a foreign country. He got a job feeding pigs, but he was still hungry. He was so hungry, he wanted the pigs' food, but he couldn't eat it. No one would give him anything.

Then he remembered his father. He thought, "The men who work for my father have plenty of food. I will go home to my father. I will say to him, 'Father, I have done what was wrong. I am not good enough to be your son. But please give me a job and let me work for you.'" Then he started walking home.

He walked for many days. When he was still far away, his father saw him coming. The father ran to meet his son on the road and threw his arms around him and kissed him.

"Father," said the son, "I have done what was wrong. I am not good enough to be your son. But please give me a job and let me work for you."

"Hurry," said the father to the servants, "Bring the best robe and put it on him. Put a ring on his finger. Put shoes on his feet. Kill the fat calf and let's have a party. For my son was dead, but now he is alive. So they began to have a big party.

Now the older brother was working out in the field. He heard music and saw people dancing. He asked, "Why is there music? Why are people dancing?"

They answered, "Your brother has come home, and your father killed the fat calf because he is so happy."

Then the older brother was angry and would not go into the house. His father went out and said, "Please come in!"

The older son answered, "For many years I have worked hard, but you never give me anything for a party. Then this son of yours who spent all your money on wild living comes home and you kill the best calf for him.

continued

"My son," answered the father, "Everything I have is yours, but today we must be happy because your brother was dead but now is alive. He was lost, but now he is found."

Notes on the Story
This story is adapted from the Biblical parable of the Prodigal Son (Luke 15:11–32).

Marking a story's events on a map

Class level: High-beginner to intermediate
Group size(s): Whole class
Objective(s): To provide a context for students to be able to
demonstrate listening comprehension without being required to
speak, to provide a new context for preteaching vocabulary, and to
connect language with the life skill of map reading
Approximate class time: 10 to 15 minutes plus time to tell the story

The activity

PREPARATION

Make a simple map showing the key places in the story. (A map with
both simple pictures and written descriptions of the places is most useful
for helping teach new vocabulary, pictures without any text force
students to remember what the different items are, and a map with only
text is easiest to create if you can't draw well. A sample of each is
provided – see pages 67 and 71.) Put some places on the map that aren't
in the story; choose items or places that you want to review from previous
stories. Make a copy for each student, or draw a map on the board or
display it on an overhead and have students copy it by hand. You could
also make the creation of the map an extra listening activity: Dictate the
locations of the various items on the map while students try to create a
map from your instructions. For example, to create a map for *Mother
Holly* (see page 149) you might give instructions something like this:

OK. Now I want you to draw a map. In the middle of the bottom of the page,
I want you to draw a house. . . . Don't make it too big because we need to
leave room for the other places on the map. Now you should have a house
near the bottom of the page, and I want you to draw a wall with a door
behind the house. On the right side of the house, I want you to draw a well.
Now draw another house near the top left corner of the page. In the middle of
the page I want you to draw a meadow with grass and flowers. Put an oven to
the right of the meadow. In the top right corner of the page draw an apple
tree, and then put some apples on the tree and a basket under the tree. And the
name of the story we are going to hear is Mother Holly, so write "Mother
Holly" across the top of the page.

Your instructions would likely include more repetition and also
explanations of any new vocabulary. (For example, I would not expect
students at the right level for this activity to know "well," "meadow,"
etc.) You might also add some nonessential items to review other recent
vocabulary. For example, if students had recently been introduced to

these words, you could add a bucket and a rope by the well, or a forest to the left of the meadow. These items are not needed for the story, but if you can make them fit on the map, they provide good review. In addition to drawing the pictures, you could also have students write the names of the various items to associate the written words with the items.

Having students create their own maps provides a good opportunity to preteach vocabulary. If you do have students make their own maps, make sure that you show them a "good" map to check this first activity, because the main activity may be impossible if they don't have a valid map to work with.

USING THE ACTIVITY

1. **If necessary, talk about the items on the map.** This provides a good context to preteach key vocabulary like "mountains," "river," "village," "bridge," or whatever else is represented.
2. **Explain to students that they should mark the events of the story on the map.** For the lowest levels, this might be a line tracing the main character's path to the different places. It could also involve putting a number on the map in each place the main character goes, that is, writing a "1" in the first place the main character went, "2" in the second place, and so on. You could ask more advanced students to write a short description of what happened at each place. (For beginning students, this is one of those activities that is harder to explain than to do. If necessary, demonstrate what you want the students to do using a different story, or help students with the first few places until they get the idea.)
3. **Tell the story orally** (or have students listen to it on tape in a language lab or read it for homework). Students should mark their maps during the telling.
4. **Retell the story, marking the events on a map on the board or overhead.** This adds a built-in review while also letting students check that they understood the story correctly. You might also have one or more students retell the story and/or mark the events on the map for the rest of the class while you retell it.

Variations

Variation 1: Instead of providing students with a map, tell the story and have them create a map based on the story. Then compare the different versions.

Variation 2: Create self-access materials. Record the story on tape or have students read the story, and then have them do this activity.

Provide a completed map for students to check their work. See page 38 for more on creating self-access materials.

Stories to use with this activity

This activity works well with any story that takes place in a number of locations. Some examples in this book are

The Greedy Old Spider	see page 75
The Boy Who Went to the North Wind	see page 238
The Fourth Question	see page 68
The Princess's Suitors	see page 122
The Wise Judge	see page 221
Goldilocks	see page 185

Notice that the last of these stories (*Goldilocks*) doesn't fit with a map per se, but the events happen in multiple places that can be represented visually (in this case, a floor plan of the house with different furniture items marked).

The Man, the Boy, and the Donkey

One morning, a man and his son left their house and started walking toward town. They walked along next to their donkey. A man passed them. He said, "You are fools. A donkey is to ride on. Why are you walking?"

So the man put the boy on the donkey. They went on down the road. Soon they passed a group of men. One man said: "See that lazy boy. He rides on the donkey while his old father walks."

So the man said to the boy, "Get off." Then he got on the donkey. They walked a little more. Soon they passed two women. One women said, "See that lazy man. He rides on the donkey while his young son walks."

The man didn't know what to do. At last he picked the boy up and put him on the donkey. Then he sat on the donkey behind the boy. Soon they came to the town. Some people pointed at them and said, "See that man and boy. The donkey is small and the man and boy are both big. They are too heavy. The poor donkey . . . they are very mean."

The man and boy got off the donkey. They cut a pole. Then they tied the donkey's feet to it. Then they put the pole on their shoulders and carried the donkey between them. They went along down the road. Everyone who saw them laughed. They walked until they got to the Market Bridge. Then the donkey got one foot loose. The donkey began to kick. The boy dropped his end of the pole. The donkey fell off the edge of the bridge and into the water. Since his feet were tied, he drowned.

An old man had followed them the whole way. "That will teach you," said the man. "If you listen to everyone, you will have trouble and no one will be happy."

Notes on the Story
This story is also especially good for work on spacial vocabulary (*toward, next to, on, off, behind, on the edge of*, etc.).

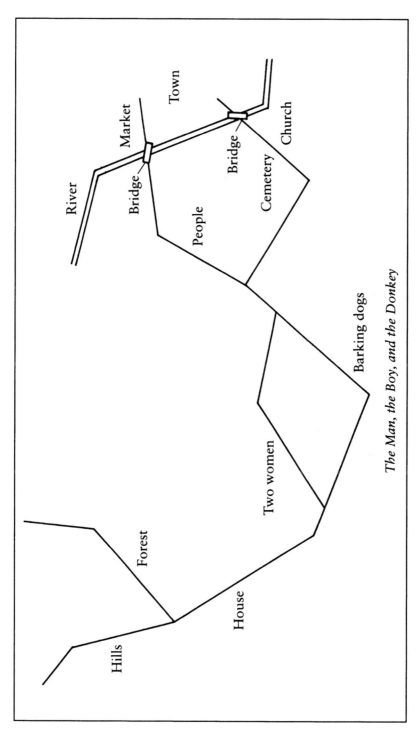

The Man, the Boy, and the Donkey

A map for high-beginner/low-intermediate students.

The Fourth Question

Once a young man lived with his elderly mother. He always worked very hard, but he was still always poor. Finally he decided to find the wise man who lived on top of the holy mountain. So he asked a friend to look after his mother and then set out.

At the end of the day, he came to a cottage. "Please," he said to the old woman who lived there, "I am going to the holy mountain to see the wise man. Do you have a place where I could sleep for the night?"

So the woman brought food and laid a mat on the floor for him to sleep. She also asked, "Would you please also ask the wise man a question for me? My daughter, Peach Blossom, no longer smiles or laughs. Promise me you will ask him what will make her smile again."

"I promise," he answered.

After journeying for some days, the young man came to a town. The people there also begged him to ask the wise man a question. "The great tree in the center of our town once bore lovely flowers, but now it bears none. Please ask why this is so."

"I will," he promised.

At length, the young man came to the holy mountain, but a great river blocked his way. The current was strong. He was afraid he would be swept away if he tried to swim.

"How can I ask the wise man my question if I cannot cross?" he said aloud.

Now a dragon there heard him, and it spoke to him: "I have always lived a good life and done what was right," said the dragon, "but I am unable to fly up into heaven. If you will ask why I can't fly up to heaven, I will carry you across."

"I will ask this for you," answered the young man. So the dragon carried him across the river.

Soon, the young man thought, he would know why it was that he always worked so hard but was still poor. He found the wise man and humbly bowed.

"How may I help you, my son?" asked the wise man.

"I have journeyed far," began the young man, "and I have four questions to ask you."

"Wait," said the wise man. "The rule of the mountain is that you may ask only three questions. Think wisely and well, and then choose which three you want to ask."

The young man was troubled. He had promised the old woman and the townspeople that he would ask their questions. And he had agreed to ask the dragon's question in exchange for a ride, and he had already taken the ride. Yet his own question was the whole reason for his journey. He thought and thought, but at last he realized he could not break his word.

"Very well," said the young man to the wise man. "There is an old woman whose daughter is named Peach Blossom. This daughter no longer smiles or laughs. What can be done to make her smile again?"

"The girl," said the old man, "will smile again when she meets her husband."

"Thank you," said the young man. "Second, there is a town with a great and beautiful tree in the center. For many years it bore the most beautiful flowers, but now it bears none. What can be done?"

The old man answered, "Several bags of gold are buried by the tree's roots. Have the people remove these bags and the tree will blossom once again."

"Thank you," said the young man. "Lastly, the dragon by the river at the bottom of this mountain says he has always lived a good life, but he cannot fly up into heaven. He wants to know what he must do."

"The dragon wears a great pearl on his forehead," answered the wise man. "Earthly riches cannot be taken into heaven. If he takes this pearl off, he will be able to fly up into heaven."

The young man bowed in thanks, and headed back down the mountain. When he came to the river at the bottom, he found the dragon waiting for him.

"Did you ask the wise man my question?" asked the dragon.

"Yes," answered the young man, "but you must carry me back to the other side before I tell you. Otherwise you will fly up to heaven and I will have no way to get home." So the dragon carried him to the other side, and the young man told him that he must leave behind the pearl on his forehead.

"Why, that is easily done," said the dragon. "I will give it to you. Keep it well, for it brings good luck to the one who has it."

continued

He gave the pearl to the young man and flew up into the heavens.

The young man took the pearl and continued on his way. At length he came to the village where the great tree grew. When the people saw him coming, they ran to meet him. "Did you ask the wise man our question?" they asked.

"Yes," answered the young man. "You must dig around the tree's roots. Bags of gold there are preventing the tree from blooming." The people dug around the tree and found the gold. In thankfulness, they gave him a large bag of gold.

So the young man took the gold and continued homeward. At last he came to the old woman's house. "Did you ask the wise man my question?" she asked.

"Yes," he answered. "The wise man said your daughter will smile again on the day that she meets her husband." Just then a beautiful young woman came from the other room. Seeing the young man, she suddenly smiled.

The old woman smiled too. "Daughter, meet your husband." And so it was not long before they were married.

Now, with wife and gold and pearl, the young man returned home to care for his mother. He continued to work hard, and also to care for others, and he was never poor again.

The Fourth Question

A map for intermediate students.

▒▒▒▒ Completing a timeline

Class level: High-beginner to advanced
Group size(s): Whole class
Objective(s): That students improve their listening skills while writing
    down key points (summarizing, note taking)
Approximatge class time: 15 to 30 minutes

The activity

1. **Show students what a timeline is by completing one on the board.**
    Creating one for a story used in an earlier class provides good review.
    Sometimes I also create a timeline on the board based on the life of
    one of the students. I ask, "When were you born? When did you start
    school?" and so on, and write the dates and information in the
    appropriate places on the line like this:

2. **If the story is at the edge of the students' abilities, give them a partially
    completed timeline (see page 74) or write some of the phrases they
    will need on the board.** This provides a good context in which to
    preteach vocabulary.

3. **Read or tell the story; the students should fill in the timeline during the telling.** For a difficult story, you might tell it twice; ask students to just listen the first time and complete the timeline the second time.

   To help students get started, you might pause early in the story and write the first few events on a timeline on the board to make sure they understand what they should be doing:

4. **When the story is done, ask students to tell you what they have on their timelines and use this information to complete a timeline on the board.** If students had trouble with parts of the story, retell some or all of the story as you fill in the timeline.

Notes

A timeline is really a time-ordered summary that is written across the page rather than as a list or in paragraph format. For students with academic goals, you might talk about how a timeline is similar to summarizing and note taking. For these students, you may also want to talk about the difference between primary and secondary points; see the evaluating activity on page 251.

Variations

Variation 1: Have students complete timelines for stories they have read individually; this confirms that they have understood what they read and provides summarizing practice.

Variation 2: Self-access materials. Record the story on tape or have students read the story, and provide a completed timeline so students can check their own work. See page 38 for more on self-access materials.

In the multilevel classroom

Have the most advanced students create a timeline on their own. Give students in the middle a timeline with some support, like this:

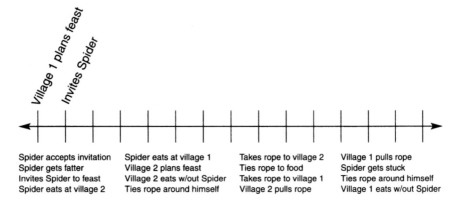

Spider accepts invitation	Spider eats at village 1	Takes rope to village 2	Village 1 pulls rope
Spider gets fatter	Village 2 plans feast	Ties rope to food	Spider gets stuck
Invites Spider to feast	Village 2 eats w/out Spider	Takes rope to village 1	Ties rope around himself
Spider eats at village 2	Ties rope around himself	Village 2 pulls rope	Village 1 eats w/out Spider

Be careful: You don't need some of the choices, and you need some more than once.

This version provides all of the language students need to complete the activity, but it is still somewhat difficult because there is too much to read it all while the story is going on; the choices at the bottom primarily help if the students are given time before the activity to prepare for what is coming, or time afterward to read through the choices and fill in the timeline then. In this example, a few extra items have been added to prevent students from completing the activity by guessing.

Give the lowest-level students a version with a great deal of support, like this:

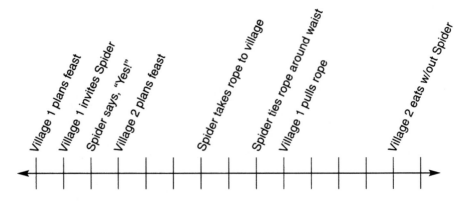

This version is the easiest: It requires students to identify only seven pieces of information, five of which are nearly identical to items that are provided.

With any of these versions, giving students time to look at them and then discussing anything they don't understand is important in helping prepare them for the listening.

Follow-up

Completing a timeline helps make sure students have a good enough understanding of the text to begin activities that look at the organizational structure of the text. (See the text structure awareness activities on page 224, the evaluating and summarizing activity on page 251, and the compare/contrast activity on page 255.)

Low-intermediate

The Greedy Old Spider

There was once a great, big, fat, greedy old spider. More than anything else, this spider liked to eat.

This greedy old spider lived in the middle of the jungle – halfway between two villages.

One day, the people in the first village decided they would have a great feast – a feast with every good kind of food they could think of. There would be fruit – papayas and mangos and oranges – and there would be rice, and greens, and chicken, and pork. The feast would be on Saturday night. Everyone in the village would be there. The people from the village also decided to invite the greedy old spider to the feast. A messenger ran along a path through the jungle until he found the old spider.

"Old Spider," said the messenger, "Please come to our feast on Saturday night. We will have every good kind of food – rice, and greens, and chicken, and pork.

"I will come," said Spider, who always loved to eat.

The people in the second village also decided to have a great feast. They also planned to have every good kind of food imaginable – fried plantains, and pounded cassava, and rice, and greens, and palm butter, and meat. The feast would be on Saturday night. Everyone in the village would be there. The people from that village also decided to invite the greedy old spider. A

continued

---

messenger ran along a path through the jungle until he found the old spider.

"Old Spider," said the messenger, "please come to our feast on Saturday night. We will have every good kind of food – plantains, and cassava, and rice, and greens, and palm butter, and meat.

"I will come," said Spider, who always loved to eat.

But now Spider had a problem. Both feasts were on the same day. He must find a way to go to both. He thought and thought. At last he had an idea.

Spider got two long, long ropes . . . long enough to reach from one village to the other. On the day of the feast, he took one rope to the first village.

"Please pull this rope when it is time for the feast," said Spider to the people in the village.

"We will," said the people. "We will pull it when the feast is ready."

Spider left one end of the rope in the village, dragging the other end to the middle of the forest. Then he went to the second village with the other rope.

"Please pull this rope when it is time for the feast," said Spider to the people in the village.

"We will," said the people. "We will pull it when the feast is ready."

Spider left one end of that rope in that village, pulling the other end behind him until he reached the middle of the forest. Then he tied both of the ropes around his belly.

"When I feel a pull on one rope," he thought, "I will run to that village and eat. I will eat until I feel a pull on the other rope. Then I will run to the other village and eat there as well."

With the ropes tied around his middle, Spider sat down to wait. He waited all through the afternoon. While he waited, he got hungrier and hungrier.

Back in the first village, the people prepared for the feast. They cooked and cooked from morning until evening. They set up tables to eat on. They got out their drums so they could dance late into the night. They set up torches to give them light. Then they remembered Spider. They pulled on the rope he gave them.

In the second village, the people also worked hard to prepare their feast. They cooked many kinds of food. They also set up tables to eat on and got out their instruments to make music with.

When all the preparations were completed, they also remembered Spider. They also pulled on the rope he gave them.

When the people in the first village saw that Spider did not come, they pulled the rope harder. When the people in the second village saw that Spider did not come, they also pulled harder. In both villages the people pulled and pulled and pulled, but still Spider did not come. "Perhaps he does not want to feast with us," they finally thought. So they started their feasts without him. They ate and ate until they could eat no more. Then they played their music and danced until they could play and dance no more.

Of course, what happened was this. Spider had felt the pull on the rope from the first village. But before he could move, he had felt a pull on the rope from the second village. He did not know what to do. Then both ropes began pulling at once. They pulled harder and harder. The knots in the ropes got tighter and tighter, and the ropes got tighter and tighter around Spider's middle.

At last the ropes had stopped pulling. But by that time, the ropes were so tight and Spider was so exhausted that he was unable to move. He fell in a heap on the ground. By the time Spider was able to struggle free from the ropes and make it to the first village, the feast had ended.

"We are so sorry," said the people when Spider arrived, "but when you did not come, we thought perhaps you had other plans. The food is all gone. There is not one grain of rice left."

Spider hurried to the second village. There too the feast had ended.

"O Spider," said the people when they saw him, "We pulled and pulled the rope, just as you told us. Why didn't you come? Alas, not a single bite is left."

And so, the greedy old spider, who hoped to have two feasts at once, instead ended up with nothing at all.

Notes on the Story

This is a West African story, retold based on a version I heard in Liberia. Spider, sometimes known as Anansi, is a common trickster in West African tales.

Note the number of spacial relational elements in this story: *in the middle, between, on the edge, around.*

5 Focus on speaking

These activities focus on getting students speaking, but many other activities in this book also involve considerable speaking. The interactive activities in Chapter 6, the drama activities in Chapter 10, and the compare/contrast activity starting on page 255 are also especially good speaking activities.

Eliciting stories from students

Class level: Beginner
Group size(s): Pairs, individuals
Objectives: To work on speaking and basic literacy skills
Approximate class time: Varies

The activity

This activity is based on the language experience approach (LEA), which assumes that students learn most effectively when they are working with materials they are attached to and interested in, and that they are most attached to and interested in materials that are about their own lives or that they have composed themselves – that is, some form of self-expression. Folktales are often an important part of people's heritage and cultural identity. This activity requires a fair amount of individual attention for each student.

1. Ask the student to tell you a story from his or her culture.
2. As the student tells the story, write it down, correcting only basic grammatical mistakes. An aide or a more advanced student can also help with this step.
3. Give the story back to the student and have him or her read it. This helps the student with beginning reading since the material is very familiar to the student.
4. Have the student revise and expand the story to work on writing.
5. If possible, publish selected stories by each student. See page 178.

Oral retelling by students

Class level: Low-beginner to high-beginner
Group size(s): Whole class
Objective(s): To review a story to help students who didn't completely
  understand and to provide an opportunity to produce language for
  those who are more advanced
Approximate class time: 10 to 15 minutes (not counting the original
  telling)

The activity

After telling a story to students (or after they have read a story), ask the
class to tell the story back to you. Especially with mixed levels, some
students can listen to a story, even with a lot of miming, sketches, and
explanation by the teacher, and still miss key parts (or the whole point).
By having students tell the story back to you, you provide one more review
for the students who didn't quite get it while at the same time providing
an opportunity to use the new language encountered in the story. It also
gives you an opportunity to find out what students understood.

1. **Tell students that you want them to tell the story back to you.** (The
   first time you do this, especially with lower levels, it may take some
   prompting before they figure out what you want.)
2. **As students tell the story back to you, write key words and phrases
   on the board;** this helps students associate oral and written forms and
   helps more visual learners. Ask questions so that all students are
   included (see page 49). Drawing simple sketches during the telling
   helps associate words with meanings for lower-level students who
   may still be missing some of what they are listening to.
3. *(Optional)* **Group students' statements by episode** (see *Building
   Awareness of Text Structure* on page 227 for an example); this begins
   to draw students' attention to the underlying structure.

This activity is most useful in contexts where it is clear that some of
the students understood the story and others didn't. This provides a
reason for students to retell: They are helping others in the class to
understand, not just repeating it for the teacher.

Because this activity can be done with basically no preparation, it can
be a nice filler if you run out of material with 10 minutes of class left, but
don't overuse it or it will become boring.

Other stories to use with this activity

This activity can be used with any story that isn't too long.

Oral telling with a repeated refrain

Class level: Beginner to low-intermediate
Group size(s): Whole class
Objective(s): To use repetition to help students remember vocabulary and other language from the story, to provide beginning opportunities to produce language, and to work on stress, rhythm, and intonation in pronunciation
Approximate class time: 15 to 40 minutes

The activity

1. **Optional: Teach about stress and rhythm first.** In syllable-timed languages like Japanese and Spanish, every syllable receives the same stress. In contrast, English is stress-timed, which means important content words are stressed while connecting words are shortened and squeezed in.
2. **Preteach essential vocabulary, especially vocabulary that is repeated.** For example, "Imagine that!" appears over and over in this telling of *Stone Soup*. Some students may not be able to figure out this expression from context, gestures, or pictures, so teach it first. Repetitions are more useful if students understand them.
3. **Begin reading or telling the story.** If practical, bring in real objects (e.g., carrots, a stone) or pictures, and point to the appropriate items to help memory and reinforce the connections between the words and the objects they represent.
4. **When you get to the first refrain, read or chant it twice, and then ask students to repeat it after you.** Clap to emphasize the rhythm. If the refrain is long, you can write either the whole refrain or key words on the board to help students until they get it. If you write the refrain, write the stressed words in large letters and the shortened words in smaller letters, like this:

So the **man** stirred the **pot** with the round yellow **onion**;
and the fine, white **flour**; and the long, red **bone**;
and the leafy, purple **cabbage**; and the long, orange **carrots**;
and the **salt** and the **pepper**; and the round, grey **stone**.

81

5. **Each time you get to the refrain, ask students to join in.** If necessary, provide a few words to get them started. For example, you might supply, "So the woman said . . ." and the students then finish, "Imagine that! Soup from a stone." Students might also join in with other repetitions, for example, the woman's "I think I have some _____."

Notes

- Because the refrain has a chanted, rhythmic quality, pay attention to where students are putting stress and how the rhythm of the language goes. You may want to exaggerate these elements in your own pronunciation.
- Since production is mostly choral rather than individual, this activity is helpful for beginners who are reluctant to speak alone.
- As stories have been passed on from person to person, they have been updated to reflect changes in language. However, because the refrains are formulaic, they tend to be preserved unchanged, so they sometimes reflect language that is no longer standard. Since our goal is to teach language that is currently useful, we must be careful in deciding whether to use such pieces as is or to adapt them. Some nonstandard items are still worth teaching. For example, "not by the hair of my chinny-chin-chin" is not exactly ordinary conversational English, but I have heard it several times in native speaker conversations when the speaker was informally conveying that there was not a chance he or she would consider a particular option. Common refrains that are part of the standard cultural upbringing need to be taught, since native speakers assume that listeners will know them.

Follow-up

This activity can be followed by having students retell the story as a class (see page 80), or retell the story in pairs with cut-out figures (see page 86).

Other stories to use with this activity

It Could Always Be Worse (see page 88). Adjust the story so it includes a refrain that begins something like this:

Oh rabbi, please help me! My house is too noisy. My children are crying; and my wife, she is shouting. It's driving me crazy.

and builds to something like this:

Oh rabbi, please help me! My house is too noisy. My children are crying; and my wife, she is shouting. The chickens are all clucking and there are feathers in our soup. The geese are all honking; the goat, it is pushing; and the cow, it is stepping on us all. It's driving me crazy.

The Gold in the Chimney (see page 269). This refrain does not build, but a nearly identical refrain is repeated eight times during the story (the only thing that changes is the creature or object being addressed).
Jack and the Beanstalk (see page 246).
The Fisherman and His Wife (see page 232).

(Low-intermediate)
Stone Soup

Once a beggar knocked on an old woman's door.

"Excuse me," said the beggar, "but could you share some of your food with me? I'm very hungry."

"I have nothing to share," said the woman. "My food is all gone."

"Well then," said the man, "I will feed you. All I need is a large pot, some water, and a stone. I will make you Stone Soup."

"Imagine that," said the woman. "Soup from a stone!" Then she went to get a pot.

The woman brought a pot of water and put it over the fire, and the man dropped in a round gray stone and began to stir.

After a little while the man tasted the soup.

"This soup is good," said the man, "but it would be better if we had some salt and pepper."

"I think I have some salt and pepper," said the woman, and she went and got some.

So the man stirred the pot with the salt and the pepper and the round, gray stone.

And the woman said, "Imagine that – soup from a stone."

After a little while the man tasted the soup again.

"This soup is tasty," said the man, "but it would be tastier if we had some carrots."

"I think I have some carrots," said the woman, and she went and got some long, orange carrots.

continued

So the man stirred the pot with the long, orange carrots; and the salt and the pepper; and the round, gray stone.

And the woman said, "Imagine that – soup from a stone."

After a little while the man tasted the soup again.

"This soup is delicious," said the man, "but it would be more delicious if we had some cabbage."

"I think I have some cabbage," said the woman, and she went and got a leafy, purple cabbage.

So the man stirred the pot with the leafy, purple cabbage; and the long, orange carrots; and the salt and the pepper; and the round, gray stone.

And the woman said, "Imagine that – soup from a stone."

After a little while the man tasted the soup again.

"This soup is hearty," said the man, "but it would be heartier if we had a bone."

"I think I have a bone," said the woman, and she went and got a long, red bone.

So the man stirred the pot with the long, red bone; and the leafy, purple cabbage; and the long, orange carrots; and the salt and the pepper; and the round, gray stone.

And the woman said, "Imagine that – soup from a stone."

After a little while the man tasted the soup again.

"This soup is thick," said the man, "but it would be thicker if we had some flour."

"I think I have some flour," said the woman, and she went and got some fine, white flour.

So the man stirred the pot with the fine, white flour; and the long, red bone; and the leafy, purple cabbage; and the long, orange carrots; and the salt and the pepper; and the round, gray stone.

And the woman said, "Imagine that – soup from a stone."

After a little while the man tasted the soup again.

"This soup is wonderful," said the man, "but it would be more wonderful if we had an onion."

"I think I have an onion," said the woman, and she went and got a yellow onion.

So the man stirred the pot with the yellow onion; and the fine, white flour; and the long, red bone; and the leafy, purple cabbage; and the long, orange carrots; and the salt and the pepper; and the round, gray stone.

After a little while the man tasted the soup again.

"This soup is rich," said the man, "but it would be richer if we had some butter."

"I think I have some butter," said the woman, and she went and got some creamy, yellow butter.

So the man stirred the pot with the creamy, yellow butter; and the yellow onion; and the fine, white flour; and the long, red bone; and the leafy, purple cabbage; and the long, orange carrots; and the salt and the pepper; and the round, gray stone.

And the woman said, "Imagine that – soup from a stone."

After a little while the man tasted the soup again.

"This soup is just right," said the man. "Let's eat!"

So the woman got two bowls, and they ate the soup. It was delicious.

"Imagine that," said the woman, "Soup from a stone."

"Imagine that," said the man.

Notes on the Story

Stone Soup is a European story with many variants. *Nail Soup* and *Ax Soup* are Scandinavian and Russian variants. *Stone Soup,* by Marcia Brown (1947), has pictures that provide fairly good support for the text. Although it does not have the repeated refrain, the story repeats the negative conditional structure: "If . . . then. . . , but [not], so. . . ."

Notice that this story is also rich in food vocabulary, colors and shapes, and comparatives (*good, better,* etc.).

Retellings with cut-out figures

Class level: Beginner to low-intermediate
Group size(s): Whole class first, then pairs or small groups
Objective(s): Through repetition and the support of small pictures, to help students use the language taught to retell a story and to help students who learn best with hands-on involvement
Approximate class time: 25 to 45 minutes
Notes: Ideal for children; can be used with older groups

The activity

PREPARATION

1. **Draw a simple picture showing the main places in the story, and then make copies for each group.** The pictures don't need to be great (students laugh at mine), just identifiable. You might also photocopy key pictures from a book, adapt pictures cut from magazines, or ask artistic students to draw for you.
2. **Draw simple sketches of key characters and objects and make copies for each group so students can cut them out.** To save paper, these can be on the bottom or side of the sheet with the background picture. (Instead of drawing pictures, you could cut approximate shapes out of colored construction paper; for example, for *Stone Soup*, make a thin orange triangle for the carrot, etc.)
3. **If you have more than about 25 students, create a larger picture set for your presentation to the class.** Copy the pictures onto an overhead, enlarge them on a photocopier, or draw a large version on the board.

VARIATION

Instead of providing pictures to the students, dictate drawing instructions to them.

OK, draw a room that fills the top right quarter of the page. This room should have two windows, a stove, and six beds. You should also draw a small table with a lamp in this room. Now put two women and five children in this room. Stick people are fine. Draw a vertical line, that is, a line going up and down, about 2 inches from the left side of the page. On the right side of this line, near the bottom of the page, draw a table and a man sitting at the table. The man should have a very long beard and a black hat. On the left of the vertical line, draw a chicken, a goose. . . ."

Now students have their own materials. Aside from saving photocopying costs, this provides an extra listening task and a good context to preteach key vocabulary. To skip paper altogether, students could work at the board. If you use this variation, increase the time for the activity by 10 or 15 minutes.

USING THE ACTIVITY

1. **Tell the story to the class.** Involve students as much as possible in repeating refrains (see page 81), predicting what will happen, and helping tell the story.
2. **Move the cut-out pieces to the right places on the background as you tell the story, to help reinforce the story.**
3. **Using the copies of the background picture and cut-out pieces, have each pair retell/act out the story with them.** If a story has two main characters, each student can take the part of one character, or students can take turns telling scenes.

   With very low beginners who are not ready to tell the story, tell it yourself a second time and have the students move the cut-out pieces around the picture as appropriate, with the sheet visible to you so that you can see whether they are on track. This provides a nonverbal way for students to demonstrate comprehension.

   In contexts with very limited resources, one set of students could move the cut-out pieces in front of the class while a different set of students told the story. This saves having to generate materials for each group.
4. **If time allows, have one pair of students retell the story to the whole class to review the material again.** Other students should listen to make sure that all details are correct and that nothing is left out.

Other stories to use with this activity

This activity works well with stories that include a fair amount of repetition so students can remember them fairly easily. To keep things simple, it is also helpful if the story has a limited number of people, places, and objects. (*It Could Always Be Worse* revolves around two people and two places; *Stone Soup* revolves around the woman's house and the pot, but it could be told around just the pot.)

Materials are included here for

Stone Soup	see page 83
It Could Always Be Worse	see page 88
The Greedy Old Spider	see page 75

Other stories to use with this activity

Salem and the Nail   see page 104
The Judgment of the Rabbit   see page 228

The stories with *Marking a story's events on a map* (starting on page 63) can also be used for this activity.

Low-intermediate

It Could Always Be Worse

There was once a poor, unhappy man. He and his wife, and his mother, and his seven children all lived in a one-room house. The house was always noisy and crowded, and someone was always fighting or yelling. When the poor, unhappy man could stand it no longer, he went to his rabbi for help.

"Wise and holy rabbi," said the poor, unhappy man, "please help me. My house is too small and too noisy, and someone is always fighting or yelling. I can't stand it any longer."

"Tell me," said the rabbi, stroking his beard, "do you have a chicken or two?"

"Yes," said the man. "In fact, I have four."

"Good," said the rabbi. "Go home and take them into your house to live."

So the poor, unhappy man went home and took the chickens into the house.

After a few days or a week had gone by, things were much worse. The chickens squawked, the children yelled, and the house was noisier than before. So the man went back to the rabbi.

"Wise and holy rabbi," said the poor, unhappy man, "please help me. The chickens are squawking, the children are yelling, and my house is noisier and more crowded and smaller than before. I can't stand it any longer."

"Tell me," said the rabbi, stroking his beard, "do you have a goose?"

"Yes," said the man, wondering why the rabbi asked.

"Good," said the rabbi. "Go home and take the goose into your house to live."

So the poor, unhappy man went home and took the goose into the house.

After a few days or a week had gone by, things were much worse. The goose honked, the chickens squawked, the children yelled, and the house was noisier than before. So the man went back to the rabbi.

"Wise and holy rabbi," said the poor, unhappy man, "please help me. The goose is honking, the chickens are squawking, the children are yelling, and my house is noisier and more crowded and smaller than before. I can't stand it any longer."

"Tell me," said the rabbi, stroking his beard, "do you have a goat?"

"Yes," said the man, feeling very worried.

"Good," said the rabbi. "Go home and take the goat into your house to live."

So the poor, unhappy man went home and took the goat into the house.

After a few days or a week had gone by, things were much worse. The goat butted, the goose honked, the chickens squawked, the children yelled, and the house was noisier than before. So the man went back to the rabbi.

"Wise and holy rabbi," said the poor, unhappy man, "please help me. The goat is butting, the goose is honking, the chickens are squawking, the children are yelling, and my house is noisier and more crowded and smaller than before. I can't stand it any longer."

"Tell me," said the rabbi, stroking his beard, "do you have a cow?"

"Yes," said the man, trembling.

"Good," said the rabbi. "Go home and take the cow into your house to live."

So the poor, unhappy man went home and took the cow into the house.

After a few days had gone by, things were much worse. The cow stepped on everything, the goat butted, the goose honked, the chickens squawked, the children yelled, and the house was noisier than before. So the man went back to the rabbi.

"Wise and holy rabbi," said the poor, unhappy man, "please help me. The cow is stepping on everything, the goat is butting, the goose is honking, the chickens are squawking, the children are yelling, and my house is noisier and more crowded and smaller than before. I can't stand it any longer."

continued

"My poor, unhappy man," said the rabbi, "go home and take all the animals out of your house."

"Yes, Rabbi," said the man happily. "I will do that at once."

So the poor man went home and took the cow and the goat and the goose and the chickens out of the house. The house seemed very quiet and not crowded at all.

The man went back to the rabbi.

"Wise and holy rabbi," said the man, "you have helped us very much. My house is so quiet and peaceful now. Thank you so much."

Notes on the Story

This is a Jewish/Yiddish tale. My favorite published version is *It Could Always Be Worse* by Margot Zemach (1976); the pictures in this version are quite entertaining and provide good support for the text.

For students who don't know what a rabbi is, you may want to substitute the word "teacher."

Notice that this story has some good farm animal vocabulary. It also repeats comparatives (noisier, more crowded, etc.).

Sketches for *It Could Always be Worse* (see page 88).

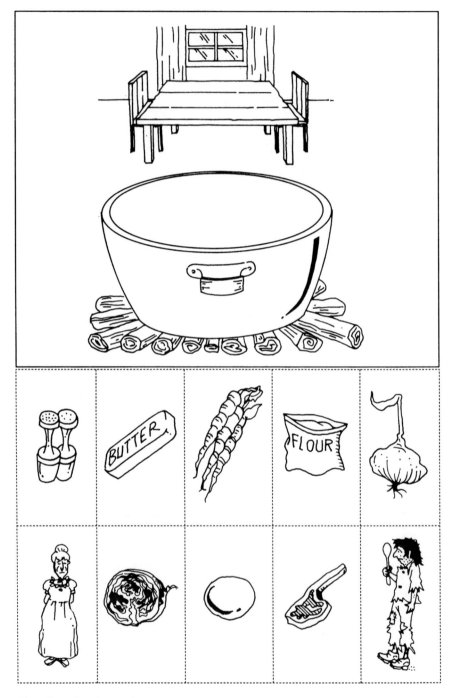

Sketches for *Stone Soup* (see page 83).

Sketches for *The Greedy Old Spider* (see page 75).

▨ Discussion activities

Class level: Intermediate to advanced
Group size(s): Whole class, small groups
Objective(s): To practice speaking, listening, conversational turn-taking, negotiating, and to relate literature to real life (compare/contrast; analyzing; drawing inferences)
Approximate class time: Varies

The activity

GENERAL COMMENTS

A number of other activities potentially involve a considerable amount of discussion. For example, negotiating a new ending for an existing story requires students to talk. Working together to create a dramatic version of a story requires a certain amount of discussion. And so on. Yet the discussion itself can also be an activity—not a means to an end but an end in its own right. The ability to share and discuss ideas is important, and folktales raise many issues that are worth discussing.

PREPARATION

Create discussion questions, and if appropriate, a specific, demonstrable task to complete through the discussion activity. For example, if you tell students, "Discuss the ways the stepmother mistreated the children in this story," you will probably get a lot less interaction than if you tell them, "Find at least five ways that the stepmother mistreated the children in this story. Then place them on a continuum from least objectionable to most objectionable." Following the general sample questions (under *Types of issues to discuss*) are some additional sample questions for a few specific stories.

IN THE CLASSROOM

1. **Tell a story or have students read one.**
2. **Unless the discussion questions involve an information gap, give the students the discussion question(s) and have them write answers individually.** This forces all students to generate something, and brings each student to the group with something to share, making it more likely that all members will contribute.
3. **Have students discuss the issues and complete the task in groups.**
4. **Give students a chance to share their conclusions with the class.**

Types of issues to discuss

SOCIOCULTURAL ISSUES

In this story, the people ate potatoes and cabbage for supper; what do people normally eat in your country? What do they serve at a feast? How does one settle a disagreement? How does one dress for different occasions? What are the differences between the rich and the poor? How are weddings celebrated? Folktales provide a natural context for discussing cultural similarities and cultural differences.

PERSONAL ISSUES

How would you have felt if . . . creates an opportunity for students to express their own feelings. Questions can be nonthreatening—*What would you wish for if you were given three wishes?* Or they can be more deeply personal—*The main characters in this story were deserted by their parents. Have you ever felt deserted by anyone? Who/when (if you wish to share)?*

You can discuss the story itself, or you can generate a variety of spin-off questions based on the story: *If a genie offered you one wish, what would it be? If a fairy were going to dress you for a ball in anything that you wanted, what would you wear? If you were Cinderella, what would you have done to the stepsisters once you were queen? Why?*

ETHICAL/MORAL/VALUE CLARIFICATION ISSUES

In one story, Cinderella is beautiful, in another, she is deformed but honest, and in yet another, she is a good poet. What values might be important in these different societies based on these differences? Which of these values do you think are most important? What other values are very important?

Is there a time when you should/should not (would/would not) help a person in need? How are the elderly regarded in your culture? In the United States, the elderly are sometimes cared for in nursing homes, often with little or no contact with relatives. In other societies, the elderly are cared for by families until they die. What values are reflected in these differences? In considering the needs of the elderly, what factors do you think should be most important?

Is there ever a time when lying or deceiving someone is acceptable? Understandable? Is there a difference between "white" lies and other lies? Do you think the lying in this story was justifiable?

What are the most important qualities you would look for in a husband or wife? Identify three negative and three positive values reflected in this story, and indicate how important you think each is in a spouse.

Such questions engage students in critical thinking about cultural differences, prepare students to notice critical items in the text, and relate the story to the issues of real life. This type of questioning can also potentially help students see that they can question and disagree with the ideas and values presented in a written text.

Sample questions for The Riddle (page 22)

You wouldn't typically use all of these questions with any particular class; a number of questions are provided just to illustrate the variety of possibilities that exist for any given story.

SOCIOCULTURAL QUESTIONS

In the story, the man expressed an obligation to care for his elderly mother, and he expected his son to care for him. What responsibilities or expectations are there in your culture to care for one's parents (or the elderly in general)?

In the United States, nursing homes often care for elderly people, some of whom have little or no contact with their children. List five advantages and five disadvantages of this approach to caring for elderly parents.

Give examples of three riddles that are popular in your country.

The story presents a king who is very rich, and a charcoal maker who is very poor; what gaps are there in your country between the very rich and the very poor?

Even though the charcoal maker is very poor, he still generously shares what little food he has with the king. In some cultures, people have very specific social obligations to guests. List expectations in your culture toward guests and, if you have had any experience with families in the United States or other countries other than your own, list any differences you have discovered.

In the story, the king asks the man how much money he earns. In some countries (including the United States) this is a taboo question – something you're not supposed to ask. In other cultures, this is something you might ask in your first conversation. What topics are taboo in your culture? What topics have you discovered are taboo in this culture that are OK to talk about in your culture?

In this story, the father is expected to provide a dowry for his daughter's marriage. In your culture, what (if anything) is each set of parents expected to provide when a couple gets married?

ETHICAL/MORAL QUESTIONS

Was the charcoal maker honest in accepting the bribe, given that he was following the letter but not the spirit of the king's request?

How important are honesty and keeping promises? Is it really wrong to do something different than you said you would do? List five examples of when it would be wrong not to keep your promise, and five examples of situations when it would be OK to break your promise.

Is it wrong to offer a bribe? If giving bribes became common, identify several potential problems that you think could result.

The king's sentence was for the man to be beaten and thrown in jail for a year. Is this punishment too harsh for the offense? Why or why not? List three principles that you would use in deciding what a just sentence would be for a crime.

PERSONAL QUESTIONS

Would you be willing to have your parent(s) live with you? Would you be willing to live with your children when you get old? Why or why not?

Tell your favorite riddle. What would you have done if you had been bribed to give the answer to the riddle?

Sample questions for The Lost Son (page 61)

SOCIOCULTURAL QUESTIONS

When the father wanted to celebrate, he had a cow killed and had a party with dancing and music. List half a dozen (or more) things that would be an important part of a celebration in your culture. What differences have you noticed between parties or celebrating in this culture and parties in your own culture?

ETHICAL/MORAL QUESTIONS

In some cultures, it is common for young people to go through a wild stage. Does this happen in your culture? Do you think this is bad? Why or why not?

The young man had been given money by his father and chose to waste it and dishonor his family. Did his family have any obligation to help him? Why or why not?

PERSONAL QUESTIONS

In this story, the young man's friends deserted him once his money was gone. If you are willing to talk about it, tell about a time when someone used you for something you had and then let you down when they had no more to gain. How did you feel?

If you found yourself in the situation of the "lost" son, would you go to your parents for help? Why or why not? Who would you go to?

How would you have felt if you had been the father in this story? The older brother? The younger brother?

One sometimes sees families in which one member is very responsible and another is not. Why do you think this happens?

The younger son went from being wild to being willing to go back home and work. Do you think his change of heart will stick, or do you think that once his belly is filled, he will go back to his wild ways?

Do you think the father was fair to the older brother? Why or why not?

Variation

Instead of writing discussion questions yourself, have students generate discussion questions after reading the story.

Telling stories from students' own cultures

Class level: Beginner to advanced
Group size(s): Individuals and whole class
Objective(s): To provide speaking and listening practice
Academic skill(s): Public speaking, focused listening
Approximate class time: 30 minutes plus time for students to tell their
  stories

The activity

This activity is useful to introduce public speaking, because it provides
an opportunity to speak in front of a group without requiring students
to do research or extensive work generating the material. The material is
something that students already know; they just need to express it in
English.

PREPARATION

Create questions that students must answer during or after listening to
stories told by peers. Just a few general questions are needed to help
students to listen actively rather than passively. Questions like the ones
below require students to understand the gist of the story, provide an
opportunity for reaction, and help students focus their listening. They
can be used with virtually any story.

What was the name of the most important character in the story?
What was the problem this person faced?
What was the solution?
What was the most important value reflected in the story?
Did you like the story? Why or why not?

IN THE CLASSROOM

1. **Have the students choose a tale from their own culture that they
   would like to share with the class.**
2. **Have the students create a timeline** (see page 72) **or text structure
   chart** (see page 227) **so they have a visual representation of the story
   for themselves.** This helps them organize the material mentally, which
   helps during the telling. This part can be done as homework rather
   than in class.
3. **Have students identify any important vocabulary they need to tell the
   story.** Students may want to look up certain words in the dictionary
   and write down key phrases so they won't forget them.

4. **Discuss important aspects of public speaking and oral presentation.** For example, talk about eye contact, pauses, gestures, and avoiding nervous movement. If needed, give students time limits for the tellings. You may want to have students make outlines for the telling as described in Chapter 2; see page 26.
5. **Before students listen to the stories, hand out questions like those shown under *Preparation* on page 99.** Make sure students understand, so they will know what to be listening for.
6. **Have each student tell his or her story while the rest of the class listens.** You may want to have students tell their stories during the next class, so they can finish their preparation for homework. If you have several students from the same culture, they might do the oral telling cooperatively.
7. **Have the listeners complete questions like the ones shown on page 99.** Having questions to answer increases student attentiveness and provides an opportunity to develop focused listening skills. You might also have the listeners complete timelines or diagram the text structure to demonstrate that they understood what they heard.

6 Interactive information gaps

Long and Porter (1985), analyzing studies of group work, found that group work resulted in more language production, higher quality of production, more individualized instruction, a positive classroom atmosphere, and better student motivation. Two-way tasks generated more interaction.

Interactive group work activities can involve either optional or required exchanges of information. For example, if you ask students to share their opinions about a story, that exchange is optional: Some students may share little or nothing and the task can still be completed. In contrast, if each student has information that all others lack, and all information is required to complete the task, then each student is forced to communicate his or her portion of the information. Pica and Doughty (1986) found that group work with required exchanges of information produced significantly more interaction than optional exchanges and teacher-fronted activities.

Studies have also shown that although input that was simplified before being presented to students was easier for students to understand, more difficult input that was made understandable through interaction resulted in significantly greater gains in later production (Ellis et al., 1994; Gass and Varonis, 1994; Pica et al., 1987).

These activities have been designed to incorporate group work, interaction, and required information exchanges. They also seek to get students interacting to understand stories that have not been simplified in advance.

▒▒▒▒ Strip story

Class level: Beginner to high-intermediate
Group size(s): Pairs or small groups (3 or 4)
Objective(s): To review language from an orally presented story and to practice speaking and listening
Approximate class time: 15 to 45 minutes

The activity

PREPARATION

1. Based on the difficulty level you want and the length of the story, write from half a dozen to about twenty sentences that summarize the story. Leave blank lines between the sentences so they can be cut apart.
2. Put these sentences on a single sheet of paper in scrambled order. If you scramble the strips first, students can cut them apart instead of your having to do so. (When I haven't scrambled them first, I've also caught students ordering the strips by using the cut marks in the paper rather than the language.)
3. Make enough copies so you have one complete set for each group.
4. If you want precut strips for a small class, cut the pages into strips. Paper-clip the sets together, or put each set in a different envelope.

PREPARATION VARIATIONS

Variation 1: To make reusable sets of strips, print the page on cardstock and then cover them with clear plastic. (This keeps them in better condition and discourages students from writing on them.)
Variation 2: In contexts with limited resources, you could dictate the strips and have students write them down (providing an extra listening exercise), or you could provide sentences on the overhead or board.

USING THE ACTIVITY

1. **Tell the story orally.** (You could also have students listen to it on tape in a language lab or read it for homework. Using one of these options, this activity could also be used as self-access material.)
2. **Divide students into groups of two to four and give each student**

several strips. (Together, each group has the pieces for the complete story.)
3. **Have students talk with each other to figure out the right order for the strips.** For maximum listening and speaking practice, don't let students show their strips to others; this requires them to listen to each other instead of just reading all of the strips.
4. **When students are done, quickly retell the story, showing the correct order for the strips; or have one or more students do the retelling.**

Variations

Variation 1: Instead of having students physically shuffle strips, give them all of the sentences on one sheet and have them number the strips. (I tend to use this when I want students to complete the activity individually and when I have a reading focus, and I use the regular strip story when students are working in pairs or small groups and I want a listening/speaking focus.) In addition to reviewing language, this helps make sure that each student understands the basic outline of the story before doing other activities that require an understanding of the basic ideas (like the compare/contrast activity on page 255).

Variation 2: Include some sentences that don't fit the story to prevent students from doing the activity by guessing if they haven't understood what they heard.

Variation 3: Use a strip story as a prelistening (or prereading) activity. As students order the strips, they learn unfamiliar vocabulary and identify what the story is about: this prepares them for the listening (or reading). After they order the strips, have one or more groups share their stories with the class. Then have them listen to the "real" story to see if they got the "right" order.

Variation 4: Scramble two stories together that you have used in two previous classes so that students must figure out which strips go with which story as they order them. This is a fun way to review language from earlier classes. This can be more or less difficult depending on how similar elements in the two stories are.

Variation 5: Combine the strip story with the evaluating/summarizing activity on page 251.

Variation 6: Create self-access materials: Use a written text and the version of the activity described in Variation 1, or record the story on tape so students can listen to the tape and then do the activity on their own. See page 38 for more on self-access materials.

Interactive information gaps: Strip story

In the multilevel classroom

Make two or three sets of strips based on one story, with fewer and easier strips for the lowest-level students and more difficult and more numerous strips for more advanced students. Then group students by level so that each group is working with strips on an appropriate level. If necessary, the lowest level could do a picture sorting activity (see page 54) based on the same story instead.

Another alternative is to have the lower-level students just order the strips while the more advanced both order the strips and do the ranking for the summarization activity (see page 251).

Low-intermediate

Salem and the Nail

Once upon a time, there was a crafty merchant named Salem. His shop, and all the carpets in it, burned in a fire. Salem had nothing left but his house, and since he was a trader, he decided to sell it. With the money he could buy a new shop and more carpets. Salem's price for his house was very low, but he had a very strange condition for anyone who wanted to buy it: "I'll sell you the house, except for that nail in the wall. That remains mine!" All people who came to look at the house went away shaking their heads, wondering why he made this strange request.

A man named Abraham, however, thought that this was a chance to get a very good deal. Even though the price was fair, he argued and bargained until he got the price even lower. At last Abraham and Salem struck a deal, so Abraham bought the whole house, except for one nail, at a very good price.

A week later, Salem came to the door. "I've come to hang something on my nail," he said. He came into the house and hung a large empty bag on the nail. Then he said "Good-bye," and left.

A few days later, Salem came again. He had brought an old coat to hang on the nail. After that, Salem was forever coming and going, taking things off the nail and hanging new things up. One evening, Salem arrived dragging a dead donkey. With a struggle, he lifted it up and tied it to the nail. Abraham and his family complained, "This dead animal smells horrible, and surely you don't expect us to look at *that* in our house?"

But Salem answered: "It's my nail, and I can hang anything on it that I want to!"

Abraham begged Salem to take the donkey away, but Salem refused. Abraham took Salem to the judge, but the judge said Salem was right: The bargain was clear, and while the house was Abraham's, the nail belonged to Salem.

Abraham and his family could no longer live in the house with the dead donkey hanging there, so Salem offered to buy the house back. Abraham tried to get more, but Salem would not pay a penny more than half of what Abraham had paid him. So Salem got his house back, with enough money left to open a new shop.

Notes on the Story
This story is from the Middle East. Another version of it can be found on the *Tales of Wonder* Internet site; see page 281.)

Low-level strips for *Salem and the Nail*

Abraham bought the house.

Salem hung coats and bags on his nail.

Salem sold his house – except one nail.

Abraham had to leave.

Salem bought his house for half price.

Salem hung a dead donkey on his nail.

Interactive information gaps: Strip story

Intermediate strips for *Salem and the Nail*

Many people came to look.

Salem bought a new shop.

Abraham took Salem to the judge.

He decided to sell his house, except for one nail.

Abraham bought Salem's house.

Abraham complained that the donkey smelled bad.

Salem hung an empty bag on the nail.

Salem's shop burned in a fire.

The judge said that Salem was in the right.

Salem hung an old coat on the nail.

People went away shaking their heads.

Salem bought his old house at half price.

Salem hung a dead donkey on the nail.

Abraham argued about the price.

Abraham could not live in the house.

Intermediate activity for *Strong Wind*
(see page 108) using variations 1 and 2

Number the sentences below so that they are in the same order as the story. Put an X next to any sentence that is not part of the story.

_____ Strong Wind's sister was surprised.

_____ The older sisters turned into trees.

___x___ He said he would marry the most beautiful woman.

_____ They could not see him, but they lied and said they could.

_____ There were three sisters who all loved each other.

_____ Strong Wind's sister asked what his bow was made of.

___3___ There were three sisters. The two oldest were mean to the youngest.

___4___ The oldest sisters went to see the warrior.

___2___ He said he would marry the first woman who could see him.

___x___ Once there was a great fighter who had many wives.

_____ The youngest sister could see him.

_____ The youngest sister said she could not see him.

_____ Strong Wind married the youngest sister because she was the most beautiful.

___1___ Once there was a great fighter who could make himself invisible.

_____ Strong Wind married the youngest sister because she was honest.

_____ Strong Wind married the oldest sister because she was the most beautiful.

_____ She said that his bow was made of the rainbow.

Strong Wind

Once there was a great warrior named Strong Wind. He lived with his sister in a tent by the shores of the sea. Strong Wind was able to make himself invisible. His sister could see him, but no one else could. He had said he would marry the first woman who could see him as he came home at the end of the day.

Many women came to his tent to watch for him. When his sister saw him coming, she would ask, "Do you see him?"

Each girl would answer, "Oh, yes! I see him!"

Then Strong Wind's sister would ask, "What is he pulling his sled with?"

And the girl would answer, "with a rope" or "with a wooden pole."

Then Strong Wind's sister would know that they were lying, because their guesses were wrong.

A chief lived in the village. His wife had died, but he had three daughters. One was much younger than the other two. She was gentle and kind and beautiful, but her sisters were jealous of her and treated her badly. They cut off her long black hair and they made her wear rags. They also burned her face with coals so that she would be ugly. They lied to their father and said that she did these things to herself. But she remained kind and gentle.

The two older sisters also went to try and see Strong Wind. When he was coming, Strong Wind's sister asked them, "Do you see him?"

"Oh, yes! I see him!" each of them answered.

"What is his bow made out of?" asked Strong Wind's sister.

"Out of iron," answered one. "Out of strong wood," answered the other.

"You have not seen him," said Strong Wind's sister.

Strong Wind himself heard them and knew that they had lied. They went into the tent, but still they could not see him. They went home very sad.

One day the youngest daughter went to try and see Strong Wind. She was wearing rags, and burns covered her face. People laughed at her, but she kept going. When she got to Strong Wind's tent, she waited.

When Strong Wind was coming, his sister asked the girl, "Do you see him?"

"No," the girl answered. "I do not see him."

Strong Wind's sister was surprised because the girl had told the truth. "Now do you see him?" asked Strong Wind's sister.

"Yes," answered the girl. "Now I do see him. He is very wonderful."

"What is his bow made of?" asked Strong Wind's sister.

"The rainbow," answered the girl.

"And what is the bowstring made of?" asked Strong Wind's sister.

"Of stars," answered the girl.

Then Strong Wind's sister knew that the girl could really see him. He had let her see him because she had told the truth.

"You really have seen him," said Strong Wind's sister. Then the sister washed the girl, and all the burns went away. Her hair grew long and black again. The sister dressed the girl in fine clothes. Strong Wind came and the girl became his wife.

The girls' two older sisters were very angry, but Strong Wind turned them into aspen trees. Ever since that day, the leaves of the aspen tree always tremble with fear whenever he comes near, because they know he remembers their lying and meanness.

Notes on the Story

This story is based on a Native American Cinderella variant. This retelling is most closely based on a Canadian version, though a number of Native American groups have similar stories.

The ambiguous strip story

Class level: Low-intermediate to advanced
Group size(s): Pairs or small groups (3 or 4)
Objective(s): To practice speaking and listening while exploring a story
Approximate class time: 15 to 45 minutes

The activity

PREPARATION

Create strips as for a regular strip story (see page 102), but leave out the final strip. Also create three or four extra strips that don't belong in the story but that could fit if one didn't know the story. (For example, in *The Man Who Never Lied,* George has a reputation for never telling a lie and two men try to trick him into telling one; in the extra strips, he has a reputation for stealing and two men try to embarrass him for this. Also, in the real story, one man climbs out the window; there is an extra strip that could fit in the same spot in which one man pulls a gun on George and tells him to lie.)

USING THE ACTIVITY

1. **Ask each group to make a story from the strips.** They must order the strips, try to figure out which ones don't belong, and guess what happened in the end. You may or may not want to let students know how many extra strips there are.
2. **Have the groups share their versions with the class.** Write an outline for each on the board.
3. **Read or tell the real story, having students listen for the correct order for the strips and the correct version.**

Adapting the activity for different levels

Low-level students usually need to look at each other's strips to complete this activity; more advanced students should do this activity without looking at each other's strips to force more verbal interaction.

Variation

Combine the strips for two stories that have similar elements. Make sure that some strips in each could potentially fit with the other story. Then have students figure out what the two stories are.

The Man Who Never Lied

There was once a man named George Fox. He was a very religious man and tried to be honest and just with all men. He talked the same way to ordinary people as he did to rich men. He also had a reputation for never telling a lie.

Two men wanted to trick him into telling a lie. Together they worked out a plan. Then one of the men went to see George in his rooms, pretending that he needed to talk to him about something. While the first man was talking to George, the second man knocked on the door. George left the room to open the door. While George was out of the room, the first man climbed out the window. The second man asked George if the first man was there. George answered, "He was there when I left him."

Notes on the Story
This is based on a historical account about George Fox, the founder of the Quakers. I included it partly because I like the story, but partly also to illustrate the wide variety of places where you can find useful stories: History is full of fascinating legends, and for our purposes, it doesn't matter whether they are historically accurate or not.

Low-intermediate/intermediate strips for
The Man Who Never Lied

He had stolen something from one of them.

The second man asked if the first man was there.

He had a reputation for never telling a lie.

When George went to the door, the first man climbed out the window.

Two men wanted to embarrass George for stealing.

Two men wanted to trick him into telling a lie.

There was once a man named George Fox.

While the first man was talking to George, the second man knocked on the door.

One man went to see George in his rooms.

The first man pulled out a gun and told George to say that he was not there.

He had a reputation for stealing little things.

The King and the Baby

Once, long ago, two women lived in the same house. They each had a baby. One woman's baby died during the night. When she woke in the night and found that her baby was dead, she got up quietly and placed her baby next to the other woman and took the other woman's baby back to her own bed.

In the morning, when the other woman woke up, she saw the dead baby lying next to her. Then she looked and saw that it was not her own baby. "This is your baby," she said to the first woman. "That is my baby that you are holding."

The first woman denied it, insisting that the baby was her own. The matter was brought to the judges, but no one could settle it.

Finally, the matter was brought before the king. The one woman said, "Her baby died during the night, and now she wants to take mine."

The other said, "No. Her baby died and she took mine."

After listening to the women, the king asked his guards to bring him a sword. "Cut the child in half," said the king, "and give half to each woman. That will be most fair."

"Yes, that would be fine," answered the first woman. "Cut the child in half."

"No! Stop!" cried the other woman. "Give the child to her. She may have it . . . just let the child live."

"Yes. Stop!" said the king. "Give the child to this woman. She is the real mother, for she cares about the child."

Notes on the Story

This story is based on an account about King Solomon in the Bible (I Kings 3). In a Japanese variant of this story, the king tells each mother to pull one of the baby's arms. The true mother is recognized because she lets go when the baby begins to cry.

Intermediate strips for
The King and the Baby

One woman's baby died during the night.

The other woman said the first woman was lying.

The one woman was afraid, so she fled to the hills with her baby and lived in a cave.

After listening to the women, the king asked his servants to bring him a sword.

When the women woke up, one woman said, "This dead baby is your baby. You took my baby."

Once two women lived in the same house. They each had a baby.

The matter was brought before the king.

The king said to cut the baby in half.

Both babies grew up to be warriors.

One woman took both babies and ran away with them.

When the two warriors realized they were old friends, they suddenly stopped the war, and everyone went home.

One woman took the other woman's baby.

After many years, the first woman found the second woman.

Creating a story from strips

Class Level: Low-intermediate to advanced
Group size(s): Pairs or small groups (3 or 4)
Objective(s): To practice speaking and listening while exploring a story; to think about the relationship of ideas while also practicing language
Approximate class time: 15 to 45 minutes

The activity

PREPARATION

Create strips as for a regular strip story (see page 102), but design them so they can be ordered in different ways and still make a sensible story. You may want to leave out the conclusion or some key points. Use ambiguous pronouns and/or passive statements (e.g., "The milk was spilled" instead of "The man spilled the milk") so there are more possible ways that the strips can be arranged.

Creating strips that can be sensibly arranged in a number of ways while still being based on a real story was much harder for me than I had expected.

USING THE ACTIVITY

1. **Ask each group to make a story from the strips.** They may add as much as they want to make all the strips fit. They must discuss order and what to add so the story makes sense. Students can write their stories down or create them orally.
2. **Have the groups share their stories with the class.** Students can vote on which they think is the best story and which they think is most correct.
3. **Read the real story, asking students to listen for the correct order for the strips.**

A sample story created from strips

Here is a set of strips to create a story from:

The man was angry with his wife.

He got stuck in the chimney.

The wife went to the field.

The cider spilled on the floor.

The man tied a rope around his ankle.

The cow fell off the roof.

The man did not complain any more.

Here is one possible story based on these pieces. (The real story is found on page 244).

Once a family had a cow. As a joke, some boys put the cow on the roof. The man tied a rope around his ankle and tied the other end to the chimney so he wouldn't fall. He tried to get the cow down, but the cow fell off the roof, and the man fell down the chimney. He got stuck in the chimney. After he got out, the man wanted some cider. His wife got some, but the beer spilled on the floor. The man was angry with his wife and began to yell and scream. She went to the field so she couldn't hear him. Then the man stopped being angry and he did not complain any more, so his wife came back.

Jigsaw story reconstruction

Class level: Low-intermediate to advanced
Group size(s): Small groups of 3 to 5
Objective(s): Students will be able to write down (take notes on, summarize) a narrative based on oral information provided by classmates
Approximate class time: 15 to 30 minutes

The activity

PREPARATION

1. **Pick a story at an appropriate level and divide it into sections.** Choose the number of sections based on natural breaks in the story and on the number of groups you want to divide the class into.
2. **With a larger class, label the sections (A, B, C, D) or put each part on a different color paper.** When students regroup in step 5, this helps to make sure that each group ends up with one person who knows each section of the story rather than two people who have heard one part and none who have heard another. When labeling the sections, I prefer letters to numbers because I want to avoid suggesting that parts go in a specific order.

IN THE CLASSROOM

1. **Divide the class into as many groups as you have sections of the story.** For example, if you divided the story into four sections, you should have four groups.
2. **Give each group one section of the story.** They can either read the section or listen to a tape of it. Have students discuss unknown words and help each other understand the story. Circulate, making sure that each group understands its portion of the story.
3. *(Optional)* **For the part of the story that each group has read, have the students complete a sentence ordering activity like the one on page 107 or comprehension questions to make sure they understand their part of the story.** Once completed, this gives students an outline or summary of their part of the story; this may help with the next step.
4. **Collect the written sections of the story so that students have to work from memory and focus on speaking what they remember rather than just reading to each other.** If the class is working on note taking, you can let students take notes and then work from their notes.

117

5. **Form new groups with one person who knows each part of the story.** In these groups, students retell their sections of the story and attempt to re-create the whole story.
6. **Once students have finished reconstructing the stories, have one or more groups share their reconstructions with the rest of the class.** At points of confusion or difference of opinion, reread portions of the original text aloud and have students decide which version is most correct.

In the multilevel classroom

If you have multiple levels, put the advanced students together and make their section longer and/or harder. Give lowest-level students the first part of the story retold in easier language. (See the example on page 42.) This way, groups work at an appropriate level while trying to understand their section, yet students at different levels also work at communicating with each other while reconstructing the story.

In the large classroom

For a large class, multiple groups can work with each part of the story so that there are never more than about four in a group. For example, with 64 students and a four-part story, have four groups of four students each read part A, four groups each read part B, and so on. When students regroup to reconstruct the story, you would then have 16 groups of four doing the reconstruction.

Variations

Variation 1: Students can re-create the stories orally, write an outline or summary, or attempt to reproduce a complete text. If you opt for writing, students may not write their own section; other students must write it for them. (This forces oral work to continue rather than having one student write while the others sit silently or drift off.) If writing is a focus, have the group check for language errors in a separate step after the content is down.

Variation 2: Each group could lack one section of the story and be forced to make up something that fits. This adds some creativity to the telling without imposing the burden of generating an entire story.

Variation 3: An optional additional step with more advanced students is for students to return to their original groups with the written versions they have produced, compare their different versions with the original text, and decide which version was the best. This involves the important cognitive skills of comparing, contrasting, and analyzing. It also may lead students to go back and reread portions of the original text, an activity that has been demonstrated useful in making reading gains.

Variation 4: Provide an opportunity for students to practice note taking and summarizing by letting them take notes while they listen to or read their sections of the story and then letting them use these notes when reconstructing the story.

Variation 5: Self-access materials. This activity requires no extra preparation to do on a self-access level. When done, students can check their work by reviewing either the entire story or a summary of the story. See page 38 for more on self-access materials.

Intermediate

Wine for the Feast

Once a king decided to have a great feast. He invited everyone in the city. He asked each family to bring a bowl of wine.

On the day of the feast, everyone washed and dressed in their best clothes, and set out for the king's palace. One man looked out his window. He saw many other families walking by, each carrying a bowl of wine. He said to his wife, "I don't want to spend money for wine, but how can we go to the feast without it?"

She answered, "Fill the bowl with water. When it is mixed with so many other bowls of wine, no one will know." He agreed and filled the bowl with water. Then they went to the feast.

When people arrived at the feast, they emptied their bowls into an enormous basin. The man and his wife poured their bowl of water into the basin as well. They smiled at each other. "No one will know," they thought.

When it was time for the feast to begin, the wine was served. The man lifted the glass to his lips, and tasted the wine. He tasted it again. It was nothing but water. For each family that came thought, "With so many bowls of wine, one bowl of water will not make a difference. No one will know." And now the large pot held nothing but water, and that was all they had to drink at the feast.

When only water is brought, only water can be drunk.

Notes on the Story
A version of this story can be found in *The King's Drum and Other African Stories* by Harold Courlander (1962).

Wine for the Feast: A low-level jigsaw reading

In four parts

When people arrived at the feast, they emptied their bowls into an enormous basin. The man and his wife poured their bowl of water into the basin as well. They smiled at each other. "No one will know," they thought.

When it was time for the feast to begin, the wine was served.

The man said to his wife, "I don't want to spend money for wine, but how can we go to the feast without it?"

She answered, "Fill the bowl with water. When it is mixed with so many other bowls of wine, no one will know." He agreed and filled the bowl with water. Then they went to the feast.

The man lifted the glass to his lips, and tasted the wine. He tasted it again. It was nothing but water. Each family that came thought, "With so many bowls of wine, one bowl of water will not make a difference. No one will know." And now the large pot held nothing but water, and that was all they had to drink at the feast.

When only water is brought, only water can be drunk.

Once a king decided to have a great feast. He invited everyone in the city. He asked each family to bring a bowl of wine.

On the day of the feast, everyone washed and dressed in their best clothes, and set out for the king's palace. One man looked out his window. He saw many other families walking by, each carrying a bowl of wine.

Wine for the Feast: A low-level jigsaw reading

In three parts

His wife answered, "Fill the bowl with water. When it is mixed with so many other bowls of wine, no one will know." He agreed and filled the bowl with water. Then they went to the feast.

When people arrived at the feast, they emptied their bowls into an enormous basin. The man and his wife emptied their bowl into the basin as well. They smiled at each other. "No one will know," they thought.

When it was time for the feast to begin, the wine was served. The man lifted the glass to his lips, and tasted the wine. He tasted it again. It was nothing but water. For each family that came thought, "With so many bowls of wine, one bowl of water will not make a difference. No one will know." And now the large pot held nothing but water, and that was all they had to drink at the feast.

When only water is brought, only water can be drunk.

Once a king decided to have a great feast. He invited everyone in the city. He asked each family to bring a bowl of wine.

On the day of the feast, everyone washed and dressed in their best clothes, and set out for the king's palace.

One man looked out his window. He saw many other families walking by, each carrying a bowl of wine. He said to his wife, "I don't want to spend money for wine, but how can we go to the feast without it?"

Intermediate/high-intermediate

The Princess's Suitors: Reading C

Long ago there was a king who had only one child – a daughter. She was kind to everyone, and very beautiful. When she got old enough to marry, many princes wanted to marry her.

One prince came riding on a black horse and wearing shining armor. He was handsome and strong and brave, and a great fighter. He was very rich, and offered the princess a thousand strings of diamonds if she would marry him.

Another prince came who wore beautiful green silks and many gold rings. People said he was very wise. He was also very rich; he offered the princess 500 strings of emeralds if she would marry him.

And, from a very small kingdom, came another prince. He wore simple clothes, and he was not very rich – he could only offer the princess a gift of 100 pieces of silver – but he was kind and cheerful. Even though he was not rich, he was a prince, so we should not forget him.

"My daughter," said the king, "these princes who want to marry you are getting tired of waiting. You should make up your mind and pick one."

"My father," said the princess, giving him a kiss, "it is hard to choose. You must give me more time to think about it."

The king loved his daughter more than anything, so he decided that she could have as much time as she wanted.

The princess said, "Thank you." Then she went to her room, for she had an idea.

The Princess's Suitors: Reading A

She sent one servant to the market to buy old clothes. She sent another servant to the kitchen to pack food for a trip. Then she wrote her father a letter saying she was going on a trip but that she would be back soon.

The next morning the princess got up early. She dressed herself in the old clothes, and hid her beautiful hair under a hat. Then she got on her horse and rode to the castle of the first prince who wanted to marry her (the one who had offered her the diamonds). She got a job working in the stables, helping take care of the horses.

Early the next morning the princess started working, taking care of the horses. Soon a messenger said the prince was coming. When he came, the princess walked past him carrying a bucket of water. She stumbled, knocking the prince down and spilling water all over him.

"Look what you did, you stupid idiot," screamed the prince, getting up off the ground.

"Excuse me. Excuse me. I'm so sorry," said the princess. "Let me clean you off." She moved closer, spilling more water on the prince's leg and stepping on his foot."

"Get back, you fool, get back!"

She stepped back quickly, poking the horse with the shovel in her hand. The horse ran away, neighing fearfully.

"Get away, you worthless person! How dare you scare my horse. He is worth more than all of your father's house. Get away, whoever you are. I never want to see you again."

"Very well," thought the princess, "you will never see me again." She hurried to where her horse was, and got on and rode away.

The Princess's Suitors: Reading D

Next, the princess rode to the castle of the second prince, the one who had offered her the emeralds. There she begged for a job in the kitchen. The cook was a kind man who said he could find something for her to do. She spent the afternoon peeling potatoes and stirring soup, and when supper time came, she took a large bowl of soup and went to the tables. She was walking toward the prince when she stumbled, spilling soup all over the floor and the prince's clothes.

You graceless ninny," cried the prince. "look what you have done."

"I am so sorry," said the princess, bowing awkwardly and spilling more soup on the floor at the prince's feet.

"Get out! Get out! . . . or I shall have you tarred and feathered and dragged through the city streets."

"Not for me," thought the princess. She left quickly, and told the cook she was sorry.

Then she rode to the castle of the poor prince. Again she got a job in the stables caring for the horses. When the prince came to ride, she came with her buckets of water at just the right time – and spilled water all over him, knocking him down. She quickly stepped back, and almost fell down herself.

The prince got up.

"Are you all right?" asked the prince, looking at the clumsy stable hand.

"I am fine. Thank you."

"Well, be more careful next time." He went back into the castle to change his clothes.

The Princess's Suitors: Reading B

After he was gone, the princess went and washed. Then she begged for work in the kitchen. The chief cook gave her a job.

When it was time for supper, the princess took a bowl of soup to the dining room. When she got near the prince, she stumbled, dumping soup on the floor and spattering the prince.

The prince looked at his clothes with a frown, and then looked at the princess.

"I'm so sorry . . . so very sorry," said the princess, bowing awkwardly and spilling more soup.

"It's all right. But stop being so sorry and bring us some more soup so we can eat it. And get something to mop up the floor." The prince remained as polite and courteous as always.

So the princess got more soup, and this time she didn't spill any. Then she left the castle, and got on her horse and rode home.

When she got there, she told her father that she wanted to marry the third prince. The wedding was celebrated soon after, and the prince and princess lived happily ever after.

▨▨▨▨ Multiple story scramble

Class level: High-beginner to advanced
Group size(s): Whole class, ends up in groups of about 4 students each
Objective(s): To improve listening and speaking skills while focusing on overall textual relationships
Approximate class time: 15 to 30 minutes

The activity

This activity is similar to the *Jigsaw Reading* (see page 117) except that it involves multiple stories and some extra oral work before the jigsaw portion begins.

PREPARATION

1. **Find several short stories (fables are good for this) and divide them each into three or four parts** so that you have enough sections to give one to each student in the class.
2. **Cut the sections apart** so that you will have one for each student.

For large classes (i.e., more than about 20 students), divide the class into groups of 20 or fewer and have each group do the activity simultaneously, with a copy of the same set of story sections.

IN THE CLASSROOM

1. **Give one story section to each student.** Have students read their sections and deal with any unknown vocabulary if needed. (If you have a class that is very reliable in attendance, you can give the story sections out in advance for students to work through as homework. However, this doesn't work well if a few students don't show up, since you then have gaps in the stories and may not even know which pieces are missing.)
2. **Have students begin to talk to each other about their parts of the story, trying to locate the other students with the same story.** Showing the written versions of the story is forbidden. Even the weakest students end up finding their groups; either the better speakers find them, or the last group forms simply because there is no one else left and the remaining people must go together.
3. **Once students find all the other students with the other parts of the same story, they must then get the story into the right order.** This step is just like the *Jigsaw Reading*.

4. *(Optional)* **If using fables, write the morals for the fables on the board at the beginning and then have groups try to identify which moral goes with their story.** You may want to ask students to stand by their moral on the board; this can again help students in the last group, since they won't have to make a choice.

In the multilevel classroom

Pick stories at several different levels. Then, when you give the story sections out, give sections of the hardest stories to the highest-level students, and sections of the easiest stories to the lowest-level students. The lower-level students work more slowly, but they have less material to deal with, so if you pick stories at the right levels, everyone should still finish at about the same time. This gets all students working on the same activity, while each still works at an appropriate level. If you don't do this too often, it won't be obvious to students that you are grouping them by level.

A multilevel version of this activity is shown on page 40.

Adjusting the difficulty of the activity

In addition to the difficulty of the texts, the difficulty of the activity is affected by how similar the stories are to each other. For example, if every story has a rabbit in it, the activity is more difficult than if each story has dissimilar characters. The number of students also makes the activity a little harder (or at least take a little longer), since each student must talk to more people before finding the right group.

Variation

More advanced students can take notes for each person they talk to, and then, individually or in pairs, try to reconstruct all the stories.

Note on the accompanying sample activity

For six or nine students, take out one or two groups of three. For some other number, either give one or two students an extra part, or add a story with a different number of parts.

A low-level story scramble for 12 students
(Belling the Cat, The Fox and the Crow, The Fox and the Stork, The Frog and the Ox)

He walked up to the foot of the tree. "Good-day, Mrs. Crow," he cried. "How pretty you look today. Your feathers are shiny, and your eyes are so bright. You must have the most beautiful voice; sing me just one song so I can call you the Queen of Birds.	Then an old mouse said, "That sounds good, but who will hang the bell on the Cat?" Then the mice sadly looked at each other and said nothing.
"We should hang a bell around the cat's neck, and then we could hear her when she is coming." Everyone liked this idea.	A little frog said to a big frog, "I saw a terrible monster! It was as big as a mountain, with horns on its head, and its tail was as big as a tree." "That was only a cow," said the big frog. "And it isn't so big; I could easily make myself that big."
So the big frog blew himself out, and blew himself out, and blew himself out. "Was the cow this big?" he asked the little frog. "Oh, much bigger than that," said the little frog. Again the big frog blew himself out and asked, "Was the cow this big?" "Bigger! Much bigger," the little frog answered.	I am so sorry that you don't like the soup," said the Fox. "Don't be sorry," said the Stork. "But I do hope you will come and eat with me soon." So they set a day, and the Fox went to visit the Stork.
One bad action deserves another.	Pride can destroy you.
It is easy to suggest impossible ideas.	Do not trust flatterers.

A low-level story scramble for 12 students (continued)

At one time the Fox and the Stork were very good friends. The Fox invited the Stork to dinner. For a joke he served only soup in a very shallow dish. The Fox could easily drink from this, but the Stork could only wet the end of her long bill, and left as hungry as when she came.	The Crow lifted her head and began to caw her best, but as soon as she opened her mouth, the cheese fell to the ground. The fox quickly ate it. "That will do," said he. "That was all I wanted."
A Fox once saw a Crow in a tree with a piece of cheese in its beak. "I want that cheese," thought the Fox.	Long ago, the mice wanted to protect themselves from the Cat. They talked and talked, but no one had any good ideas. At last a young mouse said, "I have an idea."
So the big frog took a bigger breath, and blew and blew and blew, and swelled and swelled and swelled. And he said: "I'm sure the cow is not as big as. . . . " But at that moment he popped.	The Stork served soup in a very tall jar with a narrow opening. The Fox could not get his mouth in this; all he could do was lick the outside of the jar.

An intermediate story scramble
for 16 students
(The Lion and the Mouse; The Lion, the Fox,
and the Beasts; Androcles and the Lion;
The Donkey's Brains)

But when he came there, the Lion simply pounced on the Ass, and said to the Fox, "Here is our dinner for today. You watch here while I go and have a nap. Woe to you if you touch my prey."	"Why do you not come to pay your respects to me?" said the Lion to the Fox. "I beg your Majesty's pardon," said the Fox, "but while I see many hoof-marks going in, I see none coming out. Till the animals that have entered your cave come out again, I prefer to remain in the open air."
As he came near, the Lion put out his paw, which was all swollen and bleeding, and the slave found a huge thorn that was causing all the pain.	When the Lion came back, he soon noticed the absence of the brains, and asked the Fox in a terrible voice: "What have you done with the brains?" "Brains, your Majesty! it had none, or it would never have fallen into your trap."
Just then the little Mouse happened to pass by, and seeing the sad plight the Lion was in, went up to him and soon gnawed away the ropes that bound the King of the Beasts. "Was I not right?" said the little Mouse.	The Lion once sent news that he was sick unto death and summoned the animals to come and hear his Last Will and Testament. So the Goat came to the Lion's cave, and stopped there listening for a long time.
But when the Lion got close, he recognized his friend and licked his hands like a friendly dog. The surprised Emperor summoned the slave, who told him the whole story. At this, the emperor pardoned the slave and freed him, and let the Lion loose to his native forest.	The Lion was so tickled at the idea of the Mouse being able to help him that he lifted up his paw and let him go. Some time after, the Lion was caught in a trap, and the hunters, who desired to carry him alive to the King, tied him to a tree while they went in search of a wagon to carry him.

An intermediate story scramble
for 16 students (continued)

Once, when a Lion was asleep, a little Mouse began running up and down upon him; this soon wakened the Lion, who placed his huge paw upon him, and opened his big jaws to swallow him.

He pulled out the thorn and bound up the paw of the Lion, who was soon able to rise and lick the slave's hand like a dog. Then the Lion took him to his cave, and every day used to bring him meat to live on. Shortly afterwards both were captured.

The slave was sentenced to be thrown to the Lion that had been kept without food for several days. The slave was led into the arena. The Emperor and his Court watched the Lion rush roaring toward the slave.

The Lion and the Fox went hunting together. The Lion, on the advice of the Fox, sent a message to the Ass, proposing to make an alliance between their two families. The Ass came to the place of meeting, overjoyed at the prospect of a royal alliance.

"Pardon, O King," cried the little Mouse to the Lion. "Forgive me this time. I shall never forget it: who knows but what I may be able to do you a turn one of these days?

A slave once escaped from his master and fled to the forest. As he was wandering about there, he came upon a Lion lying down moaning and groaning. At first he turned to flee, but finding that the Lion did not pursue him, he turned back and went up to him.

Then a Sheep went in, and before she came out a Calf came up to receive the last wishes of the Lord of the Beasts. But soon the Lion seemed to recover, and came to the mouth of his cave, and saw the Fox, who had been waiting outside for some time.

The Lion went away and the Fox waited; but finding that the Lion did not return, the Fox ventured to take out the brains of the Ass and ate them up.

It is easier to get into trouble than out.

Gratitude is the sign of noble hearts.

Little friends may prove great friends.

Wit has always an answer ready.

7 Focus on reading

As with a few of the other chapters, the title of this chapter may be slightly misleading, for two reasons. First, most of the activities in this book, other than the initial listening activities, can involve a fair amount of reading. Indeed, reading folktales is one of the most obvious things one can do with them, and one can do this with nearly any activity – or without any activity in particular. The second reason the title of this chapter may be slightly misleading is that these activities also include other elements: a focus on grammar (which is not specifically a reading skill), the ability to infer meaning from context, and so on.

For other activities that are potentially especially reading intensive, see Chapter 11, *Building Awareness of Text Structure* starting on page 224 and Chapter 12, *Developing Analytical Skills* starting on page 250.

Individual reading

Class level: Beginner to advanced
Group size(s): Individuals
Objective(s): To develop reading skills and vocabulary
Approximate class time: 10 to 15 minutes

The activity

Sustained silent reading (SSR) is one way to bringing extensive reading into the classroom that has been demonstrated to result in significant language gains. Key elements in this activity are:

1. **Students choose their own reading from a variety of selections.** Once students have picked something, they must read that selection for the entire reading time. Selecting their own materials improves motivation because students can choose what is interesting to them; reading a single selection prevents students from using up the time browsing through materials without ever choosing anything. Students may *not* choose materials that have been assigned for any class; the goal is *extra* reading, not doing homework during class time.

2. **Everyone, including the teacher, reads silently for a set amount of time** (usually 10 to 15 minutes). Having the teacher reading demonstrates that reading is important. Because the teacher is unavailable to them, students must struggle with the text themselves. Complete silence (this means no questions or requests for help) provides a peaceful, undistracted atmosphere for all students. And since no questions are allowed, students do not waste valuable minutes waiting for the teacher to be free to answer a question.

3. *(Optional)* **You may ask students to respond to what they read in individual journals;** other than this, *no* reports are required. Students are *not* tested or graded on what they have read.

4. **Repeat this activity on a regular scheduled basis.** This could be for the first 10 minutes of every class, or it could be less often – for example, every Friday – but students should be able to count on it. If you sometimes replace scheduled SSR with other activities, students will conclude that it is less important than these other activities and will take it less seriously. Scheduling SSR at the beginning of class is probably best – this prevents it from getting crowded out if some other activity takes longer than expected. Once students become accustomed to SSR, some students will begin to show up early to get additional reading time in. Students may also ask to take materials home so they can finish them. This should be highly encouraged.

Advantages of using folktales for sustained silent reading

SSR can be done with any type of interesting reading material, but folktales provide a particularly good source of material for several reasons:

- Folktales are short enough that students can finish them in a limited amount of time.
- Sequences of related readings appear to result in greater language gains than several unrelated readings. Because there are many folktales in the same traditions, students encounter related material and variety at the same time.
- There are a variety of degrees of difficulty and contextual support to accommodate different levels of students. There are also many kinds of stories to accommodate different tastes.
- Many students find folktales very interesting. This gives folktales a potentially high intrinsic motivation level.

Resources

See the *Bibliography* starting on page 277 for sources for material.

Readings with a focus on grammar

Class level: Any
Group size(s): Individuals
Objective(s): To provide repeated exposure to a particular grammatical
  structure in context
Approximate class time: Varies

Grammar exercises often consist of groups of unrelated sentences
illustrating some structure. This tends to be boring, and it also doesn't
show how certain tenses and structures are used or not used together in
context. The repetition and parallel episodes in folktales naturally
make structures recur many times while keeping language in context
and making the process more interesting. For example, the short version
of *The Boy Who Cried Wolf* on page 139 contains more than 20
occurrences of the regular simple past tense, and the same tense would
naturally be used if we talked about the story.

Folktales easily illustrate many other basic grammatical structures:
simple future; historic present; modals; dialog structure; adverbials of
time, place, purpose, and reason; prepositions; and so on. One also
finds more advanced structures. For example, some versions of *Stone
Soup* repeatedly present the conditional *if . . . then* followed by *but (neg)*
. . . so: "*If* you only had some barley, *then* this soup would be good
enough for a rich man. *But* you don't, *so* we'll just make do with what
we have. . . ." Folktales are well suited for providing a natural context
for a variety of grammatical structures.

The activity

PREPARATION

1. **Find a story that contains many occurrences of the structure you want
   to work on.** Sometimes it is possible to adjust or retell a story to
   include additional occurrences of the structure.
2. **Highlight or mark all the occurrences of the structure so they will
   stand out to students when they read.** If you have an electronic copy
   of the story on your computer (see the Internet sources for folktales
   on page 280 for help getting stories without typing them in yourself),
   you can bold the structure or put the words in upper case.
3. **Have students do a cloze exercise with the marked words left out.** (See
   page 147.) Create a word list that lists the words needed, but in their
   base form rather than in the form needed in the text.

135

IN THE CLASSROOM

1. **Have students read the story using text with the appropriate forms highlighted.** Some research suggests that marking structures may be enough to help students notice them, and that this noticing is enough to help them acquire the structure.
2. **In addition to whatever other activities you want to do with the story, draw attention to the structure, how it is formed, and so on.**
3. **Have students complete the cloze.** They should pay attention to putting the words in the right form when they fill in the blanks.

Stories to use with this activity

Folktales can be used to illustrate and reinforce nearly any grammatical structure. All (or nearly all) stories incorporate the simple past, articles, pronouns, possessives, conjunctions, relative clauses, infinitives, direct and indirect objects, and direct and indirect speech. For specific stories with repeated occurrences of other structures, consider the following as a few examples among many.

Adjectives
Stone Soup (page 83): many color and shape adjectives
The Three Billy Goats Gruff (page 218): many size adjectives

Comparatives
The Stonecutter (page 5): The version here uses *greater* throughout; you could use other comparatives (*either -er* or *more* ___, e.g., *happier, stronger, vaster;* or *more important, more impressive, more invincible*).
Stone Soup (page 83): "This soup is (good, tasty, rich, hearty . . .), but it would be (*better, tastier, richer, heartier* . . .) if . . .
It Could Always Be Worse (page 88): Good when working on *bad, worse, worst*
The Man and His Two Wives (page 40): *older, younger*
The Three Billy Goats Gruff (page 218)

Conditional (If . . . then)
The Stonecutter (page 5): "If I were ____, then I would be___."
Stone Soup (page 83): This can be retold with the conditional or conditional + negative: "If only we had some ___, then this soup would be ____, [but we don't, so. . . .]
The Judgment of the Rabbit (page 228)
The Fisherman and His Wife (page 232)

Degree ("too ____")
Goldilocks (page 185): *too big, too small, too hot, too cold*, etc.

Dialog/direct speech
Almost any: for example, *Stone Soup* (page 83), *The Riddle* (page 22), *Fresh Fish* (page 40), *The Lost Son* (page 61).

Gerunds ("-ing")
The Lost Son (page 61)
It Could Always Be Worse (page 88)
The Princess's Suitors (page 122)

Imperative
It Could Always Be Worse (page 88)
The Fisherman and His Wife (page 232)
The Boy Who Went to the North Wind (page 238)

Infinitives
The Unmerciful Man (page 216)

Modals (can, could, would, should)
New Patches for Old (page 214)
The Fisherman and His Wife (page 232)

Negatives
The Wise Judge (page 221)

Past perfect
The Wise Judge (page 221): Particularly at the beginning of the story

Questions
The Riddle (page 22), *The Woodcutter's Axe* (page 40)

Simple present
You can retell any story in the simple present, though see *Notes on the Story* at the end of *By Unanimous Vote* on page 140.

Spacial prepositions

The Greedy Old Spider (page 75) has many spacial elements: *in the middle, on the edge, between, around,* etc.

The Man the Boy, and the Donkey (page 66) has many spacial elements: *toward, next to, on, off, behind, on the edge of,* etc.

Goldilocks and the Three Bears (see page 185).

The Three Billy Goats Gruff (see page 218).

The Man Who Kept House (page 244).

The Boy Who Cried Wolf

Once, a little boy named Peter LIVED in a small town. He WATCHED sheep for the townsfolk. Each morning he WALKED to the hills with the sheep. He watched the sheep all day long. Each night he WALKED back to the village with the sheep. He always WALKED alone. He was lonely.

One day, he SHOUTED, "Wolf!"

All the men HURRIED from the village. They LOOKED, but there was no wolf.

"He ran away," said Peter.

The men WALKED back to the village.

The next day, Peter WALKED with the sheep to the hills again. Again he SHOUTED, "Wolf!"

Again all the men HURRIED from the village. They LOOKED, but there was no wolf.

"He ran away," said Peter again.

The men WALKED back to the village.

The next day, Peter WALKED with the sheep to the hills again. He heard a growl. He LOOKED. There was a wolf. He SHOUTED, "Wolf!"

But no one HURRIED from the village. The men STAYED in the village. And the wolf KILLED all the sheep.

Notes on the Story

Capital letters draw attention to all simple past tense verbs, and bold draws attention to the different endings. Notice too that slight manipulation of the text could make it work on irregular verbs:

Once, there **WAS** a little boy named Peter. He **KEPT** the sheep for the townsfolk. Each morning he **WENT** to the hills with the sheep. He **SAT** with the sheep all day long. Each night he **WENT** back to the village with the sheep. He **WAS** always alone. He **WAS** lonely.

One day, he shouted, "Wolf!"

All the men **CAME** from the village. . . .

I retold this story with a particular structure in mind, but even unmanipulated texts contain many natural recurrences of many structures.

By Unanimous Vote

While in a certain town, a friend of mine was walking along with one of the local residents. They came to a building with a number of people standing about outside.

"Oh," says the local man. "Today is election day. Would you like to vote?"

"I can't vote," says my friend. "I'm not a citizen."

"That doesn't matter," answers the local man. "Anyone can vote. People will be honored if you participate in our election. Come. I'll show you."

So the local man leads my slightly bewildered friend into the building. People smile at them as they walk together to the voting station.

"You see," says the local man, "anyone can vote. You just take a ballot and drop it in the box." The local man himself picks up a ballot and drops it in the voting box. "You can vote too," he says. "Just take one and drop it in. You can even vote twice if you want."

My friend picks up a ballot and looks at it. "This one's already marked," he says. He looks at the pile and discovers that others are marked as well.

"Oh," says the local man. "They are all marked before people come in. The people here do not know a lot about politics, so the ballots are all marked in advance so people will not make foolish choices. It's easier for them if they only need to put the ballot in the box."

So my friend drops his ballot in the box, and they leave together.

The next day, my friend reads about the election in the paper. Not surprisingly, one man won by unanimous vote.

Notes on the Story

This story happened to an acquaintance of mine. While not always this bizarre, real life is frequently a source for good stories. It is told here in the historic present; that is, it uses the simple present to relate a past series of events. In theory, virtually any story can be retold using the simple present, though it is generally more appropriate with more contemporary stories. For example, you wouldn't normally tell a Greek myth in the historic present: "So Zeus says to Hercules . . ." isn't what we expect. (Actually, the Greeks liked the historic present, so it's not out of the question.) Still, native speakers are more likely to use the historic present when retelling a story as if they were present when it happened, which fits more with contemporary stories than traditional ones. You can provide present-tense grammar review either by having students listen to or read stories told in this way or by having students convert a story from past to present tense.

Dealing with unfamiliar vocabulary while reading

Class level: Low-intermediate to advanced
Group size(s): Individual, pairs
Objective(s): To improve reading fluency, develop inferencing skills, and reduce dictionary dependence
Approximate class time: 15 to 30 minutes

The activity

While folktales have many characteristics that contribute to easy reading (see Chapter 1 for a discussion of these characteristics), they also often have some vocabulary that is less common. Enchantments, potions, trolls, and ogres aren't words that many language learners have previously encountered. Even words like *princess, crown, sword,* and *treasure* – while fairly common – are words that some students won't know. As students read folktales, it is important to show them that they can guess at the meaning of most of these unknown words (so they don't disrupt their reading with repeated visits to the dictionary) and still understand the story well.

Because of the predictability, redundancy, and repetition in folktales, unknown words are usually easier to guess than in many other types of texts. This makes folktales good for developing skill at inferring meaning from context – a very useful general reading strategy.

PREPARATION

Write six to ten questions about a story and copy these (along with the story) for each student. These questions can address general comprehension, reactions, opinions, and responses to the exercise itself. The purpose is partly to give you feedback on where students are, partly to help students make sure they understood the story, and partly to give the faster students something to do when they have finished the exercise while other students are still reading.

PRETEACHING

1. **If necessary, teach students that they can figure out the meaning of an unknown word without using a dictionary.** To do this, write sentences like the ones below on the board one at a time.

   She poured the water into the **tock**.
   Then, lifting the **tock**, she drank.

Unfortunately, as she was setting it down, the **tock** slipped from her hand and broke.
Only the handle remained in one piece.

(from Nuttall, 1982, p. 70)

After writing the first sentence, write students' suggestions of what the word could mean on the board. (Suggest additional ideas if students don't generate enough.) Words like *cup, sink, swimming pool, bucket, bottle, lake,* and *hole* are among the possibilities. Point out that many other nouns are possible (for example, someone could pour water into a computer as I did once, but this is rather unlikely). After writing the second sentence, cross out ideas that students now think are impossible (e.g., *holes, lakes, pools, computers*), put a question mark next to items that students now think are unlikely, and add any additional guesses. Continue writing the sentences. After three or four sentences, there should only be one or two guesses left. Point out to students that they have arrived at a fairly precise definition without touching a dictionary. (If you use a nonsense word as above, make this clear to students so they don't think it is a real word.)

You will probably have to convince students that this is usually actually better for their language learning (because not interrupting reading improves comprehension, because some unknown words are so infrequent that they are a distraction from more important words, because important words will *always* come up again and with enough occurrences the precise meaning will become clear, etc.).

2. **Model for students how you would guess at unknown words.** Put the beginning of a story on the overhead (or give copies to each student) and begin to read it aloud. Each time you come to a word that students might not know, go through your thought process aloud to show how you would tackle figuring out what the word means. For students to really get a strategy, it needs to be modeled repeatedly over time. Whenever someone asks about the meaning of a word and it is appropriate, read the text aloud, verbally express what clues in the text suggest the word could mean, and only then give an explanation of the more precise meaning if necessary.

IN THE CLASSROOM

1. **Give each student a copy of the story and questions.**
2. **Instruct students to read the whole story, circle each word they don't know, and write what they guess it means in the margin.** If you prefer, they can complete the reading before going back and writing their

guesses; this gives students a better general context to draw from in making their guesses.

3. **Have students who have finished guessing the unknown words answer the questions about the story.** The questions not only fill time for faster students; they also help demonstrate to these students that they got the overall meaning even though they didn't look up unknown words. It doesn't matter if not all the students get to the questions.

4. **About 3 to 5 minutes before you plan to wrap up the activity, tell students that if they haven't finished yet, they should stop writing guesses and just finish reading the story.** This is especially important if you plan to collect the stories to see how students did with their guessing; it can be frustrating for a student not to get to the end of the story.

5. **As a class, get students to talk about which words they had difficulty with, what their guesses were, and why.** Draw attention to the fact that there were different guesses, and even some that were incorrect, but that most were adequate for understanding the text. For guesses that are way off, draw attention to elements in the text that show this.

6. **Review the questions.** Point out to students that they were able to understand the story even though they didn't know all of the vocabulary.

Variations

Variation 1: In teaching students that they can figure out meaning without knowing all of the words, giving them a cloze passage (that is, a written text with words periodically left out) is sometimes helpful. Students must use the same basic skills to infer from context what word must go in the blank. You can delete words on a regular basis (for example, every seventh word), or you can leave out a particular type of word (for example, all the adjectives). In making a cloze passage, decide which words to delete, and then use white-out or tape pieces of white paper over those words. (If you have an electronic version of the story in your computer, you can use your word processor to replace the words with blank lines.) Normally words are not left out in the first or last sentences, and one usually doesn't leave out more than one word in seven.

Variation 2 (self-access materials): Have students do a cloze passage and provide a completed cloze for them to check their work, or have them read a story and guess at unknown vocabulary as described in this activity, and then provide an annotated text that has explanations in the margins for vocabulary that students are likely to have difficulty with.

Stories to use with this activity

This activity can be done with nearly any story. The trick is to pick a story that is beyond the students' comfort level (so that it has a moderate amount of unknown vocabulary), without being so difficult that they can't figure out what is going on (because then students would have no context for their guesses).

Example of guessing meaning in a low-intermediate story: *The Thief*

Once there was a large (mining) (company) with **some kind** a (security checkpoint) by the gate. Guards **of place** would check people and (vehicles) as they went out to make sure that no one was stealing from the company.

police

things

One evening, a man came up to the gate pushing a (wheelbarrow) mounded high with (straw.) A guard came and searched the straw but **dirt** found nothing in it, so he let the man leave.

cart

The next evening, the man came to the gate again – again pushing his wheelbarrow heaped high with straw. Again the guard searched the straw. Again he found nothing.

Day after day, the man came to the gate with his wheelbarrow (overflowing) with straw. Day after day, the guards searched the straw and checked the man himself. Day after day, they found nothing. They were (convinced) he was stealing something, but they could never find anything in the straw.

very much

thinking

Finally, the chief guard pulled the man aside. "We all know you are stealing something," he said, "but we can't figure out what it is. I am dying of (curiosity.) I stay awake at night trying to figure out what you are taking and where you have hidden it. If you will tell me what you are stealing, I promise that I will not (punish) you or even try to stop you in the future."

want to

know

say you go

to jail

The man (leaned) close to the guard. "Wheelbarrows," he said.

came

Amin and the Eggs

Once upon a time there lived a peasant named Amin. He owned a miserable little plot of land that he managed to survive on, but one year he lost all his crops in a drought, so he decided to seek his fortune in another village. On credit, he got a dozen hard-boiled eggs for his journey from a merchant, and then off he went on his donkey.

Seven years later, Amin returned to his village. This time he was riding a fine black horse, followed by a servant on a camel laden with gold and silver. Amin had become a rich man.

News of Amin's riches soon spread through the village. Right away the merchant who had given him the dozen eggs on credit came knocking at Amin's door, insisting that Amin owed him five hundred silver pieces in payment of this old debt. Amin of course refused to pay such a large sum and so the matter was taken before the judge.

At the appointed time on the day of the hearing, the merchant was there in court, but of Amin there was no sign. The judge waited impatiently for a quarter of an hour, and was ready to adjourn the hearing, when Amin rushed in, out of breath.

The judge began the hearing, and the merchant presented his case against Amin. "Seven years ago Amin bought twelve eggs from me on credit. If I had kept those twelve eggs, twelve chickens might have hatched. They would have grown to be hens and roosters, which would have laid more eggs, which in turn would have hatched. By now, seven years later, I would have had a large flock of chickens, and so I demand from Amin a payment of five hundred silver coins to compensate for my loss.

"This sounds very fair and just," agreed the judge. He turned to Amin with a scowl, since he was still angry with Amin for being late. "What have you to say for yourself?"

"Please pardon my lateness," began Amin humbly, "but I had a plate of boiled beans that I needed to plant in my garden right away so that I would have a good crop next year!"

"Fool!" exclaimed the judge. "Since when do boiled beans grow?"

To this Amin answered: "And since when do hard-boiled eggs hatch into chickens?" And so he won his case.

Notes on the Story
This story is from the Middle East.

Amin and the eggs: An intermediate sample for the cloze variation

Once upon a time there lived a peasant named Amin. He owned a miserable little plot _____ land that he managed to survive _____ , but one year he lost all _____ crops in a drought, so _____ decided to seek his fortune in _____ village. On credit, he got a _____ hard-boiled eggs for his journey _____ a merchant, and then off he _____ on his donkey.

Seven years later, _____ returned to his village. This time _____ was riding a fine black horse, _____ by a servant on a camel _____ with gold and silver. Amin had _____ a rich man.

News of Amin's _____ soon spread through the village. Right _____ the merchant who had given him _____ dozen eggs on credit came knocking _____ Amin's door, insisting that Amin owed _____ five hundred silver pieces in payment _____ this old debt. Amin of course _____ to pay such a large sum _____ so the matter was taken before _____ judge.

At the appointed time on _____ day of the hearing, the merchant _____ there in court, but of Amin _____ was no sign. The judge waited _____ for a quarter of an hour, _____ was ready to adjourn the hearing, _____ Amin rushed in, out of breath.

_____ judge began the hearing, and the _____ presented his case against Amin. "Seven _____ ago Amin bought twelve eggs from _____ on credit. If I had kept _____ twelve eggs, twelve chickens might have _____ . They would have grown to be _____ and roosters, which would have laid _____ eggs, which in turn would have _____ . By now, seven years later, I _____ have had a large flock of _____ , and so I demand from Amin _____ payment of five hundred silver coins _____ compensate for my loss.

"This sounds _____ fair and just," agreed the judge. _____ turned to Amin with a scowl, _____ he was still angry with Amin _____ being late. "What have you to _____ for yourself?"

"Please pardon my lateness," _____ Amin humbly, "but I had a _____ of boiled beans that I needed _____ plant in my garden right away _____ that I would have a good _____ next year!"

"Fool!" exclaimed the judge. " _____ when do boiled beans grow?"

To _____ Amin answered: "And since when do _____-boiled eggs hatch into chickens?" And _____ he won his case.

A high-intermediate story for guessing meaning from context

Read the story below. While reading, circle any words that you don't know. Guess what these words mean and write your guess in the margin. Do *not* use a dictionary! Then answer the questions at the end of the story. After you are done, use your dictionary to look up any words that you think are important.

Mother Holly

Once upon a time there was a widow who had two daughters. One of them – who was actually her stepdaughter – was pretty and clever; the other was ugly and lazy. But since the ugly one was her own daughter, the woman liked her better than the other, and so the pretty one had to do all the work of the house, and was treated as if she were their maid. Every day she had to sit by a well next to the road and spin till her fingers were so sore that they often bled.

One day some drops of blood fell on her spindle, so she dipped it into the well, meaning to rinse it. But as luck would have it, it slipped from her hand and sank to the bottom of the well. She ran weeping to her stepmother and told her what had happened.

The old woman was so merciless in her anger that she scolded the girl harshly, and she said, "Well, since you dropped the spindle, you must just go down after it yourself, and don't let me see your face again until you bring it with you.

Then the poor girl returned to the well, and not knowing what she was about, in the despair and misery of her heart she leapt into the well and sank to the bottom. For a time she lost all consciousness, but when she came to herself, she was lying in a lovely meadow with the sun shining brightly overhead and a thousand flowers blooming at her feet. She got up and wandered through this enchanted place, till she came to an oven full of bread.

The bread called out to her as she passed, "Oh! Take me out, take me out, or I shall be burnt to a cinder. I am quite done enough." So the girl stepped up quickly to the oven and took out all the loaves

Mother Holly (continued)

one after the other. Then she went on a little farther and came to a tree laden with beautiful, rosy-cheeked apples.

As she passed by, it called out to her, "Oh! Shake me, shake me! My apples are all quite ripe. My branches will likely break if some-one doesn't shake off this load." She did as she was asked, and shook the tree till the apples fell like rain and none were left hanging. After she had gathered them all up into a heap, she went on her way again.

At length she came to a little house, at the door of which sat an old woman. The old dame had such large teeth that the girl felt frightened and wanted to run away, but the old woman called after her, "What are you afraid of, dear child? Stay with me and be my little maid, and if you do your work well I will reward you handsomely. But you must be very careful how you make my bed – you must shake it well till the feathers fly; then people in the world below say it snows, for I am Mother Holly."

She spoke so kindly that the girl took heart and agreed readily to enter her service. She did her best to please the old woman, and shook her bed with such a will that the feathers flew about like snowflakes. So she led a very easy life, was never scolded, and lived on the fat of the land. But after she had been with Mother Holly for some time she grew sad and depressed, and at first she hardly knew herself what was wrong. At last she realized that she was homesick, so she went to Mother Holly and said, "I know I am a thousand times better off here than I ever was in my life before, but nonetheless, I have a great longing to go home in spite of all your kindness to me. I can remain with you no longer, but must return to my own people."

"Your desire to go home pleases me," said Mother Holly, "and because you have served me so faithfully, I will show you the way back into the world myself." Then Mother Holly took the girl by

Mother Holly (continued)

the hand and led her to an open door. As the girl passed through it, a heavy shower of gold fell all over her, till she was covered with it from head to toe.

"That's a reward for being such a good little maid," said Mother Holly, and she also handed the spindle that had fallen into the well back to the girl. Then she shut the door, and the girl found herself back in the world again, not far from her own house.

When she came to the courtyard, the old hen, who sat on the top of the wall, called:

Click, clock, clack,

Our golden maid's come back.

Then the girl went in to her stepmother, and since she had returned covered with gold she was welcomed home. She proceeded to tell all that had happened to her. When the stepmother heard how she had come by her riches, she was most anxious for her own idle, ugly daughter to secure the same good fortune, so she told her to sit at the well and spin.

To make her spindle bloody, the lazy girl stuck her hand into a hedge of thorns and pricked her finger. Then she threw the spindle into the well and jumped in after it. Like her sister, she came to the beautiful meadow and followed the same path.

When she reached the baker's oven the bread called out as before, "Oh! Take me out, take me out, or I shall be burnt to a cinder. I am quite done enough."

But the good-for-nothing girl answered, "A pretty joke, indeed. As if I should dirty my hands for you!"

On she went. Soon she came to the apple tree, which cried out, "Oh! Shake me, shake me! My apples are all quite ripe. My branches will likely break if someone doesn't shake off this load."

"I'll just move along,' she answered, "for one of them might fall on my head." And so she continued on her way.

Mother Holly (continued)

When she came to Mother Holly's house she wasn't the least afraid, for she had been warned about her big teeth, and she readily agreed to become her maid. The first day she worked hard enough, and did all her mistress told her, for she thought of the gold the woman would give her, but on the second day she began to be lazy, and on the third she wouldn't even get up in the morning. She didn't make Mother Holly's bed as she ought to have done, and never shook it enough to make the feathers fly. So her mistress soon grew weary of her, and dismissed her, much to the lazy creature's delight.

"For now," she thought, "now the shower of golden rain will come."

Mother Holly led the girl to the same door she had led her sister to, but when she passed through it, instead of the gold rain, a kettle full of pitch came showering over her.

"That's a reward for your service," said Mother Holly, and she closed the door behind her.

So the lazy girl came home all covered with pitch, and when the old hen on the top of the wall saw her, it called out:

Click, clock, clack,

Our dirty girl's come back.

The pitch stayed on her, and never came off for as long as she lived.

Of the words that you circled, which ones do you think are important enough to look up in a dictionary?

How difficult was it to guess the meaning of the words you didn't know? Which words were hardest to guess? Why?

Why did the girl's mother treat them so differently?

Why was the first girl covered with gold and the second with pitch?

Are there any stories like this from your country? If yes, what is the name of the story? How is it the same and how is it different?

Did you like this story? Why or why not?

8 Focus on writing

These activities involve extensive writing. The process of converting folktales into drama (see page 212) and the activities for developing analytical skills in Chapter 12 can also involve a fair amount of writing. Lesser amounts of writing are integrated into many of the activities in this book.

You may notice that there are no self-access variations for these activities. This is because, although writing activities can be done independently, they are virtually impossible to self-correct. If you have students who particularly like writing and who are also good at giving and incorporating peer feedback, or if you don't mind doing some extra work to read and give feedback on what is written, they could be done as self-access activities; see page 38 for more on self-access activities.

Using pictures to introduce story writing

Class level: Beginner to intermediate
Group size(s): Individuals, pairs, or small groups
Objective(s): To help students generate material for writing and to
  introduce them to the basic questions that many kinds of writing
  address. This activity provides a good opportunity for students to
  work on question forms.
Approximate class time: 15 to 40 minutes

The activity

PREPARATION

Pick a story that can be reflected in about four to eight pictures. You can
draw the pictures and copy them for each student, draw or hang larger
pictures on the board or overhead, or show several pictures from an
illustrated book.

IN THE CLASSROOM

1. **If necessary, preteach vocabulary.** One possible way to do this is
   through the *Discussion of story pictures* activity (see page 48). It is
   important to make sure that students have the words they need to do
   the writing, and the writing provides a good opportunity to use words
   they have learned. If possible, leave new words written on the board
   while students do the activity so they can see and review them when
   they need a word.
2. **Depending on the clarity of the pictures, the familiarity of the story,
   and students, you may need to tell some or all of the story.** For a
   familiar story like *The Tortoise and the Hare,* this probably isn't
   necessary since most students know the story. Likewise, if the pictures
   are clear enough for students to figure out the whole story, you don't
   need to tell it. For a longer, more complex story, however, students
   may not be able to complete the next step without some input.
3. **For each picture, have students answer the questions who, what,
   when, where, and why.** These are the same types of questions that
   journalism attempts to address; being conscious of these questions can
   help students write journalistic-type articles and also help them read
   newspaper articles more effectively. Several of these questions are also
   important for certain types of scientific and academic writing. If you
   have more pictures, don't have students answer every question for
   every picture: Pick those that will yield meaningful answers.

4. **Once students have answered these questions for each picture, have them write a story based on the information they have generated.** This might be as short as one sentence per picture for beginning students, or a whole paragraph for each picture for more advanced students. Using pictures to generate the content for the writing prevents students from getting stuck because they don't know what to say, and also frees more energy to focus on the language. A sample activity sheet for *The Tortoise and the Hare* is shown on page 156.

It does not matter if the stories students come up with are even similar to the original story; the goal is simply to use the pictures to generate content for students to express in English.

Variations

Variation 1: To make the activity a little harder and also to give more room for creativity, give the pictures in mixed-up order so students must decide how to order them before writing about them.

Variation 2: To work on question forms, have students write one or more questions for each of the pictures instead of or in addition to answering them. For example, for the pictures on page 157, the students might write, "Who is the man with the invitaton? What is the Spider doing? Why does Spider have two ropes around his waist?" and so on.

Adapting the activity to different levels

For beginners, you can make the activity easier by filling in some of the information for them. (For example, the first column is filled in for the activity on page 156.) More pictures, more complicated pictures, and the amount or writing you expect students to generate can make the activity more suitable for higher levels.

Stories to use with this activity

Many of Aesop's fables are especially good for this activity. Many illustrated folktales could also be used by selecting a half-dozen key pictures. In this book, the stories and pictures in the *Picture sorting listening activity* can also be used (giving the pictures to the students in the right order). See examples for *Jack and the Beanstalk* on page 157 and *The Fox and the Stork* on page 158.

The Tortoise and the Hare

Who: a rabbit and a turtle

What: a race

Where: don't know

When: a long time ago

Why: because the rabbit wanted

to show he was faster

Now write sentences about the pictures:

Once, a long time ago, a

rabbit and a turtle decided

to have a race. The rabbit

said that he would win.

Writing stories from pictures for *The Tortoise and the Hare.*

The Greedy Old Spider (see page 75)

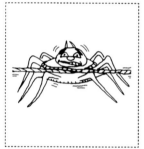 

Writing stories from pictures for *The Greedy Old Spider.*

Jack and the Beanstalk (see page 246)

Writing stories from pictures for *Jack and the Beanstalk.*

The Fox and the Stork (see page 128)

Writing stories from pictures for *The Fox and the Stork*.

Writing stories using a list of items to include

Class level: High-beginner to advanced
Group size(s): Small groups of 3 or 4, pairs, individuals
Objective(s): To have students write an original story (and to work on brainstorming skills)
Approximate class time: 30 to 50 minutes

The activity

Students should have been exposed to a number of folktales before trying this activity so they know something about the types of things that happen in folktales.

IN THE CLASSROOM

1. **Give students a list of objects, people, and places they must incorporate into a story.** See the lists on pages 161–162 and 165–167 for some ideas. You can give the same list to everyone in the class, or you can give each group a different set. (One option that creates an interesting beginning is to have a half-dozen bags, each containing many pieces of paper with a different item written on each; students must pick one paper from each bag.) For example, students might get a list like this:

   a poor boy, a princess, a talking donkey, a flying stick, a mountain, a dragon, a key, a lantern

2. **Either in small groups or as a class, have students brainstorm about possible ways to use all of the items in a story.** If students haven't brainstormed before, do this with the class as a whole the first time to give the idea.

3. **Students must create a story that uses all of the items they have been given.** I usually have students do this in small groups, but it can be done in pairs or individually. Students may add as many objects as they want, as long as they use everything on the list. Students can create the stories orally or in writing. If you choose writing and students are working in groups, you may want to make a rule that no one may write down his or her own ideas – this keeps more oral interaction going and increases the chance that everyone will follow what is going on.

4. **Have students share their stories with the rest of the class.** If students had the same list, it is interesting to see the variety that can come from the same objects; if students had different lists, then the stories will be completely new.

5. **If writing is a focus, you can have the students give feedback to each other on the stories, and then have students revise the stories.** After doing this a few times, you could let students pick their favorite stories and "publish" a book so each class member can have a copy. (Depending on how the activity went, students may not be particularly attached to stories created in this way, so you might do better saving the book creating for stories from the students' own cultures; see page 178.)

Adapting the activity for different levels

Making sure that the items go together makes the activity easier; likewise, choosing items that don't typically go together requires more thinking and discussion, probably results in a longer story, and hence makes the activity more difficult. For example, it is usually easier to generate a story from a group of items like *a king, a dragon, a mountain, a magic sword, and rescuing a princess* than from a group like *a king, a talking donkey, a swamp, a beggar, and a key*. The difficulty of the actual items also helps adjust the activity for different levels; items like *king, trees,* and *pot of gold* are quite suitable for beginners; items like *wandering minstrel, a jeweled casket,* and *an enchanted potion* are more suitable for advanced students.

Focus on writing: Writing stories using a list of items to include

These lists are by no means exhaustive; they merely suggest a few possibilities as a starting place. Note that adding adjectives can change many of the items below (a fat cook, a skinny cook, a beautiful princess, an ugly princess, a poor king, a handsome young king, a blind king, a clumsy thief, an honest thief, etc.). I have included mostly traditional sorts of items, but there is no reason you couldn't also occasionally include one or more contemporary elements: a used car salesman, a computer programmer, a telescope, a mousetrap, etc. (This may make the activity harder for some students.)

You may not always want to use all of these categories. For example, I often don't give a task, since this limits the scope of the story students can produce. Although a few of the words listed are not very common (e.g., alchemist), discussion of what these words mean provides some very good language input.

Places	Creatures	Tasks
a castle/palace	an ogre (troll, etc.)	to make the princess
a mountain	a witch/fairy	laugh
a swamp, bog	a dragon	to kill a dragon (ogre,
a cave, pit, tunnel	a giant	giant, etc.)
a road infested with	a jinn	to marry the princess
robbers	an elf, a dwarf, a fairy	to find three people
a fountain	an angel	more foolish than
a poor man's cottage	a snake	one's spouse
a stable	a pack of wolves	to make dragon soup
a forest, wood, field	a dog	to find a missing ring
a dungeon	a goat, a fox, a lion	to pick up 1,000,000
an inn, tavern, etc.	a talking donkey	pieces of spilled rice
the moon	a horse with wings	in one day
a lake/ocean	a singing frog	to answer a riddle
a well	a spider	to compose a poem
a maze	an ant, a grasshopper	to catch the wind in a
the end of the rainbow	the wind	jar
a bakery	a horse with two heads	to trick the king
a marketplace	a mermaid	to find the truth
a bridge	a cat	to win a race/contest
a ship	a swan	to find one's father
an island	a hawk/eagle	to find an honest man
a great city	a tiger in a pit	to find two lost
a tower	a camel	brothers
a desert	the devil	to break an
the bottom of the sea	a goose (or other	enchantment
heaven/hell	animal) that, once	
a rooftop	touched, one can't let	*Note:* You may want to
a city gate	go of	skip giving a task,
a courtyard		since this often con-
	(any other animal or	siderably narrows
(any other place)	*creature)*	what students can do.

161

Focus on writing: Writing stories using a list of items to include

People	Things	Magical things
a woodcutter	a stick	a crystal ball
a shepherd, etc.	a pot of gold	a flying carpet
a wise (or foolish) old woman	a precious jewel	a purse that is never empty
a king/queen	a key	a ring (cloak, etc.) that makes one invisible
a prince/princess	a locked chest (with no key)	a bow and arrow that cannot miss (or that cannot hit)
three sons/daughters	a pair of old shoes	
a thief	a sword	
a wizard/fairy/witch	a bucket (with a hole)	a horn that summons help
a priest/rabbi/etc.	an old hat	
a dwarf	a nail	a harp that plays itself
a mean/kind stepmother	an axe	a hen that lays golden eggs
a poor boy	a rope	
a man with one leg	a stone	a wishing well
a swordsmith	a flagon of wine	three wishes
a princess who can't laugh/cry	a bone	a gate that opens and shuts itself
a cook	a long black cloak	a pot that makes food until told to stop
a wandering minstrel	a silver cup	
an innkeeper	a pot of pitch	a bag that can never be filled
a beggar	a drum	
a crafty merchant	a brass lamp	an enchanted potion
a band of plunderers	a leaky boat	a magic mirror
an alchemist	a pot of soup	a love potion
a knight in rusty armor	a feather bed	magic seeds
a baby	a candle	something you can't let go of once touched
a wise man	an iron ring	
a blind man	a shovel	a ring (hat, etc.) that makes the wearer always tell the truth
a pirate	a kiss	
a poet	a pen and ink	
a peddler	a wheelbarrow	an instrument that makes the hearers dance
a leper	a cheese	
a man who can turn into a bear	a barrel	a lamp that makes the room darker
	a net	
a son/daughter who will do no work	a wooden bowl	a wand that grants one wish but does the opposite of the next
	a blank scroll	
a scholar	a shovel	elixir of life
a judge	a harp (or other instrument)	
a juggler	a bell	
a trickster	a piece of ice	
a marriage broker	a map	
a midget	a loaf of bread	
		Note: Any ordinary object can become magical in a folktale
(any other class or occupation)	*(any other tool, food, or object)*	

Writing stories using a stack of item cards

Class level: High-beginner to advanced
Group size(s): Small groups of 3 or 4, pairs
Objective(s): To have students write an original story
Approximate class time: 30 to 50 minutes

The activity

This activity is similar to the previous activity except that here students get a stack of cards with items on them and they must deal with the items in the order that they draw the cards. Since students must deal with items in a specific order and without knowing what other items they will subsequently have to deal with, it requires more "on the fly" creation as opposed to the planning and negotiation that the previous activity provides. Because of this, this activity has a different feel and so provides more variety in the classroom.

PREPARATION

1. **Write down six to twelve items on a sheet of paper so it can be cut into pieces with one item on each.** You may want to use vocabulary that has been recently introduced to provide some recycling and review.
2. **Copy the sheet onto cardstock so you have one for each group, and cut each into cards with a single item.** (You can also use regular paper if you wish.) You may want to shuffle the cards so that each group will get them in a different order.

Before doing this activity for the first time, demonstrate the activity for the class by doing it yourself on the board for part or all of a story. As you pick up each card, ask for input on how the item could be added to the story, and then write the sentences on the board. As you are trying to put things together mentally yourself, think out loud so that students can view the mental process that you are going through. If you're feeling a little adventurous, have half a dozen or more students each write one item on a card that they would like to see you include in a story. (They should not consult with each other.) Then collect the cards and use them so students can see that you really are dealing with completely unexpected material (just as you'll be asking them to do).

Focus on writing: Writing stories using a stack of item cards

1. **Divide the class into groups of three or four students and give each group a stack of cards.** Some sample cards are provided on pages 165–167; see also pages 161–162 for additional items to use.
2. **In each group, one member takes the top card. That person must produce the initial sentence(s) of a story, somehow including the item on the card.** The group should be encouraged to discuss ideas, but the person who drew the card has the final say and must dictate the sentence(s) so the person on his or her right can write them down.
3. **Once that section of the story has been written down, the next member (going clockwise) draws a card. That member must add one or more sentences to the story so that the item on the card is included.** Again, discussion is encouraged, but the member who drew the card must produce the sentences and the person on his or her right must add them to the written story. Students may add whatever they wish in addition to what is on the card.
4. **Continue until all the cards in the stack have been used.** Give students the option of adding an ending if they think their story needs it. If time runs out before the cards run out, give students a 5-minute warning and tell them to finish the story.
5. *(Optional)* **If writing is a focus and some interesting stories have emerged, let students revise and rewrite the earlier portions of the story after the initial writing is finished.** These stories tend to have more of a "thrown together" feel to them than those created in the previous activity, so the stories may not be ones students care enough about for them to feel that revising is worthwhile.
6. **Once everyone is done, some or all of the groups should share their stories with the class.**

Adapting the activity for different levels

If the items go together, the activity tends to be easier; items that fit together less readily require more thinking and discussion, probably result in a longer story, and make the activity more difficult. (For example, a stack that contains *a boat, a bridge, a river, a castle, a road,* and *a horse* will usually be easier to tie together than a stack with *a dog, a sword, a bucket, a pin, a bird, a swamp,* and *a crown.*

Letting students look through the whole stack of cards before shuffling them also makes the activity easier; even though students don't know which order items will come in, knowing what is coming helps them generate ideas and plan more effectively.

The difficulty of the actual items also helps adjust the activity for different levels; items like *castle, forest,* and *gold* are quite suitable for beginners; items like *wandering minstrel, a jeweled casket,* and *an enchanted potion* can be used with more advanced students.

In the multilevel classroom

Group students by level and give more and harder cards to the upper levels.

A set of cards for creating a story

a locked door	a precious jewel	a pair of old shoes	a wise man
a crooked stick	a bucket	a mirror	a giant
a palace	an old woman	a fountain	a poor man's cottage

A set of cards for creating a story

a deep and swiftly flowing river	a rickety bridge	a dark and foreboding castle	a king clothed in rags
an evil enchantress	a jeweled crown	a long and twisty secret passage	a rusted key

A set of cards for creating a story

a cracked jar	a sack with a hole in it	a large stick	a witch
a king	a golden chest	a rope	a tall tower
a key	a rich prince	a poor boy	a beautiful princess

A set of cards for creating a story

a flying carpet	a king with a dying daughter	an evil spirit	a large iron cage
a bottle with a stopper	a wandering teacher	a bell	a strong young man who is afraid of the dark

A set of cards for creating a story

a poor woman	a crooked judge who loved bribes	a thieving merchant	a small copper bowl with a cross etched into the bottom
a wise king	a dark, damp, drippy prison cell	a truthful beggar	a diamond ring that had been lost in the mud

Finishing existing stories

Class level: Low-intermediate to advanced
Group size(s): Small groups of 3 or 4, pairs, individuals
Objective(s): To help students learn to write an original story ending
Approximate class time: 20 to 30 minutes

The activity

This activity is similar to having students compose complete original stories, except that it gives all of the students the same beginning place. This may be harder for some students, since it is more limiting, but it is also easier in that students have something existing to work with.

1. **Read or tell the beginning of any story.** (Try to choose stories for which a single ending is not too easy to anticipate from the beginning; otherwise all the stories generated will be too similar.)
2. **In small groups or with the class as a whole, let students brainstorm about directions the story could take.**
3. **Let students, either individually or in groups, create endings for the story.**
4. **Provide some context, either in groups or with the whole class, for students to share the endings they have created.** Talk about the different endings and which ones students like best and why.
5. *(Optional)* **Tell the complete original story.** Get student feedback on whether they liked the "real" ending as well as the ones they created.

Adapting the activity to different levels

Aside from the difficulty of the language used for the beginning of the story, the difficulty of providing acceptable endings affects how easy the task is to complete. For example, *The Missing Brothers,* on page 170, leaves an enormous number of possibilities: The older brothers could have been waylaid by thieves (or a dragon, an ogre, etc.), turned into toads, married to domineering wives and not allowed to leave, locked in prison, lost in an enchanted forest, lost at sea, etc. It is not hard to come up with ideas, and less mental energy devoted to generating content means more energy free to focus on language. In contrast, the problem in *The Princess Who Never Smiled* (page 171) is much more difficult: Given that so many prior attempts at humor have failed, there are no immediately apparent solutions. Because the task is more difficult, students must focus more attention on this problem than on language. This does not mean the latter sort of beginning isn't useful, but only that it is not usually suitable for lower-level students. For more difficult stories, helping students explore some *why* questions can help generate ideas. For example, *Why does the princess not smile? Is there some external situation that saddens her? Was there something about the other men who tried that bothered her?*

In the multilevel classroom

Provide a beginning that is suitable for the lowest-level students. More advanced students can easily generate a more complex story for a simple beginning if they wish, but a beginning that is too hard will frustrate the lower students. You can also give different groups different beginnings at different levels.

A sample student completion

For *The Missing Brothers* (a version without the donkey, fishing pole, and sack), a low-level immigrant student generated this:

After one year the yongest brother got some money and he came back to the intersection looked for his brothers. The yongest brother waited for his brothers 1–2 weeks until a month but no one show up. Then he turn left side looking for the oldest brother.

At last he hearded that his brother get married with a Vietnamese girl and they rich and they went back to Vietnam and started a new life there, they got two car dealers in Vietnam, that business get him so busy, so that why he can't came back to Unitied States. After that he went back to the intersection and he went to straight way, and looking for his other brother, the other brother was a beggar, so he stopped and talk, then he gave to his brother some money and bought a air plane ticket because they will come back to Vietnam look for their brother, after few days they did see each their faces, and they both helped the oldest brother to sales auto vehicles.

Other stories to use with this activity

This activity can be used with the beginning of many folktales. Here are a few possibilities:

Salem and the Nail (see page 104). Stop after the judge decides that Salem is in the right but before Salem buys his house back, and see if students can come up with a way for Abraham to get the best of the deal.

Wine for the Feast (see page 119). Stop right after the man announces that he wants to go to the feast without buying any wine.

The Rabbit's Judgment (see page 228). Stop after the scholar pulls the tiger from the pit and the tiger announces that he is going to eat the scholar.

The Princess's Suitors (see page 122). Stop after the princess announces
that she has a plan, but before anyone knows what the plan is.

The Fourth Question (see page 68). Stop after the wise man tells the
young man that he may ask only three questions. Students must not
only decide which three to ask but must also come up with the wise
man's answers.

The Missing Brothers

Once there were three brothers. Their father and mother had died,
and had left them nothing but a donkey, a fishing pole, and a large
empty sack. The oldest brother took the donkey, the second
brother took the fishing pole, and the youngest brother got only
the empty sack. Together they set out to make their way in the
world.

After they had walked some ways, they came to a place
where three other roads joined the road they were on. The oldest
brother said, "Let's each take a different road and see what we
find. But let us meet here in a year and a day to share our fortune
with one another." The brothers agreed, and so they each took a
different road.

When the year and a day had passed, the youngest brother
returned. He waited and waited, but his other brothers did not
come back. At last he said, "Perhaps something bad has happened
to my brothers. I must see if I can help them, or avenge their
deaths if they have died." So he set out on the road that the second
brother had taken.

When he had gone some ways down this road. . . .

Notes on the Story
Although it is similar to "real" tales, I just made up this
beginning one day when I needed it for an activity; this story
has no "authentic" ending. A sample student ending is shown
on page 169.

The Princess Who Never Smiled

Once upon a time, a king had a daughter who was beautiful and kind and wise. The only problem was that she had never smiled. This so bothered the king that he said that whoever could make her smile could have half the kingdom.

Many men came to the palace. They told jokes and stories; they did stunts and tricks; a few even tried to tickle her, but nothing they did made her smile.

At last the king grew weary of this. He announced that, from now on, whoever tried to make the princess smile and failed would be covered with tar and feathers and led about the city square with a bucket on his head.

Many more men came to try and make the princess smile – each sure that his stories were the funniest, but each of them also failed and was covered with tar and feathers and led about the city square with a bucket on his head.

Now it happened that one day the son of a poor farmer was in the city, and he saw a man being led by who was covered with tar and feathers, with a bucket on his head.

"Why," the boy asked a stranger, "is that man covered with tar and feathers and being led about with a bucket on his head?"

"You must be from far away," the man answered. "The king has a daughter who has never smiled. The king has said that anyone who makes her smile can have half the kingdom, but anyone who tries and fails will be covered with tar and feathers and be led about the city square with a bucket on his head."

"I see," said the young man.

The next day, the young man went to the palace. . . .

Notes on the Story
This is another beginning that I made up; there is no "correct" ending.

The Teacher's Jar

Once upon a time, there was a traditional Korean school. The teacher was a greedy, stern, lean, unkind old man with a mustache.

One day, a friend came to see him. He ordered the students to review until he returned. A few minutes later, he returned holding a jar. He said, "This is very dangerous! If you taste even a drop of the contents of this jar, you will die at once." But this was not true; he lied because he wanted to eat it all by himself.

A few days later, he had to leave hastily, so he told the students to do homework. As soon as he left, they began to play. While they were playing, one student suggested that they explore the closet. When they opened it, they noticed the jar immediately. . . .

Notes on the Story

This is the beginning of a Korean story. It was originally told to me by one of my students. In the real story, the students open the jar, discover that it is honey, eat it, and then realize they are going to get in trouble for doing so. One bright student then shatters the teacher's most precious inkstone, and the other students think he is mad until he explains his plan. When the teacher returns, hs is astonished to find his inkstone shattered and all of his students lying on the floor. The student who came up with the plan explained that he had tripped and knocked the inkstone off the desk. Because they were so sorry about the loss of his treasure, he explains, they all wanted to die, so they ate the poison in the closet. The teacher finds himself unable to punish the students, is forced to tell them the truth about the jar, and never lies to them again.

What Hershel's Father Did

Once Hershel of Ostropol stopped at an inn and asked for some dinner. The innkeeper looked at his shabby clothes and thought, "This man is a tramp. He has no money to pay for a meal." After talking with his wife, they pushed him out the door. Shortly after, they heard a knocking at the door. They looked out. It was Hershel.

"If you don't give me something to eat," he called out, "I will have to do what my father did!" . . .

Notes on the Story

Hershel is a common trickster in Jewish tales. Sometimes he is very crafty, other times just foolish. In the original version of this story, after a great deal of ranting outside, he terrifies the innkeeper and his wife into giving him as much as he can eat. Once Hershel is full, they timidly ask what his father did. "Oh," he replies, "when my father had nothing to eat . . . why he went to bed hungry."

▨▨▨▨ Writing original stories

Class level: Beginner to advanced
Group size(s): Individuals and whole class
Objective(s): To practice all language skills while developing original
 stories
Academic skill(s): Brainstorming, organization of ideas
Approximate class time: Parts of several classes

The activity

1. **Brainstorm to generate ideas that could be included in the stories.**
 Write every idea on the board, regardless of how trivial or bizarre. It
 may be worth talking about some of the more unusual ideas and how
 they might be workable so students see the value in not immediately
 rejecting unusual ideas when working on their own. Brainstorm for
 ideas about when and where the story could take place, about possible
 elements in the story, and about possible outcomes. Brainstorm as a
 whole class, or have students brainstorm in small groups and then
 share the ideas generated by the groups and continue brainstorming
 as a class. If students get stuck, you can get things going again by
 either providing an idea or two in a different vein than students have
 been thinking in, or asking questions like "Where will the story
 happen?" and "Is there anything magical that might help?"

2. **Use semantic mapping to group the ideas.** Sort the ideas from the
 brainstorming into categories. For example, you might put all the
 settings together, all the heroes together, all the problems together, and
 so on. (You may also want to draw attention to categories that no
 ideas were generated for.) This shows how to organize a collection of
 ideas and is useful in many contexts.

    The sorting can be done either by the students or by the teacher on
 the board. If students do it, as you go over it, see if you can find
 different students who used different organizational schemes, to
 illustrate that there is more than one way to organize the same
 material. Another option is to do the mapping as ideas are generated:
 Write each new idea under the appropriate category.

3. **Have students write their own stories.** If any students really have
 trouble inventing a story, you might privately give them the option of
 writing a story from their own culture instead.

4. **Have peers read the stories and provide feedback.** They should make
 comments on ideas that might be developed in the stories, on points
 that were confusing, and on grammatical issues. (If you have time for
 an extra draft, allow comments only on ideas in the first round, and

allow grammatical corrections in the second round.) I have students put their names on the drafts they commented on and sometimes collect their comments to see what type of feedback was given; students sometimes make comments more carefully if they know the teacher will be checking (and possibly grading) what they have done.

5. **Have students implement peer comments and revise as needed.**
6. **Provide teacher feedback on the stories.** Usually, if I catch grammatical errors, I just mark the problem point without explaining what was wrong. Then I let students work in pairs to try to figure out what the problem was. (If they can't figure it out, I provide a time at the end of class when they can ask me for clarification.) I also write comments on the ideas and pose questions that suggest ways the stories might be further developed or clarified.
7. **Have students revise the stories a final time.** Giving a chance to revise after teacher feedback increases the chances that the feedback will be looked at carefully rather than just passed over on the way to finding the grade. When students submit the final version, you may require that they submit all drafts so you can see the amount of revision, willingness to incorporate comments, and degree of improvement from the first draft to the final. I grade more based on progress than on the actual quality of the final draft.
8. **If possible, publish a book of student stories and/or display the final products publicly** (e.g., in the school library). See page 178 for help producing a book of stories.

Variation

Give students the beginning of a story or even all of a story except for the ending, and have them complete the story (see page 168). This provides students with the opportunity to be creative while giving them a starting place. If you want, offer several beginnings and let students choose which one they want to finish.

Sample brainstorming – partial results

Once upon a time
when the tiger smoked
a king and a princess
ugly princess
beautiful princess
marry the princess
marry a rich prince
get a lot of money
a dragon
it burns up all the crops
a bad witch
an oni
steals king's daughter
three sons

lazy sons-father angry
a stupid boy but nice
old lady
a drink that makes some-
    one love you
two brothers – one mean,
    one nice
a small town
a big city
big castle
hidden room where lots
    of gold is
China, Korea, America
today
long time ago

getting enough food
becoming thieves
becoming honest
thrown in a dungeon
being asked a hard riddle
king says you must die
beggar becomes king
pick up 1,000 grains of
    rice spilled on ground
big party
everyone drinking
magic stick – does
    anything you want

Sample semantic mapping for the same material

Beginnings
Once upon a time
When the tiger smoked

When
today
long time ago

Characters

– Good –
a king
ugly princess
beautiful princess
a stupid boy but nice
old lady
three sons
two brothers – one mean,
    one nice

– Bad –
a dragon
a bad witch

an oni
lazy sons-father angry

Problems
get rid of dragon
crops burned up
king's daughter missing
getting enough food
being asked a hard riddle
king says you must die
pick up 1,000 grains of
    rice spilled on ground
thrown in a dungeon

Goals
marry the princess
marry a rich prince
get a lot of money
becoming thieves
becoming honest

Tools/Helps
magic stick – does
    anything you want
a drink that makes
    someone love you

Places
a small town
a big city
big castle
hidden room where lots
    of gold is
China, Korea, America
big party – everyone
    drinking

Endings
beggar becomes king

Writing stories in shifts

Class level: Low-intermediate to advanced
Group size(s): Individuals
Objective(s): To provide a fun context for writing practice
Approximate class time: 30 to 40 minutes

The activity

IN THE CLASSROOM

1. **Have each student write the beginning of a story.** If necessary, precede this with some brainstorming. Convey to students that the goal is *not* grammatical accuracy, but to write as much as they can in 5 or 10 minutes. Let them know they are *not* supposed to finish the story in that time, just to write a beginning. You can give students the beginning of a story to work from if you wish (see page 168), but if you do this, make groups of 3 to 5 students and give each group member a different beginning.
2. **After students have been writing for 5 or 10 minutes, ask them to finish the sentence or thought that they are on and then pass the story to the student to their right.** Each student will then have a story beginning that someone else wrote.
3. **Have students read the beginning of the story that they received and let them know that they will have 5 or 10 minutes to add to the story before passing it on to someone else.** If needed, let them get clarification about what was written.
4. **Every 5 or 10 minutes, have students pass the story again, read the new story that they have received, and continue it.**
5. **On the final round, let students know that they should try to bring the story to a conclusion if they can.** (Having four or five students contribute to each story is generally appropriate; less than this does not add enough variety to the story; more than this makes the activity too long.)
6. **Have a few students share their stories with the class.** If students are not good oral readers, you might want to read them aloud yourself.

▨▨▨ Creating a book of student stories

Class level: High-beginner to advanced
Group size(s): Individuals; some pair or small group work
Objective(s): To produce a book of student stories, to give students a
  writing purpose (especially a purpose for revising and incorporating
  teacher and peer feedback), and to provide a demonstrable
  accomplishment for their efforts
Approximate class time: Extensive, part of a number of classes

The activity

IN THE CLASSROOM

1. **Have students write stories from their own cultures or original stories.**
   See the preceding activities for more on having students write the
   stories. If students are writing stories from their native cultures and
   you have many students from the same culture, you may want to begin
   by getting them to brainstorm and list all the folktales from their
   culture that they can think of. Then, once many tales are listed, have
   them each pick a different story. (If you don't do this, your book will
   probably end up with multiple tellings of a few stories.)
2. **Once students have edited their stories (using both peer and teacher
   feedback), collect the final drafts.** Notice that the teacher feedback
   comes before students are done with the activity and before they get
   a grade; they are expected to evaluate and respond to this feedback
   rather than just reading it. If you don't plan to type up the stories for
   the final booklet, make sure that students all use the same size paper
   so you won't run into problems when you copy the pages into
   booklets. On the final version submitted, make sure each story has a
   title and the name of the author or reteller. If the class includes
   multiple nationalities, also have students include the national origin
   of the tale if it is a tale from their own culture.
3. **Have students write introductions for themselves.** This is explained
   on the next page.
4. *(Optional)* **Have students illustrate their stories.** Some older students
   will not care for this idea, so feel free to skip this. If a few students are
   interested in illustrating all of the stories, this can still be used
   productively. They will get a lot of reading practice reading the stories
   to illustrate, and you can then get other students to read the texts
   again to make sure that the pictures are consistent with the texts.
5. **Collate the stories into booklets.**

WRITING "ABOUT THE AUTHOR" SELF-INTRODUCTIONS

Preparation: Go to a library and copy about half a dozen "about the author" pages (sometimes found on the inside of the back of the cover jacket). Make sure that the ones you choose are at an accessible level for the students. (Juvenile and adolescent books are more likely to be useful than most adult books.) Also make sure that a variety of styles are reflected. For example, one jacket will tell the facts of the author's past (where she grew up, what degrees she has, etc.). Another will tell about the author's interests (e.g., "He lives with his wife, and has three cats. He loves to play the violin and hunt water buffalo in his free time."). Still others will convey aspects of the author's dreams and philosophy of life. Some will be personal and informal, others not. Make sure that each introduction reflects a different style and type of information.

1. Give copies of the introductions to the students and have them read each of them.
2. Have students identify which they liked best and why. Also have them list types of information that were included – for example, schools attended, pets, family, favorite foods, and hobbies.
3. Once students have completed the above steps individually, review what they found as a class. Write the different observations on the board.
4. Have students individually list information about themselves that they would like people to know if they were to write a book. Then have them use this information to write an introduction for themselves.
5. Using both peer and teacher feedback, get students to revise and polish these introductions. Follow the same steps as when revising the stories; see page 178.

Grammatical exercise option: Have students initially write their introductions in the first person, and then have them convert them to the third person.

PRODUCING THE BOOKS

1. Copy the students' stories and introductions, or, if you have time and wish to do so, type them up. I like numbering the pages and creating a table of contents as well, though this isn't essential.

   If your students are proficient with the computer, they can submit stories on computer disks, but if they don't already know how to use word processors or have a definite need to learn, this ends up being a distraction from their language learning goals.
2. If possible, get a photograph of the class and include a copy of this in the "About the Authors" section. Put a title on the page like "The

Authors," and put a caption under the photo that lists the students' names.

3. Give a copy (or two) of the book to each student. Also try to find a public place (e.g., school library, bulletin board) where you can display the book so others can see it as well.

Note: If you want to produce a nicer-looking booklet, a local printer, graphic designer, or typesetter may be able to help.

9 Folktales and language games

In one sense the activities in this chapter are not exactly folktale activities; they are general activities that are used here to review and reinforce the language encountered in folktales. Yet I have found that language games generally fit well into the kinds of classes that one can incorporate folktales and storytelling into, and the fun review is a useful addition to the classroom.

Concentration matching game

Class level: Beginner to intermediate
Group size(s): Small groups, pairs
Objective(s): That students will understand and be able to produce a
   number of potentially new vocabulary items
Approximate class time: 15 to 20 minutes

The Activity

PREPARATION

1. **Make fifteen to twenty pairs of cards based on the language in the
   story.** (When creating the cards, I divide a sheet of paper into 20
   squares [4 across by down], and use two sheets for a set. Don't cut the
   original set apart; see the next step.) See *Options for creating the cards*
   below for suggestions on what to put on the cards.
2. **Copy these sheets of cards so that you will have one set for each group
   of students.** After copying the sheets, cut the copies into cards with a
   paper cutter and put each set in a separate envelope. This lets you save
   the cards for later use without getting them scrambled. If you plan to
   reuse them many times, you might laminate them.

IN THE CLASSROOM

1. **Form groups of two to four students.**
2. **Have students shuffle the cards and lay them face down in straight
   rows.**
3. **One student in the group turns over two cards so all players can see
   them.** The student must read what is on the cards aloud (or say the
   name of the item if the card has a picture). It is acceptable to get help
   from other group members if a student does not know some word or
   item.
4. **If the cards match, the student keeps that pair and takes another turn.
   If the cards do not go together, the student turns them face down again
   in the same places that the cards were originally. It is now the next
   student's turn.**

Options for creating the cards

Depending on the level of the students, these pairs could include:

A word with a corresponding picture. These are best for beginners.
   Unless you are really good at drawing, concrete nouns are easiest to

draw. You can also photocopy pictures from illustrated stories or picture dictionaries and cut out the related part of the picture and paste it on the card.

A word from the story with a synonym, antonym, or related word. These are good for vocabulary development for high-beginner to intermediate students, and the cards are quick to create. Examples: synonyms – forest, wood; bad, wicked. Related words – marriage, wedding; king, crown. Opposites – mother, child; brother, sister; lost, found.

A word from the story with a more general or more specific related word. Examples: animal, wolf; building, house; child, girl. Helping students network these various meaning relationships is important both because these relationships are an important part of knowing the meaning of a word and also because understanding these relationships is often important in understanding discourse-level connections.

A word from the story with a short definition. These are good for vocabulary development, and the cards are quick to create. Examples: forest, place where many trees grow; porridge, hot cereal eaten for breakfast.

A sentence from the story with a blank replacing one word paired with a card that has the missing word. These are good for intermediate to advanced students and are fairly quick to create. With this or the following option, create sentences for a strip story (see page 102), and then use these sentences to create the cards. Then, if some groups finish before others, have them order the pairs just as they would do with a strip story.

Half of a sentence from the story on one card with the other half of the sentence on the matching card. These are good for intermediate to advanced students and are fairly quick to create. For example, "Little Red Riding Hood went to" could be on one card and "her grandmother's house" on another. You need to be conscious of the fact that some sentence halves may potentially fit with more than one other piece. This is not necessarily bad, since it can require students to reread the previous matches at the end to figure out how things could have been matched differently if something doesn't work out. Sentence-half pairs can simultaneously work on grammatical structures. For example, these pairs from *The Boy Who Went to the North Wind* (see page 238) require grammatical knowledge of the appropriate use of prepositions:

The widow sent her son	*to the barn.*
The boy got some meal	*from the barn.*
The boy lost his magic cloth	*at the inn.*
The North Wind gave a cloth	*to the boy.*

The landlord reached	*for the stick.*
The stick chased the innkeeper around	*the inn.*
The boy sat still	*upon his bed.*

BEFORE OR AFTER THE STORY?

This activity can be done either before or after reading or listening to the story. If done before, it familiarizes students with the vocabulary and helps prepare them for and ease them into the reading. If done afterward, it helps review the vocabulary they learned.

A USEFUL UNSUPERVISED ACTIVITY

This game is useful not only because it reviews language in a fun way and brings variety into the classroom, but also because it requires little direct teacher supervision. This activity can be used with students who have completed an activity before the rest of the class, by the whole class (working in pairs or small groups) when the teacher needs a little time to set up the next activity, or in self-access activities. (See page 38 for more on self-access activities.)

In the multilevel classroom

Create a few sets of card at different levels (for example, one set matching word to picture and another set with sentence halves) and group students by level. Another option is to create the sentence halves so they also form a strip story. Then let the lower group just do the matching while the higher group does the matching and also orders the sentences.

Stories to use with this activity

This activity works well with any story except stories that are very short (because you can't find enough vocabulary items or unique sentence halves to make enough cards). With shorter stories, you could form one set of cards that reviews several stories.

Goldilocks and the Three Bears

Once upon a time, there were three bears – a papa bear, and a mama bear, and a baby bear. They lived in a little house in the middle of a forest. One morning, mama bear had just finished making the porridge for their breakfast. She put it into bowls on the table – a great big bowl for papa bear, a medium-sized bowl for mama bear, and a little tiny bowl for baby bear. Then, since the porridge was still too hot to eat, they all went out for a short walk in the forest.

It was not long after this that a little girl named Goldilocks came along. She saw the house, with the front door open, and though no one was at home, she decided to go inside and look around.

She walked into the kitchen, and there she saw the three bowls on the table – the great big bowl for papa bear, the medium-sized bowl for mama bear, and the little tiny bowl for baby bear. She thought the porridge looked very tasty, so she decided to try it. First she took a bite of papa bear's porridge, but it was too hot. Then she tried a bite of mama bear's porridge, but it was too cold. Then she tried a bite of baby bear's porridge, and it was just right, so she ate it all up.

Then she went into the living room and saw three chairs – a great big chair for papa bear, a medium-sized chair for mama bear, and a little tiny chair for baby bear. She thought she would try them. She climbed up into papa bear's great big chair, but it was too hard. She climbed into mama bear's medium-sized chair, but it was too soft. Then she climbed into baby bear's little tiny chair, and it was just right. She rocked back and forth until it broke.

Then she went upstairs and found a bedroom with three beds. There was a great big bed for papa bear, a medium-sized bed for mama bear, and a little tiny bed for baby bear. She thought she would try them. She climbed up into papa bear's great big bed, but it was too hard. She climbed into mama bear's medium-sized bed, but it was too soft. Then she climbed into baby bear's little tiny bed, and it was just right. It was so comfortable that she fell asleep.

Now, when the three bears came back from their walk, they noticed at once that something was not right.

continued

"Someone's been eating my porridge," said papa bear in his great big voice.

"Someone's been eating my porridge," said mama bear in her medium-sized voice.

"Someone's been eating my porridge," said baby bear in his little tiny voice, "and it's all gone!"

Next they went into the living room.

"Someone's been sitting in my chair," said papa bear in his great big voice.

"Someone's been sitting in my chair," said mama bear in her medium-sized voice.

"Someone's been sitting in my chair," said baby bear in his little tiny voice, "and they've broken it!"

So they went up the stairs to check the bedroom.

"Someone's been lying in my bed," said papa bear in his great big voice.

"Someone's been lying in my bed," said mama bear in her medium-sized voice.

"Someone's been lying in my bed," said baby bear in his little tiny voice, "and she's still there!"

At this, Goldilocks woke up. She was terrified to see the three bears, and leapt through the window in her fright. Fortunately, she landed in some bushes, so she wasn't too badly hurt. Then she ran home as fast as her legs would carry her, and she never went into that forest again.

Notes on the Story

This story was written in the 1800s, but is now almost universally known among American and English children. This is a good story to use when teaching vocabulary related to furniture and rooms of the house.

Sample high-beginner cards for the matching activity

The cards below are based on *Goldilocks and the Three Bears* (see page 185). These are based on concrete nouns and are suitable for early beginners.

Bowl	Porridge	Spoon	Path	Forest
Table	Chair	Rocking chair	Bed	Bear
House	Stairs	Door	Window	Goldilocks

Sample high-beginner cards for the matching activity

The cards on this page are also based on *Goldilocks and the Three Bears* (see page 185), but these sentence cards are based mostly on adjectives and common irregular past tense verbs. These cards are suitable for high-beginner or low-intermediate students.

Papa bear's porridge was too _____ .	Mama bear's porridge was too _____ .	Papa bear's chair was too _____ .	Mama bear's chair was too _____ .	Papa bear's voice was very _____ .
hot	cold	hard	soft	loud
Goldilocks _____ baby bear's porridge.	Goldilocks _____ baby bear's chair.	The bears went for a _____ .	Papa bear was very _____ .	Baby bear was very _____ .
ate	broke	big	walk	small
Goldilocks _____ in baby bear's bed.	Goldilocks _____ away from the bear's house.	Goldilocks _____ out the window when she saw the bears.	When the bears were around the bed, Goldilocks _____ .	There were _____ bears.
slept	ran	jumped	woke up	three

Language *Jeopardy*

Class level: Medium-beginner to advanced
Group size(s): Whole class, equal-ability small groups
Objective(s): To improve vocabulary, review language (including grammar) presented previously, and provide opportunity for students to process aural input quickly
Approximate class time: 15 to 30 minutes

The activity

CREATING THE ACTIVITY

1. **Write down the names of five stories you have used recently, or five categories that fit with stories you have worked with.** Choosing five stories and letting each story be its own category is usually easiest. Categories might also include topics like *stupid actions, things that got lost, magical things, actions by women, modes of transportation, animals, surprises, things people found, character qualities, winners, what happened in the end, items of clothing,* or any other topic that showed up in the stories. If you lack better categories, you can occasionally get away with categories like *actions, things, places, problems, people,* etc.
2. **For each story or category, write down five key vocabulary words.**
3. **For each group of five words, rank the words from 1 to 5, with 1 being the easiest word and 5 being the hardest.**
4. **Write a clue based on the story that will help the students figure out the word.**

IN THE CLASSROOM

1. **Divide students into three teams.**
2. **Make a grid on the board like the one on page 192.**
3. **Read one 10-point question** (that is, the question for a word that you ranked no. 1 [i.e., easiest] for one of the categories). The first student with a hand up gets to answer the question. (If one member is answering all the questions for a team, I prohibit that person from answering again until every member of the team has answered at least one question; this requires quieter members to participate.)
4. **If the answer is right, write the answer in the square. That team gets the appropriate score and chooses the category for the next question. If the answer is wrong, another team gets to answer.** If someone gives a correct answer that wasn't what I was looking for (e.g., I was looking for "leap" and someone said "jump"), I usually give credit

189

anyway. I sometimes do require an exact match but allow a team a second try if they had the right concept but not the exact word. Sometimes I also say, "Ten points more for the first team to give me another answer." (Real *Jeopardy* deducts points for wrong answers, but I rarely do this.) The next question is the one with the lowest point value in the category selected. Thus, within a category, you never get to the 20-point question until the 10-point question has been answered in that category, but you might get to the 50-point question in one category before any questions have been asked in another category.

5. **The game ends when all 25 answers are filled in or when the allotted time runs out.**

Adapting the activity for different levels

Choosing words of appropriate difficulty helps adjust the activity for different levels. Most stories can be used at a variety of levels. For example, using *The Greedy Old Spider* (see page 75), words like "man" and "eat" are suitable for beginners; words like "messenger" and "invite" are more appropriate for intermediate students.

Probably more important is the difficulty of the clues. "King Midas loved _____" and "The king's daughter was transformed by a touch into what?" both elicit the answer "gold," but the latter clue involves more sophisticated listening. The value of this game is not just the vocabulary that it reviews or the production of the answers; the listening students do when the clues are presented is an equally important opportunity for good language exposure.

To a lesser degree, the difficulty of grammatical structure required in the answer also adjusts the game for different levels. Low-beginning students might be expected to give one-word answers, higher beginners might have to make any kind of statement about the story, and (when grammatical focus is appropriate) intermediate to advanced students might have to make statements using a particular grammatical structure. (When scoring, if the student has the content right but gets the grammar wrong, give half-credit and have the student's team help produce the correct grammatical expression.)

Using multiple stories with categories that are not story names (see the example on page 195) also makes the activity harder, since students must listen to the clue without having a context in which to interpret it. (It can be made a little easier by including the name of the story either at the beginning or the end of the clue.)

For harder clues, you can make the activity easier by letting students discuss the clue before answering, though make sure that the best students don't do all the answering. Also, don't allow any further discussion for a team after someone on the team has raised a hand; otherwise students will raise their hands so they get the first chance to answer, and then try to figure the answer out.

Focus on grammar

Standard *Jeopardy* requires that all answers be given in question format (e.g., "What is gold?" "Who is the innkeeper?"), but you can ask students to present the answer using any structure you are working on. For example, you might require students to express the answer as a tag question ("It's gold, isn't it?"), a statement using modals ("It might be gold"), a statement with a passive verb ("Gold was desired by the king"), and so on. You can also work particular structures into your clues.

You can also work on certain aspects of grammar by making all the words you are looking for fit a particular grammatical category. For example, all the answers might be plural nouns, gerunds, irregular past tense verbs, or adverbs that have been formed from adjectives. This provides repeated exposure to the structure while being much more pleasant than grammar exercises.

Focus on pronunciation

To work on pronunciation while playing *Jeopardy*, pick answers that all (or mostly) include the sounds or clusters you are working on. For example, for beginners working on the correct pronunciation of plural nouns, all the answers might end with a consonant followed by the sounds /s/, /z/, or /ɪz/. With Japanese speakers, you might choose words that all include /l/ or /r/. When working on pronunciation with *Jeopardy*, require correct pronunciation for a full score. (The right answer with poor pronunciation gets half-score and another chance to pronounce it correctly.)

As an independent small-group activity

Rather than having the teacher lead this activity, a small group of intermediate (or higher) students could play with one of the students acting as the moderator. In a multilevel classroom, this could provide a way for one group of students to profitably occupy themselves while you are working with another group of students, or this could serve as a variation in the self-access classroom (see page 38 for more on self-access materials).

Folktales and language games: Language Jeopardy

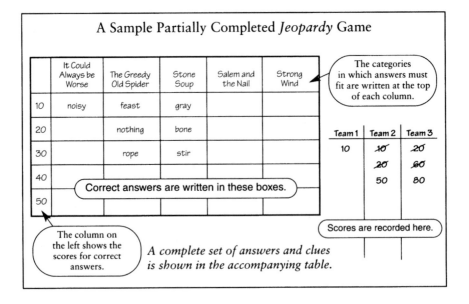

A Sample Partially Completed *Jeopardy* Game

	It Could Always be Worse	The Greedy Old Spider	Stone Soup	Salem and the Nail	Strong Wind
10	noisy	feast	gray		
20		nothing	bone		
30		rope	stir		
40					
50					

The categories in which answers must fit are written at the top of each column.

Team 1	Team 2	Team 3
10	10	20
	20	60
	50	80

Correct answers are written in these boxes.

The column on the left shows the scores for correct answers.

Scores are recorded here.

A complete set of answers and clues is shown in the accompanying table.

ANSWERS AND CLUES FOR THE *JEOPARDY* GAME

Answers for a high-beginner/low-intermediate language Jeopardy game

	It Could Always Be Worse	*The Greedy Old Spider*	*Stone Soup*	*Salem and the Nail*	*Strong Wind*
10	noisy	feast	gray	empty bag	trees
20	chicken	nothing	bone	house	invisible
30	crowded	rope	stir	dead donkey	rainbow
40	outside	pull	delicious	burned	honest
50	peaceful/quiet	messenger	beggar	merchant	warrior

192

Clues for the moderator to read

	It Could Always Be Worse	The Greedy Old Spider	Stone Soup	Salem and the Nail	Strong Wind
10	The poor man's house was too ___	A large meal	Color of the stone	The first thing Salem hung on the nail	What happened to the two older sisters
20	The first animal the rabbi told the man to bring in	What Spider got to eat	The long, red ___	What Salem sold to Abraham	Something that you can't see is ___
30	When too many people are in one place	What Spider took to each village	To mix what's in the pot	The awful thing Salem hung on the nail	What Strong Wind's bow was made of
40	Where the man took the animals in the end	What people did with the rope	Tastes very good	What happened to Salem's shop	Someone who always tells the truth is ___
50	What the house was like at the end	Person sent to invite Spider to the feast	Someone who doesn't work but asks other people for food or money	Someone who sells things	What Strong Wind was

Folktales and language games: Language Jeopardy

Words students must use in their answers

	Animals	Losers	Used for the trick	Character qualities	Where it happened
10	turtle	Spider	rope	greedy	in the middle of the forest
20	donkey	oldest sisters	nail	honesty	on the roof
30	pig	hare	stone	crafty	in the barn
40	goat	innkeeper	water	arrogant	in a tent/ by the sea
50	cow	Abraham	bucket/water soup/disguise	diligent/ persevering	near the stable

Note: The fifth column illustrates combining content with a grammatical point, in this case spacial prepositions. (This grammar focus is more appropriate for lower-level students than the clues in the other columns are designed for, but it still illustrates how a grammar point can be worked in.)

Clues for the moderator to read

	Animals	Losers	Used for the trick	Character qualities	Where it happened
10	Won the race with the rabbit (*The Tortoise and the Hare*)	Tried to get two meals and got nothing (*The Greedy Old Spider*)	What Spider used to try to go to two feasts at once (*The Greedy Old Spider*)	The problem with Spider (*The Greedy Old Spider*)	Where Spider lived (*The Greedy Old Spider*)
20	Was hung on a nail (*Salem and the Nail*)	Tried to get a husband and ended up as trees instead (*Strong Wind*)	The part of the house that wasn't sold (*Salem and the Nail*)	The characteristic that won Strong Wind's heart (*Strong Wind*)	The unusual place the cow was put to feed (*The Man Who Kept House*)
30	The creature that spilled the cream (*The Man Who Kept House*)	Lost a race he could have won (*The Tortoise and the Hare*)	The key ingredient in the beggar's soup (*Stone Soup*)	The quality that enabled Salem to buy a new shop (*Salem and the Nail*)	The place the flour was kept (*The Boy Who Went to the North Wind*)
40	The North Wind's second gift (*The Boy Who Went to the North Wind*)	Helped himself to magical things but got beaten in the end (*North Wind*)	Substituted for wine because no one would know (*Wine for the Feast*)	The quality that caused the hare to lose the race (*The Tortoise and the Hare*)	Where Strong Wind lived (*Strong Wind*)
50	Pulled a man up the chimney (*The Man Who Kept House*)	Bought a house and had to sell it back for half price (*Salem and the Nail*)	How the princess found out what the princes were like (*Princess's Suitors*)	Describes the boy who went to the North Wind (*The Boy Who Went to the North Wind*)	Where the princess's first test took place (*Princess's Suitors*)

Crossword puzzles to review vocabulary

Class level: High-beginner to advanced
Group size(s): Individuals, pairs, small groups
Objective(s): To review vocabulary and language from a story in a fun
  way, and to provide an opportunity for rereading some or all of a text
Approximate class time: 10 to 20 minutes
Notes: Preparation time can be extensive, though a quick variation is
  included. Because of the time involved, you will probably want to
  create full crosswords only for stories you plan to reuse.

The activity

PREPARATION

The likelihood of finding ready-made puzzles suitable for ESL lessons is
minimal, so the only alternative seems to be to create one's own. (If you
know other teachers who are interested in using crosswords, you can
each create a few and then share them.) Crossword puzzles can take a
fair amount of time to create, though a quicker variation is given on the
next page. If you create puzzles for stories that you plan to reuse, you can
use them repeatedly (with different classes) and get a better return for
your time investment.

I have tried several methods of creating crossword puzzles, ranging
from pencil and graph paper to using computer programs that generate
puzzles. I have had the most success with the following technique:

1. **Brainstorm to create a list of words that could go into the puzzle.** For
   a good puzzle, you will normally need at least twice as many words
   as you ultimately want in the puzzle, since you won't be able to make
   every word fit.
2. **Use Scrabble letters to form the words you have created.** (If you want,
   you can use the board to keep things lined up, but this isn't necessary.
   Use your longest words first, and the most important shorter words
   next. If you only have one set of Scrabble letters and are creating a
   large or complex puzzle, you may need to create the puzzle in sections.
   (For example, you may need to create half of the puzzle, write what
   you've done, and then use the same letters again to create the rest of
   the puzzle.) Once you have fit in as many words from your list as you
   can, you can call the puzzle done if you wish.
3. **If you want a more complete puzzle with fewer black spaces, use a
   word processor with a spelling checker that lets you look up words
   with undetermined characters.** (For example, WordPerfect lets you
   do this.) Find every place where a word could fit and look up the

196

different letter combinations. For example, you could look up "f?r?" and get all the four-letter words that begin with "f" and have "r" as the third letter. (Notice that this won't find any three-letter words. If you were interested in potential three-letter words for this same spot, you would also have to look up "f?r.") Then read down the list and see if any of the words are related to your puzzle topic. I also fill in with common little words (like prepositions, conjunctions, and pronouns) that students should know.

4. **Create a copyable version of the puzzle.** Although the computer programs for creating crossword puzzles that I have seen are unfortunately not that great for creating good puzzles, they are very handy for printing out a nice looking copy of the puzzle. If you don't have access to a program like this, writing them on graph paper is the next easiest option.

5. **Write clues for the puzzle.** (Or see the next activity!) When possible, base the clues on the story; this increases the chance that students will go back and reread some of the text to find the answers. Bear in mind that the difficulty of the clues contributes to the difficulty of the activity as much as the difficulty of the words you selected. For example, "middle" is the answer for both "Spider lived in the _____ of the forest" and "equidistant between two points," but the latter makes the activity much more difficult.

QUICK PUZZLE

If you don't have time to create a full puzzle, just interlock as many words as you can in a few minutes. For example, a puzzle for *The Riddle* (see page 22) that takes only 10 minutes to create might look like the one shown here.

IN THE CLASSROOM

1. **Tell the story, have students listen to it on tape, or have them read it.** You don't have to tell the story just for this activity; you could

use the story with other activities first and then use this activity to follow up.

2. **Have students complete the puzzle.** This can be done in the classroom, in a language lab, for homework, or as self-access material.
3. **Review the puzzle as a class or have students check their answers using an answer key.**

SAMPLE PUZZLES AND SOLUTIONS

Solutions for these puzzles are found on page 204. The story *The Greedy Old Spider* is found on page 75.

Variations

Variation 1: Self-access materials. Crossword puzzles work well as self-access materials since they are easy to do and correct independently. See page 38 for more on self-access materials.
Variation 2: If your students especially like crossword puzzles, let them try making their own from scratch.

In the multilevel classroom

Create puzzles based on the same story at a few different levels, and then give different puzzles to different students. For the more difficult puzzles, use both harder vocabulary from the story and less simply written clues. For lower-level students, you can provide a word list for them to pick their answers from. This still requires students to associate words with meanings, but provides considerable help in getting the right words.

Folktales and language games: Crossword puzzles to review vocabulary

The Greedy Old Spider – A low-intermediate crossword puzzle

Across

2. too
5. what Spider got to eat
8. Spider was _____ .
10. Pull the rope when the feast _____ ready.
11. Spider _____ to go to both feasts.
13. Spider ran _____ the first village.
14. At the feast they would have _____ food.
15. Spider took one rope _____ each village.
17. You _____ food.

Down

1. The rope was _____ .
2. Spider came _____ the feast was finished.
3. The greedy old _____
4. Spider wanted to _____ to both feasts.
6. Either . . . _____ ,
9. Not young
10. Spider lived _____ the forest.
11. Spider _____ one rope to each village.
12. Spider like to _____ .
13. Also
14. opposite of come
16. The feasts were _____ Saturday night.

Folktales and language games: Crossword puzzles to review vocabulary

The Greedy Old Spider – An intermediate crossword puzzle

Across
1. Spider told people to _____ the rope.
3. "The food _____ gone," the people said.
7. something to cook in
9. 3rd sing neut pronoun
10. what Spider got
13. to want too much is to be _____
14. food from an animal
18. The people pulled the rope when it was time _____ the feast.
19. like a string only thicker
20. Spider lived _____ the forest.
21. present tense of *did*
22. 1st person sing of *to be*
24. Both feasts were on the _____ night.
26. where Spider lived
27. Spider liked to _____ .

Down
1. something to walk on in the forest.
2. a _____ rope
4. the greedy old _____
5. participle ending
6. past form of *eat*
8. Spider didn't get _____ food.
11. either/_____
12. 3rd sing. pronoun.
14. The people pulled _____ .
15. go fast on foot
16. A _____ went to invite Spider.
17. also
18. a large meal
20. Spider had an _____ .
23. mother
25. 1st person pronoun

Folktales and language games: Crossword puzzles to review vocabulary

The Greedy Old Spider – A high-intermediate crossword puzzle

Across
2. try with difficulty
10. make
11. attempted
13. people
15. not the middle
16. food from an animal
17. There would _____ good food.
19. to cook over the fire or in an oven
20. a drink
21. a helping verb
24. prepare for eating
25. Spider fell in _____ _____ on the ground. (2 words)
27. pronoun
28. see 28 down

Down
1. what Spider likes to _____ (3rd sing)
2. who the story was about
3. you find this in the forest
4. color
5. opposite of down
6. meat from a wild animal
7. large
8. to have let someone borrow something
9. past tense ending
12. meat from the side of the animal
14. very tired
16. songs
18. comes from thinking
22. what the people pulled
23. in two parts
26. belonging to a man
27. casual greeting
28. 1st person sing. pronoun

Crossword puzzles to practice description and paraphrasing skills

Class level: Low-intermediate to advanced
Group size(s): Individuals, pairs, small groups
Objective(s): To review vocabulary and language from a story in a fun
   way, to provide an opportunity to reread some or all of a text, and to
   develop the skills of describing, paraphrasing, and defining (strategic
   competence)
Approximate class time: 20 to 30 minutes in one class, and then 10 to 25
   minutes in a following class

The activity

PREPARATION

1. **Create at least two different crossword puzzles.** (See the steps on page
   196.) Either full puzzles or quick ones (see page 197) will do. These
   can be based on the same story or on two or more different stories
   that you plan to use close together. You can use some of the same
   words in both puzzles.
2. **Make copies of the** *completed* **puzzles so each individual or group will
   have one puzzle but no clues.** Roughly equal numbers of students
   should get each puzzle.

IN THE CLASSROOM

1. **Tell the story, have students listen to it on tape, or have them read it.**
   You don't have to tell the story just for this activity; you could use it
   with other activities first and then use this activity to follow up. If you
   are working on note taking, you can have students take notes while
   listening or reading.
2. **Divide the class into groups of two or three and give each group a
   different completed puzzle.** (Dividing the class alphabetically [e.g.,
   last names A–M get puzzle 1; N–Z get puzzle 2] makes it easier to
   remember who's had what.)
3. **Have students write clues for each of the words in the puzzle.** If you
   wish, you can let students refer back to printed copies of the story.
   You may want to assign the weakest writers to be the secretaries for
   each group. If the best student is writing the clues down, there will be
   the temptation – perhaps unconscious – for that student to offer an
   idea, write it down, and move on to the next item before anyone else
   has really understood what is going on. By having the least proficient
   student write the clues down (with as much assistance with wording
   and spelling as needed), the group is forced to go at a pace at which

everyone has a reasonable chance of understanding. This also provides the greatest potential for real peer assistance. Another option is to have students take turns creating clues, always having the person to their right (or left) doing the writing for them. This keeps each member participating and requires verbal interaction.

4. Collect the clues that students have written. After class, make copies of them with the blank puzzles.
5. In the next class, give out the blank puzzles with the student written clues so that other students can use those clues to solve the puzzles. Make sure students get a copy of a puzzle they did not write clues for.
6. Review the puzzle as a class or have students check their answers using an answer key.

The Greedy Old Spider – Solution
to the puzzle on page 199

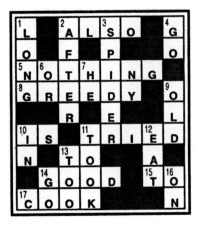

The Greedy Old Spider – Solution
to the puzzle on page 200

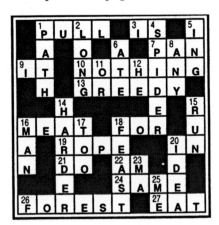

The Greedy Old Spider – Solution
to the puzzle on page 201

10 Folktales and drama

Because of their active, concrete nature, folktales are generally great for acting out. Acting folktales out has a variety of advantages: It helps those who learn best by active, physical, hands-on involvement, it forces students to interpret feelings and motives that may not be stated explicitly in the text, it integrates many language skills, and it is often quite fun.

▨▨▨ Presenting folktales with drama

Class level: Beginner to low-intermediate (this can be done with higher levels too, but for them the next activity, in which they convert the tale to drama themselves, is more appropriate)

Group size(s): Small groups (either mixed or equal ability)

Objective(s): To give students an opportunity to use English for communication in both producing and presenting simple dramatic presentations of folktales

Approximate class time: Depends on class size (about 20 to 25 minutes for groups to prepare and practice, and then another 5 or 10 minutes for each play to be performed)

The activity

PREPARATION

Find a few stories at appropriate levels and edit the texts into a short plays. Guidelines for doing this are found on page 212.

IN THE CLASSROOM

1. **Divide the class into groups and give each group a different folktale play.**
2. **Let students read their play, assign parts, identify any props they would like to use, and then practice briefly.** Converting words to actions helps in relating stories to life and drawing inferences. For example, students must decide whether characters are angry or sad or indifferent. Often this is not stated directly; students must infer this from the text. Students may need to have their attention drawn to this, so encourage them to think about what the characters would be feeling if it were real life. When students do this play, sketches or simple props to give a little context are sometimes helpful. For example, for *The Boy Who Cried Wolf*, someone could sketch a few houses on the board and write "the town" over it (where the men wait) and sketch a hill with grass and a few trees with "hill" written over it (where the action with Peter takes place). Simple signs – for example, one reading "the next day" or "later" – can provide transitions and at the same time bring in a little reading for a beginning audience.
3. **Have each group perform its play for the rest of the class.** If you do this in a following class, students can bring in simple props if they want. You may need to give students 5 or 10 minutes to review their parts at the beginning of class. Remember that the purpose is language

practice, not a polished production, so if students need to use scripts during the production, that may be OK. (Or there can be some ad libbing.) Depending on student interest, there are often other contexts in which student drama could be performed if desired. It could be done for another class, and places like nursing homes often provide willing audiences. (Polish the productions a little if you go "on the road" with them.)

4. *(Optional)* **Follow the plays with exercises involving written texts that use the same stories.** This reviews the new language that students encountered in watching others' plays and connects written and spoken forms. Activities like a cloze passage (see page 148), concentration matching cards (see page 182), or a strip story (see page 102) are all options.

Converting a very short story (like *The Boy Who Cried Wolf*) to a play is relatively straightforward. *The Princess's Suitors* illustrates how a more involved story might be adapted to drama. Depending on the audience and how much contextual support could be created though the use of simple props, more redundancy and repetitions might be useful.

The Boy Who Cried Wolf

Characters

      Narrator   Peter   Wolf   Townsmen   Sheep

Narrator: Peter lived in a small town. He watched sheep for the people in the town. Every morning he walked to the hills with the sheep.

Man 1:   You must watch the sheep. If you see a wolf, shout and we will come.

[Peter walks from town toward hill.]

Sheep: Baa. Baa. Baa.

Narrator: He watched the sheep all day long. Each night he walked back to the village with the sheep. He always walked alone. He was lonely.

[Peter walks back and forth looking bored, then looks toward the town.]

Peter: Wolf!!

[Three men run from village and look at Peter and the sheep.]

Man 2:   Where is the wolf?

Peter: It ran away.

[Men look at Peter and then walk back to village.]

Narrator: The next day, Peter watched the sheep again. He was still lonely.

[Peter walks back and forth looking bored, then looks toward the town.]

Peter: Wolf!!

[Three men run from village and look at Peter and the sheep.]

Man 3:   Where is the wolf?

Peter: It ran away.

[Men look at Peter and then walk back to village shaking their heads.]

Narrator: The next day, Peter watched the sheep again. As he watched, he saw a wolf coming.

[Wolf enters and growls.]

Peter: Wolf!! Wolf!! Wolf!!

[No men come and wolf attacks and carries off the sheep.]

The Princess's Suitors, **intermediate**

Characters

| Narrator | Princess | Three Princes | Messenger |
| King | Stable Master | Cook | |

[King, sitting on throne (chair, up high if possible), daughter standing nearby]

Narrator: Long ago there was a king with a beautiful daughter. Many princes wanted to marry her.

[Three princes enter]

Narrator: First, there was a strong, brave prince who was a great fighter.

Prince #1: Good day my king. I am strong and brave. I want to marry your daughter. I will give you a hundred horses and a thousand diamond necklaces if you let me marry her. Surely you can't say no.

Narrator: Next, there was a handsome prince who was very wise.

Prince #2: Good day my king. Your daughter is more beautiful than the sun. If you let me marry her, I will give you a golden chariot and five hundred strings of emeralds. Surely you will not say no.

Narrator: Next, there was a prince who was the second son of a king from a small and somewhat poor kingdom in the North.

Prince #3: *[smiling]* Good day my king *[bows]*. Good day Princess *[bows to princess]*. I have been moved by your daughter's wisdom and kindness. *[to princess]* I would be very honored to have you as my wife.

King: And what would you give?

Prince #3: Of riches I have only little, but I would share all that I had with her.

King: Very well, you may all go for now.

[The three princes leave]

King: So, Daughter, which one would you pick?

Princess: I don't know yet. You must give me a few days to decide.

[King and princess both exit, then princess returns.]

Princess: *[Speaking to audience]* First, I will put on a disguise. *[puts hat on, different coat, etc.]* Then I will go to the castle of the strong, brave prince and ask for a job.

Narrator: So the princess went to the first prince's castle and asked for a job in the stable taking care of the horses.

[Enter stable master.]

≫→

The Princess's Suitors, intermediate
(continued)

Princess: Please let me work in your stable taking care of the horses. All I want is a little food for my work.

Stable Master: You may clean the horses' stalls and brush the horses.

[Princess mimes the actions.]

Messenger: Get the prince's horse ready. He is coming.

Narrator: The prince comes in, but he does not recognize the princess because of her disguise.

[Enter Prince #1. The princess comes along carrying a bucket. She stumbles, knocks the prince down, spills water all over him. Note: If you put confetti in the bucket, the princess can really spill something on the prince without getting him wet.]

Prince #1:   *[Screaming]* Look what you've done, you stupid fool.

Princess: Excuse me. Excuse me. I'm so sorry. *[She moves closer, spilling more water on the prince, banging him with the bucket, and stepping on his foot.]*

Prince #1:   *[Screaming]* Get back, you fool, get back! You have dumped water all over me, knocked me in the mud, stepped on my feet, and scared my horse. You are worthless. *[He shoves the princess away.]* You are fired. I never wish to see you again.

Princess: Very well, it shall be as you wish.

Narrator: So the princess left and went to the next castle, where she asked for a job in the kitchen.

[Prince #1 leaves, and princess walks to next castle.]
[Enter Cook.]

Princess: Please sir, could I work in your kitchen? You would only need to pay me a little food to eat.

Cook: OK, you may have a job. You may cut vegetables for my soup.

[Enter Prince #2, who sits at a table as if waiting for a meal.]

Messenger: Hurry. The prince is hungry and wants his food right away.

[The princess runs with a bowl of soup, and dumps soup all over the floor and the prince.]

Prince #2:   You clumsy fool! Look what you have done.

Princess: I am so sorry. I am so sorry. *[The princess bows awkwardly and spills more soup on the prince]*

Prince #2:   Get out! Get out! . . . or I will have you covered with tar and feathers and dragged through the streets.

The Princess's Suitors, intermediate
(continued)

Princess: [To audience] Not for me. Not for me.

Narrator: Next the princess went to the castle of the poor prince in the small kingdom in the North. Again she disguised herself so no one would know who she was. Again she got a job taking care of the horses.

[Prince #3 enters. Princess comes along as before with bucket and stumbles into prince, dumping water all over him, knocking him down, and falling down herself.]

Prince #3: Are you all right? [Prince smiles at her.]

Princess: [Getting up] I am fine. But aren't you angry?

Prince #3: Not really. Anyone can have an accident. But please do be more careful.

Narrator: After he was gone, the princess went to the kitchen and asked for work there.

[Enter Cook.]

Princess: Please sir, could I have some work in exchange for a bit to eat?

Cook: Yes, you may work for me. Please take this bowl to the prince.

[Prince enters and sits down at a table as if ready to eat. Princess comes in and stumbles, dumping soup on the floor and on the prince. The prince looks at his clothes with a frown, and then shrugs.]

Princess: [Bowing awkwardly and splashing more soup from the bowl] I'm so sorry . . . so very sorry.

Prince #3: You are most certainly forgiven. But now stop being so sorry and bring us some more soup so we can eat it. Then get something to mop up the floor.

Narrator: The prince remained as polite and courteous as always. At this, the princess was satisfied and did as she was told. When she brought the next bowl of soup, she did not spill a drop. Then she slipped out and quickly headed for home.

[Princess mimes actions as narrator speaks. Princess leaves stage and then reenters with the King.]

Princess: Father, I have made my choice. I want to marry the prince from the small kingdom in the North.

King: Very well. Let us prepare for the wedding at once.

[Prince #3 enters and stands next to princess.]

Narrator: And so the princess married the poor but kind prince, and they lived happily ever after.

Converting folktales to drama

Class level: Low-intermediate to advanced
Group size(s): Small groups (either mixed or equal ability)
Objective(s): To give students an opportunity to use English for communication, in both producing and presenting simple dramatic presentations of folktales
Approximate class time: Depends on the complexity of the stories (some time is needed to convert the text to dramatic form, then about 20 to 25 minutes for groups to prepare and practice, and then another 5 or 10 minutes for each play to be performed)

The activity

1. **Divide students into groups and give each group a different story.** The story you give should have a good amount of action.
2. **Have students convert the story into a play.** Convert thoughts and indirect speech into direct speech. Convert past tense into present tense. Decide how to represent narrative comments with direct speech or actions.
3. **Have students assign parts, identify any props that they would like to use, and then practice briefly.** See page 206 for elaboration of this and the following steps.
4. **Have each group perform its play for the rest of the class and/or for others.** If students are interested in doing the play outside the classroom (for another class, at a nursing home, etc.), provide feedback on places where the play could be filled in and smoothed out.
5. *(Optional)* **Follow the plays with exercises involving written texts that use the same stories.** This reviews the new language that students encountered in watching others' plays and connects written and spoken forms. Activities like a cloze passage (see page 148), concentration matching cards (see page 182), or a strip story (see page 102) are all options.

In the multilevel classroom

The different lengths of parts in many tales usually makes it easy for different levels to work together to produce a single play. You can also assign a difficult story to an advanced group and an easy story to a low-level group and have them perform them for each other. A little preteaching combined with the visual support of the acting can make the higher group's presentation intelligible to the lower-level students.

Stories to use with this activity

This activity works well with nearly any story that has a good amount of action. A few stories are included here, and additional stories that are good for drama are included with both the next and previous activities.

Intermediate

The Tiger and the Dried Persimmon

Once upon a time, a grandmother and her young grandson lived together. One evening, he would not stop crying. There was also a tiger who lived and hunted in the mountains nearby. At that time, food was scarce, and the tiger was very hungry, so he stealthily crept down to the village, hoping to capture some food there. He slipped into their house. The baby was still crying. Hoping to silence him, the grandmother said, "If you keep crying, a tiger will capture you."

The tiger was surprised to hear this. He thought the old woman knew he was there. He became tense and ready to spring.

Though the woman had said this, the baby still cried. So she said, "If you stop crying, I'll give you a dried persimmon."

At this he stopped crying and looked at her expectantly.

When the tiger heard this, he was afraid. When the old woman had mentioned a tiger, the child paid no mind, but when she mentioned a dried persimmon, it fell silent at once. A dried persimmon must be a fearful thing, perhaps much fiercer than himself. So the tiger prepared to slip out of the house.

At just that moment, a thief broke into the house, hoping to steal a cow. Because it was dark, and because he did not expect to find a tiger in the house, the thief thought the tiger must be a cow and grabbed the tiger's tail. The tiger became even more frightened, thinking that the thief must be the fierce dried persimmon. So the tiger sprang through the window and ran away as fast as he could.

Meanwhile, the thief too was terrified. He realized that this was no cow and that he had somehow come to be holding on to the tail of a huge tiger. In terror he continued to hang on, but eventually he let go and fell to the ground. And the tiger didn't stop running until it was very far away, and it never came near that village again.

Notes on the Story
This story was told to me by one of my Korean students.

New Patches for Old

It was the day before a holiday, so a man decided to leave his shop a little early. He went and bought presents for his wife and his mother and his daughter. He still had some money left when he found a new pair of pants for himself. The trousers he wore now were old and patched; it would be nice to have new ones for the holiday. He tried them on and found that they fit perfectly except for being four fingers too long. That could be easily mended, so he bought the pants.

Then he went home and gave the presents to his family. After giving the gift to his wife, he said, "My dear, I need to have these trousers shortened by four fingers. Would you be willing to do it for me?"

"I'm sorry, my dear," she answered, "but I don't have time. I still must finish the holiday meal for tomorrow."

So the man went to his old mother and gave her his gift. Then he asked her, "Dearest Mother, I need to have these trousers shortened by four fingers. Would you be willing to do it for me?"

"I'm sorry, my son," she answered, "but I don't have time. I still must finish preparing for tomorrow."

So the man went to his daughter and gave her his gift. Then he asked her, "Daughter, I need to have these trousers shortened by four fingers. Would you be willing to do it for me?"

"I'm sorry, father," she answered, "but I don't have time. I still must help mother with the preparations for tomorrow."

So the man sighed and cut off four fingers' width of material from the bottom of each leg and then hemmed them. "There," he thought, "now they are ready to wear for tomorrow." Then he went to sleep.

Now, once his wife finished her work, she thought, "My husband was so kind to bring me a gift, and I did not help him. What I will do is I will hem his new trousers for him so they will be ready for him tomorrow." Then she quietly got the trousers and cut off four fingers' worth and hemmed up the bottom and placed them back where he had left them.

In the same way his mother thought that she too would like to bless her son, for he was always kind to her, and so she got the trousers and cut off the bottoms and hemmed them up again.

His daughter did the same. Each of them went to bed happy,

214

thinking how pleased he would be in the morning when he woke and found the job done.

In the morning, the man woke and pulled his trousers on. He could not believe his eyes. They were twelve fingers too short. "How could I have made such a mistake?" he asked his wife. "I was sure I cut off the proper amount."

Then the wife and mother and daughter each explained how they had decided to help him the night before. And so, they got the pieces they had cut off and sewed them back on, and when they were done, the trousers were exactly the right length.

"Well," said the man, "I am thankful for a wife and mother and daughter who all love me. And I am also thankful that at least now my patches are new patches."

And so they enjoyed the holiday together.

Notes on the Story
This is a Turkish tale. A nice illustrated version of this tale can be found in *New Patches for Old,* by Barbara Walker and Ahmet E. Uysal (1974).

Low-intermediate

The Unmerciful Man

Once there was a man who owed the king millions of dollars. The king sent for the man but he was not able to pay. So the king said, "Sell this man, and sell his wife, and sell his children, and sell his house and everything else that he owns, so that I may at least get something."

The man begged the king to spare him and his family. He promised that he would pay everything in time.

The king decided to have mercy, so he cancelled his debt and let the man go.

When this man went out, he saw another man who owed him a few thousand dollars. He grabbed this man and began to choke him. "Pay me what you owe me at once," he shouted.

This second man fell to his knees and begged, "Please be patient with me and I will pay you back." The first man refused, and instead had him thrown into prison until he could pay.

The king's servants saw all this and went and told the king what had happened.

In anger, the king sent for the man. "You wicked man! I cancelled all of your debt because you begged for mercy. Shouldn't you have had mercy on someone else who only owed you a little, just as I showed you mercy? Then in anger the king had the man thrown into prison, saying that he would not come out until he had paid the last penny.

Notes on the Story
This story is a retelling of a Biblical parable found in Matthew 18:23–34.

Multipart story drama

Class level: High-beginner to advanced
Group size(s): Groups of 3 to 5
Objective(s): To practice language while presenting part of a story through drama and watching other students perform other parts of the story
Approximate class time: 30 to 40 minutes

The activity

PREPARATION

1. **Choose a story with a good amount of action and preferably about three to five main characters.** (With smaller classes, it is fine to have only two or three characters.)
2. **Divide the story into four or five parts.**
3. **For large classes, make enough copies so that each group gets one section of the story.**

IN THE CLASSROOM

1. **Divide the class into groups of three to five students and give each group one section of the story.** For example, if you have 20 students and 4 parts, make four groups of five. If you have 60 students, form 12 groups and give each part to three groups. For some stories, you might want to have different size groups for the different parts.
2. **Give students 20 or 25 minutes to read their section of the story together and prepare to act out their part of the story.** Students may make one person a narrator if needed, and they may assign roles in any way they wish. They may also freely add dialog to help them present the story, and they may leave out details that they don't think are essential. They may also make hasty props or use whatever they have to help them act out their part of the story. Once students have roles worked out, they should practice acting their part out.
3. **Once each group has prepared its section of the story (i.e., when the 20 or 25 minutes is up), call groups to the front of the class in the right order to act out their parts of the story.** Other students watch until it is their group's turn to perform. If you have more than one group preparing each part, select one to present that part to the class. Try to move from one group to the next as seamlessly as possible so the story flows smoothly.

Stories to use with this activity

This activity can work well with nearly any story that has a good amount of action. Some I suggest include:

A High-Beginner Multipart Story Drama

The Three Billy Goats Gruff, Part 1

Once there were three goats – a little, tiny goat, a medium-sized goat, and a great big goat. They were brothers. They lived on a green, grassy hill in the mountains, and they liked to eat grass.

One day, the little, tiny goat said to his two bigger brothers, "I am going to cross the bridge over the river. The grass is greener on the other side."

The little, tiny goat trotted down to the river and started walking over the bridge. His feet made a soft "clip, clop" on the boards.

"Who's walking on my bridge?" said a loud, mean voice from under the bridge. It was the voice of a troll.

"I am," said the little goat with his little voice.

"I will have to eat you up," said the voice from under the bridge.

"Please don't," said the little goat. "My big brother is coming. He is much bigger than I am, and he will be much better to eat."

"OK," said the troll. "You may go across."

The Three Billy Goats Gruff, Part 2

Soon the medium-sized goat said to his older brother, "I am going to cross the bridge over the river. The grass is greener on the other side."

So he trotted down to the river and started walking over the bridge. His feet made a loud "clip, clop" on the boards.

"Who's walking on my bridge?" said a loud, mean voice from under the bridge. It was the voice of the troll.

"I am," said the medium-sized goat.

"I will have to eat you up," said the voice from under the bridge.

"Please don't," said the goat. "My big brother is coming. He is much bigger than I am and will be much better to eat."

"OK," said the troll. "You may go across."

The Three Billy Goats Gruff, Part 3

Soon the great big goat decided that he too would cross the bridge over the river. He thought, "The grass is greener and thicker and longer on the other side."

So he trotted down to the river and started walking over the bridge. His big feet made a very loud "CLOP, CLOP" on the boards.

"Who's walking on my bridge?" said a loud, mean voice from under the bridge. It was the voice of the troll.

"I am," said the great big goat.

"I will have to eat you up," said the voice from under the bridge.

"Come and try," said the great big goat.

So the troll came up on the bridge and ran toward the goat. But the great big goat just lowered his head and butted the troll into the river. The river carried him away, and the troll was never seen again.

Then the great big goat crossed over the bridge and joined his brothers on the other side. There they all ate grass until they got very fat, and if they have not gone somewhere else, then they are still there.

Notes on the Story

Notice that this story has many spacial prepositions (*on, over, under*) and a number of comparatives (*greener, bigger, better*). This story could have been divided into four parts by splitting Part 3 where the troll comes up on the bridge.

A Short Intermediate Multipart Story Drama

The Good Neighbor, Part 1

Once there was a man who was journeying from Jerusalem to Jericho. As he traveled along, robbers attacked him and beat him up. They took his clothes and everything else that he had and left him half-dead by the side of the road.

The Good Neighbor, Part 2

As the man lay bleeding by the side of the road, a priest came walking along the same road. He saw the bleeding man lying on by the road, so he crossed over to the far side of the road and quickly went by, leaving the wounded man lying there.

The Good Neighbor, Part 3

A little while later, a religious teacher came along. He also saw the man lying bleeding by the side of the road. He too crossed to the other side of the road and walked by, leaving the man lying there in the dirt.

The Good Neighbor, Part 4

Finally a Samaritan, a man from a different country and a different religion, came along. He saw the man lying bleeding by the side of the road. He stopped and picked the man up and bandaged his wounds. Then he put the man on his own donkey and took the man to an inn. All night long he cared for the man.

The next day, the traveler gave two silver coins to the innkeeper. "Please take care of this wounded man for me," he said. "When I come back, I will pay you back if it costs you more than this."

Notes on the Story

This story is taken from the Biblical parable of the Good Samaritan found in Luke 10:30–35.

An Intermediate Multipart Story Drama

The Wise Judge, Part 1

The good widow Yemswitch, had lost most of her hearing many years ago, but now she had also lost all of her sheep. She had been washing her clothes in the river, and the sheep had wandered off, and she now had no idea where they had gone. She set off to find them.

As she went along, she met an old farmer, Mr. Mulugeta. "Mr. Mulugeta," she cried, "Have you seen my sheep?"

Now Mr. Mulugeta was also very nearly deaf, and he could not understand a word that she said, so he guessed she was telling him how well his crops were growing.

"Yes," he answered, pointing back at his fields. "The crops are doing very well. We have had very good weather this year, and I have also worked very hard."

She did not hear a word that he said, but she thought he had seen her sheep and was pointing in the direction they had gone. "Thank you, Farmer Mulugeta," she shouted. "If I find them there, I will bring you one for your supper."

They smiled at each other and bowed politely. Then the widow Yemswitch headed off in the direction that he had pointed. It happened that the sheep really had gone that way, and so she soon found them. She was very thankful to Farmer Mulugeta. She found that one of the lambs had an injured leg, and decided to give that one to him. She returned to his house.

continued

The Wise Judge, Part 2

"Mr. Mulugeta," she said loudly, "I found my sheep exactly where you said. I would like to give this one to you for your supper to express my thanks." She held out the lamb to him.

"No! I did not hurt your lamb," he answered loudly, "so I will not pay for it."

Widow Yemswitch only heard the word "No" and thought that he wanted her to give him a better lamb.

"Don't be greedy," she shouted. "All you did was show me the direction to look in, so this is payment enough. I will not give you a better one. This one is good enough." She tried to push the lamb into his arms.

He refused to take it, insisting that he had not hurt the lamb and that he would not pay for it. Soon they were shouting angrily at each other, though this made little difference since neither one could hear much of what the other said. They made so much noise that a police officer came to see what the problem was. He insisted that they must go to the judge at once to settle the matter.

The police officer took them to Judge Yasu. Judge Yasu was known everywhere for being very wise and very fair.

The Wise Judge, Part 3

When they were standing before Judge Yasu, the widow Yemswitch cried out, "I lost my sheep and he showed me what direction they went, so I tried to thank him by giving him this lamb. He wanted me to give him a better one, but I think this is enough thanks for his help. He should not be greedy."

Farmer Mulugeta explained, "I am a kind man and would do nothing to hurt a lamb. I do not know how it got hurt, but I had never even seen it before. I was working in my field all day. I had never seen it until she accused me. I did not do it, so I will not pay for it."

Now Judge Yasu listened carefully, but he was also quite deaf, so he could not understand a word that they said. He was also mostly blind. He peered at them intently and decided that he was looking at an old man and an old woman. He saw the lamb and thought that it was a baby. The judge had dealt with people's problems for many years, so he thought he understood. The man and woman wanted a divorce, but they could not agree who should get the child.

"How many years have you been married?" asked the judge.

Widow Yemswitch thought he was asking how many sheep she had, so she shouted, "Twenty" at the top of her voice.

The Wise Judge, Part 4

Judge Yasu was able to hear this answer, and this helped him reach a quick decision. He said, "You should be ashamed. You have lived together for twenty years and still not learned to live together peacefully? This is my decision: You must continue to live together and make a good home for this little one. If you do not, I will have you both thrown in prison. Case dismissed!"

After some time, the bailiff was finally able to make Farmer Mulugeta and Widow Yemswitch understand what Judge Yasu had decided.

"But how can we live together?" cried Widow Yemswitch. "We are not married!"

"Then you had better get married right away," answered the bailiff, "or else the judge will have you thrown in prison!"

So a priest was called, and Farmer Mulugeta and Widow Yemswitch were married that very night. Since Widow Yemswitch was a very good cook, and since Farmer Mulugeta was a very good farmer, and since neither of them could hear what the other was saying, they lived very happily together. And the fame of the wise Judge Yasu spread even more widely through the land.

Notes on the Story

This is an Ethiopian tale, very loosely adapted from *The Lion's Whiskers and Other Ethiopian Tales,* by Brent Ashabranner and Russel Davis (1997).

11 Building awareness of text structure

Patricia Carrell (1985) reviewed the work of Bonnie J. F. Meyer and others to provide some good support that being conscious of the underlying structure of texts helps readers better understand and remember what they have read. The activities here introduce and help students notice the three most basic and common underlying bases for arranging texts: chronological order, problem–solution arrangements, and cause–effect arrangements. These activities can be useful for virtually all levels, from high beginners to advanced students with academic goals.

Introductions, episodes, and conclusions

Class level: High-beginner to advanced
Group size(s): Any
Objective(s): To build awareness of the various possible basic arrangements of ideas that can exist in texts. (*Optional:* To use structural awareness to help with summarizing.)
Approximate class time: 20 to 30 minutes

The activity

1. **If students are not familiar with words like "introduction," "conclusion," and "episode," teach these words.** Teaching them early will make discussing stories and literature easier later. (For "introduction," I start by explaining what it means to introduce a person [e.g., Lam, this is Hosea] and move from that to the introduction of the story. For students who watch TV, the use of the word *episode* to describe one day's show is sometimes helpful.)
2. **Orally tell a story (or have students read it).**
3. **Have students identify the main sections.** If the students list too many events (i.e., many individual actions rather than whole episodes), list all the events on the board and then ask the students to break the list into the appropriate number of groups. Providing students with some type of chart to help them generate some visual representation of the story's structure is helpful. Many types of graphic organizers can be used; examples are shown on pages 227 and 230.
4. **Once the main events are filled in, have students tell the main events for each episode.** Add these to the chart as shown on page 227.
5. **Draw attention to the parallelisms and similarities between episodes.** For example, in *The Judgment of the Rabbit,* in each episode, the scholar asks for someone else's verdict, the tiger agrees, the scholar tells the story, and the animal gives a judgment. Similarly, in *The Boy Who Went to the North Wind* (see page 238), each episode repeats the same events: The boy goes to the North Wind, the North Wind gives a gift, the boy heads for home and stops at the inn, etc. Being aware of parallel structure helps students better understand future stories.
6. **If you had students complete this activity individually or in groups, review the activity on the board.** Discuss any differences of opinion.

The first time or two you do this activity, work through the structure of the story on the board with the whole class. The diagram on page 230 shows another way to represent text structure. Once students are familiar with it, have them complete this activity individually, in pairs, or in small groups.

Adapting the activity for different levels

As with the timeline graphic organizer shown with *The Greedy Old Spider* (see page 75), you can provide a partially filled-in version of the chart, a blank one with a list of items to be inserted in the appropriate places, or a blank chart, or you can give advanced students nothing at all and let them create their own organizational chart. This provides different levels of assistance so all students can complete the activity at their own level.

Follow-up

This activity fits well either before or after exploring problem–solution and/or cause–effect relationships (see pages 236 and 242). Since doing the timeline activity (see page 72) helps students get a good understanding of the events of the story, that activity may be a good one to do before doing this activity. Since the chart used in this activity involves writing a series of summary statements, this activity can also be connected to instruction on note taking, summarizing, and outlining.

For students who plan to do university-level work, this activity is a good way to lead into exploring the structure of arguments in essays. By teaching students to notice the arrangement of ideas in major sections in folktales (where it is relatively easy to see), you prepare them to notice such structures in more difficult pieces of writing.

Other stories to use with this activity

Since any story has an underlying structure, this activity can be used with nearly any story. Different graphic organizers may be more appropriate for some stories.

Some stories that I particularly like for this activity are:

The Boy and the North Wind	See page 238
The Princess's Suitors	See page 122
Mother Holly	See page 149
The Fourth Question	See page 68

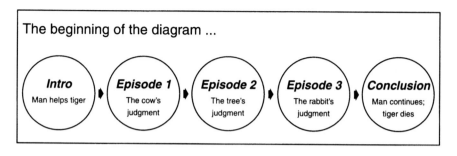

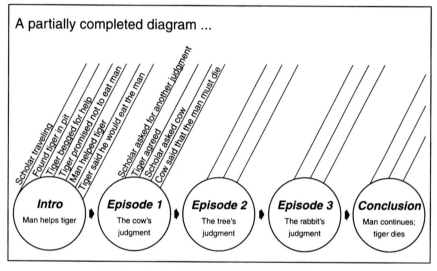

Diagrams for exploring the structure of *The Judgment of the Rabbit*.

The Judgment of the Rabbit

Once upon a time, when the tiger smoked, there was a scholar who was kind to everyone. One day, he left home to go to the palace to take the exam to become a government official.

While he was climbing a mountain, he heard a distant scream: "Help me! Help me!" The scholar hurried in the direction of the scream. He was surprised to find a big tiger in a deep hole. "Help me! Help me, please!" As soon as the tiger saw the scholar, it began to scream more loudly. The scholar hesitated, deliberating over whether or not to pass the tiger by.

The tiger begged more loudly, "Please don't leave me in this terrible hole, please!"

"If I save you, you will eat me," said the scholar.

"No, I'll not eat you if you save my life," cried the tiger. "I promise."

So the scholar pulled the tiger out with a stick. "Hu-woo. . . !" The tiger rested for a while.

"Now, I must go my way," said the scholar.

The tiger's face suddenly became threatening. "You can't go because I must eat you."

Th scholar was surprised to hear this and said, "What? Why? I saved your life, and you promised not to eat me."

Then the tiger laughed, "But man is a wicked creature. I know that all the animals and plants hate man. So I must eat you."

The scholar didn't know what to do, but after a moment an idea occurred to him. "OK," he said, "but before you eat me, please go and ask someone whether I must be killed by the tiger after having saved its life. If he answers 'Yes,' I'll submit to your decision to eat me." The tiger agreed, and so they left the hole and went to find someone.

A cow was working in the farmer's field. The scholar asked the cow, "I saved the tiger from a deep hole, and now he wants to eat me. Since I saved his life, do you think he should kill me?"

The cow answered, "You must be a good person. But I think man must die. He always causes me pain by treating me harshly."

As soon as the tiger heard the cow, he prepared to eat the scholar. But before the tiger could eat him, the scholar screamed, "No, please let me ask someone else. If he also says I must die, I'll submit to your decision."

The tiger agreed, "OK, one more. But then you must keep your promise."

They found a big pine tree on the hill and the scholar asked the same question that he asked the cow: "I saved the tiger from a deep hole, and now he wants to eat me. Since I saved his life, do you think he should kill me?"

Then the pine tree answered firmly, "Man is always bad. He cuts my body to pieces and burns me as firewood. So man must die!"

After hearing this, the tiger said haughtily, "Did you hear that? Now it is time for you to die."

"Oh, please give me one more chance to live," begged the scholar. "If the last one says I'm bad, then I'll let you eat me."

"Well, just one more," answered the tiger. "This is your last chance."

They went down the hill and found a rabbit running to the pond. "Wait, Mr. Rabbit! May I ask you a question?"

"Certainly," answered the rabbit. So the scholar once more explained his story from the beginning. After hearing the whole story, the rabbit thought the matter over for a moment and then said, "I can't understand your story very well. If you need my judgment, you must show me what happened from the beginning. It will help me understand and judge what you have said."

The scholar and the tiger agreed with this proposal, and they returned to the hole. The tiger jumped down into the hole and said, "I was waiting here for someone's help."

As soon as the tiger jumped down into the hole, the rabbit pulled out the stick. "And there was no stick in the hole?" continued the rabbit. "Well, I think that the tiger is bad and must die in the hole, because he was ungrateful for the scholar's kindness. That is my judgment."

Then the rabbit went on his way, and the scholar left for the palace to take his exam, and the tiger remained in the hole until he died.

Notes on the Story
This is a Korean story that was written for me by one of my Korean students. "When the tiger smoked" is a traditional beginning for Korean tales in which animals talk and do things that are usually done only by people.

Text structure of *The Princess's Suitors*	
Main events	**What happened**
Introduction Princess doesn't know who to marry	Princess is very nice and beautiful Three princes want to marry her Her father tells her to pick one She thinks of a plan to help her choose
Main event 1 Princess tests first prince	Princess goes to first prince's castle The princess gets a job in the stable The princess spills water on the prince The prince gets very angry The princess goes away
Main event 2	
Main event 3	
Conclusion	

The cyclical story

Class level: High-beginner to advanced
Group size(s): Whole class for listening; individuals or pairs for chart
Objective(s): To build awareness of the various possible basic
    arrangements of ideas that can exist in texts
Approximate class time: 20 to 30 minutes

The underlying "structure" of a cyclical story is in a different category than
the structure explored in the previous activity. In a cyclical story, we still
have an introduction, parallel episodes, and a conclusion; the characters
just happen to be in the same place at the end (at least in some ways) as
they were in the beginning. As such, what we are really looking at is
content rather than literary structure. However, this pattern occurs in quite
a few folktales and also shows up in logic arguments and in history. This
activity helps students pay attention to the text, and it also provides variety.

The activity

1. Orally present or have students read a story with a cyclical structure.
2. Have students fill in the main episodes of the story on a graphic like
   the one shown on the next page.
3. If desired, identify the main elements in each episode as in the previous
   activity.
4. Review the activity as a class.

Stories to use with this activity

The Stonecutter	See page 5
It Could Always Be Worse	See page 88

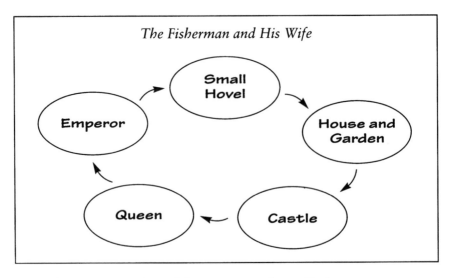

A graphic representation of the structure of a cyclical story.

Intermediate

The Fisherman and His Wife

Once upon a time a fisherman and his wife lived in a small hovel by the sea. The fisherman was quite happy doing the best he could, but his wife was always wanting something that they didn't have and continually complaining about it.

One day the fisherman was out fishing when he caught a large fish. When he pulled it out of the water, it spoke to him, saying, "Please set me free. I am really not a fish but an enchanted prince."

"Gladly," said the fisherman, and placed the fish back into the water.

When the fisherman went home, he told his wife what had happened.

"You foolish man," she cried. "Surely the fish would have granted a wish if you had asked."

"I'm sure that we have what we need. Why should I have asked him for anything?"

"Because we live so wretchedly. Now go back at once and tell him that I want a nice house with flowers and a garden."

So the man went back to the sea. It was not quite its normal color but was a yellowish-green, but still the fisherman stood by the shore and called,

> Fish of the sea, fish of the sea,
> I need your help, so come to me.

So the fish came and said, "What is it that you want?"
"My wife wishes for a house with flowers and a garden."

"Go home," said the fish, "and you will find what you have asked for."

And so the fisherman went home and there was the house and the flowers and the garden. "Well, wife," he said, "now we can be content."

"We will see," she said. "We will see." After about a week passed, the wife said, "Husband, this house and this garden are much too small. What we need is a castle. Go back to the fish and tell him to give us one."

"Wife," said the fisherman, "he might be angry if I go back. Besides, this house is quite nice enough and I think we ought to be content with it."

"Nonsense," said the wife. "If we don't look out for what we need, we will never get anywhere in life. Now run along at once."

So in the end the husband agreed, and off he went back to the sea. It was now a deep, dark gray, and the water looked troubled. But still the fisherman stood by the shore and called,

> Fish of the sea, fish of the sea,
> I need your help, so come to me.

So the fish came and said, "What is it that you want?"
"My wife wishes for a great stone castle surrounded by a vast estate."

"Go home," said the fish, "and you will find what you have asked for."

And so the fisherman went home and there was the castle surrounded by trees and lawns and gardens, with servants coming and going. "Well, wife," said the fisherman, "surely this is enough. Now we can be content."

"We will see," she said. "We will see."

But a few days later the wife said, "Husband, this castle is not enough. What we need is to be king and queen of this land. Go back to the fish and tell him to make us king and queen."

"Wife," said the fisherman, "he might be angry if I go back.

continued

233

Besides, I have no wish at all to be king. We ought to be content with what we have."

"Nonsense," said the wife. "If we don't look out for what we need, we will never get anywhere in life. If you don't want to be king, then I still must be queen. Now go."

So in the end the husband agreed, and off he went back to the sea. The waters were even darker now, and the waves crashed on the rocks. But still the fisherman stood by the shore and called,

> Fish of the sea, fish of the sea,
> I need your help, so come to me.

So the fish came and said, "What is it that you want?"

"My wife wishes to be queen."

"Go home," said the fish, "and you will find what you have asked for."

And so the fisherman went home, and there was his wife wearing a golden crown and seated on a throne in a great hall. Courtiers and officials were coming and going. "Well, wife," said the fisherman, "surely this is enough. Now you can surely can be content."

"We will see," she said. "We will see."

But the next day the wife said, "Husband, being queen is not enough. What we need is to be emperor. Go back to the fish and tell him to make me emperor of all the world."

"Wife," said the fisherman, "he might be angry if I go back. This is too much. Be content with what you have."

"Nonsense," said the wife. "If we don't look out for what we need, we will never get anywhere in life. Now go before I summon my guards."

So in the end the husband agreed, and off he went back to the sea. The waters were nearly black now, and the waves rose like mountains. But still the fisherman stood by the shore and called,

> Fish of the sea, fish of the sea,
> I need your help, so come to me.

So the fish came and said, "What is it that you want?"

"My wife wishes to be emperor of the whole world."

"Go home," said the fish, "and you will find what you have asked for."

And so the fisherman went home, and there was his wife on a throne that looked like a small mountain. Kings were there to beg her favor, and crowds of people were coming and going. "Well, wife," said the fisherman, "surely now you must be content. There is nothing more to ask for."

"We will see," she said. "We will see."

But the next morning the wife said, "Husband, being emperor is not enough. Go back to the fish and tell him to make me lord of the sun and moon."

"Wife," said the fisherman, "he might be angry if I go back. This is too much. Be content with what you have."

"Nonsense," said the wife. "If we don't look out for what we need, we will never get anywhere in life. Now go before I summon my armies."

So the husband agreed, and off he went back to the sea. The waters were black as the darkest night now, and the waves reached up to the heavens. The fisherman feared that the waves would sweep him away. But still the fisherman stood by the shore and called,

> Fish of the sea, fish of the sea,
> I need your help, so come to me.

So the fish came and said, "What is it that you want?"

"My wife wishes to be lord of the sun and moon."

"Go home," said the fish. "She will have what is due her."

And so the fisherman went home, and there was his wife in the same old miserable little shack that they had always lived in, and there they lived for the rest of their days.

Notes on the Story
This is a common western European tale.

A Thrilling Tale

One night, in the heart of the Harz Mountains, a band of robbers set out. And the chief of the robbers said, "Scotty, my boy, tell me a thrilling tale."

So Scotty began, "One night, in the heart of the Harz Mountains, a band of robbers set out. And the chief of the robbers said, Scotty, my boy, tell me a thrilling tale.'"

So Scotty began, "One night, in the heart of the Harz Mountains. . . ."

Notes on the Story
This is an example of an endlessly cyclic story; it can go on forever.

▨▨▨ Problem/solution stories

Class level: High-beginner to advanced
Group size(s): Whole class, individuals, pairs
Objective(s): To build awareness of the various possible basic
    arrangements of ideas that can exist in texts
Approximate class time: 20 to 30 minutes

The activity

1. **Begin by talking about problems and solutions in general to make sure students understand the idea.** For example:

Problem	Solution
Flat tire	Gas station
No money	Get job
Raining	Umbrella
Don't know English	Taking class

    Note that some solutions lead to new problems or fail to achieve the desired results. (For example, problem: no money → solution: get job → problem: no transportation → solution: buy car → problem: no money → etc.)

2. **Tell a story that has an underlying problem–solution structure.** Aside from being chronological, most folktales are either problem–solution or cause–effect (or some combination of these) in their orientation.

3. **On the board or on paper, create a problem–solution chart like the one on the next page.** The sample is for *The Boy Who Went to the North Wind* (page 238.) The first time you may have to identify the problems and do some prompting to get students to offer solutions. An alternative to creating a chart for students to fill in is to create a matching exercise with problems on one side and solutions on the other; this provides an extra level of support for lower-level students since no production is required and all answers are visible. See the sample matching exercise with the cause-and-effect activity on page 244.

Problem	Solution	Results
Lost flour	Went to the North Wind	Got magic cloth
Cloth didn't work	Went to the North Wind	Got magic goat
Goat didn't work	Went to the North Wind	Got magic stick
Innkeeper a thief	Stick beat innkeeper	Got cloth and goat back
		Lived happily ever after

4. Each time that you use a problem–solution story, draw attention to the structure, expecting students to contribute more and more each time. Advanced students who have looked at other structures should fairly soon be able to identify that the story is addressing problems and solutions without your telling them.

Follow-up

This activity can be followed up by having students analyze the structure of the text (that is, breaking it into introduction, episodes, and conclusion; see page 225). After you have done this activity a few times, you can also have students examine a problem–solution text that is not a folktale.

Once students are aware of problem–solution relationships, you can also use this as a foundation for students writing original stories: Students choose a general problem for the characters to solve (a plundering dragon, three lazy sons who won't work, needing to meet impossible demands to marry the king's daughter, etc.), and then create a series of lesser problems and solutions that are part of reaching that goal.

Other stories to use with this activity

It Could Always Be Worse (see page 88). Problem: too noisy; solution: animals into house; result: things got worse; etc.

The Wise Judge (see page 221). Problem: lost sheep; solution: search and ask Farmer M.; problem: Farmer M. deaf; result: answered different question; etc.

The Boy Who Went to the North Wind

Once there was a boy named Peter who lived with his poor old mother. One day Peter went to the barn to get some flour. As he walked back to the house, the North Wind blew the flour away.

So Peter went back to the barn to get more. Again the North Wind blew the flour away. Peter went back again . . . and again, until at last there was no more flour.

"Well," said Peter, "I must get our flour back."

He went to the house and said, "The North Wind has taken away all our flour, so I must get it back. Good bye, Mother." Then he left.

He walked, and he walked, and he walked, until at last he came to the North Wind.

"Good day," said Peter.

"Good day," said the North Wind. "What can I do for you?"

"Well," said Peter, "you blew all our flour away. We are very poor. We need it, so please give it back."

"I don't have your flour," said the North Wind, "but I will give you this cloth instead. "Say, 'Cloth, Cloth, give me food,' and the cloth will give you food."

"Thank you," said Peter. He took the cloth and started home.

He walked and walked, but he got very tired, so he stopped at an inn to rest. He spread the cloth on the table and said, "Cloth, Cloth, give me food." At once the cloth was covered with as much delicious food as Peter could eat.

Now the innkeeper was watching as Peter did this, so he saw the cloth covered with food.

"This must be a magic cloth," thought the innkeeper. "I must have it." So he waited until Peter was sleeping, and then he crept very quietly into his room. He took the cloth and put another one in its place.

In the morning, Peter got up and took his cloth and headed for home. When he reached home, he cried, "Look, Mother! I went to the North Wind, and he gave me a magic cloth. If you say, 'Cloth, Cloth, give me food,' the cloth gives food."

"Let me see," said his mother.

So Peter spread the cloth on the table and said, "Cloth, Cloth, give me food." But there was no food.

"The cloth does not work," said Peter. "I must go back to the North Wind." So he left to find the North Wind again.

He walked, and he walked, and he walked, until at last he came to the North Wind.

"Good day," said Peter.

"Good day," said the North Wind. "What can I do for you now?"

"Well," said Peter, "You blew all of our flour away. You gave me a cloth, but the cloth does not work. We are very poor. We need food, so please give our flour back."

"I don't have your flour," said the North Wind, "but I will give you this goat instead. "Say, 'Goat, Goat, give me gold,' and the goat will give you gold."

"Thank you," said Peter. He took the goat and started home.

He walked and walked, but he grew very tired, so he stopped at the inn to sleep. He took the goat to the stable. Once the door was closed, he said, "Goat, Goat, give me gold." Gold came out of the goat's mouth. Peter gathered the gold and went to pay for his room.

Now the innkeeper was watching Peter, so he saw the goat give gold.

"This must be a magic goat," thought the innkeeper. "I must have it." Once Peter was sleeping, he went to the stable and took the goat and put another one in its place.

In the morning, Peter got up and took his goat and headed for home. When he reached home, he cried, "Look, Mother! I went to the North Wind, and he gave me a magic goat. If you say, 'Goat, Goat, give me gold,' the goat gives gold."

"Let me see," said his mother.

So Peter patted the goat and said, "Goat, Goat, give me gold." But there was no gold.

"The goat does not work," said Peter. "I must go back to the North Wind." So he left to find the North Wind again.

He walked, and he walked, and he walked, until at last he came to the North Wind.

"Good day," said Peter.

"Good day," said the North Wind. "What can I do for you now?"

continued

"Well," said Peter, "You blew all of our flour away. You gave me a cloth, but the cloth did not work. You gave me a goat, but the goat does not work. We are very poor, and we need food, so please give our flour back."

"I don't have your flour," said the North Wind, "but tell me, did the cloth never give food?"

"No," said Peter, "It gave food at the inn. But it did not work when I got home."

"Hmm," said the North Wind. "And did the goat never give gold?"

"No," said Peter, "It gave gold at the inn. But it did not work when I got home."

"Hmm," said the North Wind. "I have one more gift for you. Here is a stick. Say, 'Hit, Stick, hit,' and it will keep hitting until you say, 'Stop, Stick, stop.'"

"Hmm," said Peter, "Thank you!" Then he took the stick and started home.

He walked and walked, and by evening he came to the inn.

Now the innkeeper saw the stick in Peter's hand, and he thought, "This must be a magic stick. I must have it." So he waited until Peter was sleeping, and then crept quietly into Peter's room to take the stick.

Now Peter was not really sleeping, and as soon as the innkeeper was ready to take the stick, he shouted, "Hit, Stick, hit!"

The stick began to hit the innkeeper. The innkeeper ran, but the stick chased him. "Make it stop! Make it stop!" the innkeeper cried.

But Peter said nothing, and the stick kept hitting the innkeeper.

"Make it stop, and I will give your cloth and your goat back," cried the innkeeper.

So Peter said, "Stop, Stick, stop."

The stick stopped hitting the innkeeper, and came to Peter's side. The innkeeper brought the cloth and the goat.

Then Peter took the stick, and the cloth, and the goat, and headed for home. When he reached home, he cried, "Look, Mother! I went to the North Wind, and he gave me a magic stick."

"Let me see," said his mother.

"Oh no, Mother," said Peter, "I will not show you how the

stick works. But here are the cloth and the goat. I will show them to you."

Peter spread the cloth on the table and said, "Cloth, Cloth, give me food." And the table was full of good food. He patted the goat and said, "Goat, Goat, give me gold." And gold came from the goat's mouth.

And Peter and his mother were never hungry again.

Notes on the Story
This is a Norse tale. I have told it here at a high beginning level. A published version that is particularly good for beginners because of fairly easy text and strong support from the pictures is *Peter and the North Wind,* by Freya Littledale, illustrated by Troy Howell (1988).

Cause-and-effect stories

Class level: High-beginner to advanced
Group size(s): Whole class for listening; individuals or pairs for chart
Objective(s): To build awareness of the various possible basic
arrangements of ideas that can exist in texts
Approximate class time: 20 to 30 minutes

For students who plan to do university work in English, awareness of
cause-and-effect relationships is critical because many academic arguments involve cause–effect (and problem–solution) relationships.

The activity

PREPARATION

If needed, create a cause–effect chart or a matching activity like the ones
shown on pages 243 and 244. The first several times you will probably
have to identify causes and let students fill in the effects; with practice
and as students become more advanced, they should be able to identify
causes on their own. The matching chart can be a helpful form of support
for lower-level students, since it requires no production from the
students. In addition, all answers are provided, so students just have to
find the one they need. This also provides more written text that directly
corresponds to what is being presented orally, so it can be helpful in
connecting oral and written forms.

IN THE CLASSROOM

1. **Begin by talking about causes and effects in general to make sure
   students understand the idea.** For example:

Cause	Effect
Forgot umbrella	Got wet
Slept late	Missed breakfast
Brought flowers	Girlfriend happy
Didn't do homework	Did badly on test
Exercised every day	Got stronger and faster

   Get students to contribute examples until everyone understands.
2. **Tell a story that has an underlying cause-and-effect structure.** (In
   addition to being chronological, most folktales are either problem–
   solution, cause–effect, or a mix of these.)

3. **Either while you are telling the story or after you are done, have students fill the chart in.** If you use the matching activity, students should complete it afterwards.
4. **Review students answers as a class.**

Instead of or in addition to doing this activity, you can take a few minutes while doing other activities to point out or ask students to identify cause-and-effect relationships in stories that are read or listened to.

Other stories to use with this activity

This activity works well with many folktales. A few possibilities are:

Cause-and-effect relationships in *The Man Who Kept House*

Cause	Effect
The man was angry.	He grumbled at his wife.
The man grumbled at his wife.	They traded jobs.
The man was thirsty.	
The man heard the pig in the kitchen.	
The man chased the pig.	
The man didn't want to take the cow to the field.	
The man didn't want to spill the cream again.	
The man got water with the churn on his back.	
The man was afraid the cow would fall.	
The cow fell.	
The wife saw the cow and cut the rope.	
All of these troubles . . .	

Cause and effect in
Jack and the Beanstalk

Match the events from the story on the left with the effects these
events had. The first one is done for you.

Cause

Effect

Mother discovers they have no food, or money.

Jack finds out about giant's gold.

Peddler offers Jack magic beans.

Beanstalk grows.

Jack shows beans to his mother.

Mother gets angry.

Mother throws beans out the window.

Mother decides to sell the cow.

Jack climbs beanstalk.

Jack trades cow for beans.

Jack hides in the castle.

Jack discovers castle in the sky.

Intermediate

The Man Who Kept House

Once there was a man who was always angry. He worked hard
every day, and he thought that his wife did too little. He was
always grumbling at her that her life was too easy. "If you only
went to the fields and worked like I did," he said, "then you
would see what real work was like and how easy your life is."

One day she answered, "Husband, if you would like,
tomorrow we can trade jobs. I will go to the fields with the scythe
and cut the hay, and you can stay here and do my work. Then I
will better understand your work."

The husband agreed to this, so the next day the wife headed
off to the field with the scythe, and the man set about to do the
daily chores.

"I'd like some butter for my lunch," thought the man, "so
I'll do that first." So he got some cream and put it in the butter
churn. Then he thought, "I'm thirsty. I think I'll go to the
basement for a mug of cider before I begin." So the man got a
large mug and went down in the basement to the barrel of cider.

He had just pulled the stopper and begun filling his mug when he heard a scuffling sound upstairs. It sounded as though the pig was in the kitchen. He raced up the stairs and found the cream spilled all over the floor. The pig was lapping it up. He gave a shout and began to chase the pig. He gave it a kick as it raced out the door, and then noticed that he still held the stopper for the cider barrel in his hand.

He raced back to the basement, but by that time most of the cider had spilled on the floor. He sighed and went upstairs, and began to clean up the cream on the floor. Then he remember that the cow was still in the barn. It needed to be taken out to pasture. He didn't want to take the time to lead it the whole way up to the pasture, so he got some boards and made a ramp up to the roof and then pushed the cow up there so it could eat the thick grass growing there.

Then he got some more cream because he still wanted butter for his lunch. He had not finished making the butter when he remembered that he needed to put the water on to boil to make the porridge for lunch. The jug in the house was empty, so he would have to go to the well to draw some more. He didn't want the baby to knock the churn over and spill the cream, so he tied the churn to his back and set off for the well.

He lowered the bucket into the well and then bent down to haul it up. As he bent over the well, the cream poured from the churn on his back, spilling all over his head and into the well.

As he looked up, he saw the cow grazing near the edge of the roof. He was afraid it would fall off, so he rushed and got a rope, climbed onto the roof, and tied one end around the cow's neck. Then, realizing it was almost lunch time, he threw the other end down the chimney and rushed down into the house to make the porridge.

Once in the house, the man tied the end of the rope around his ankle, and then set about to make porridge. He had set the pot on the coals in the fireplace and was beginning to stir it when the cow stepped off the edge of the roof. The rope pulled the man halfway up the chimney, where he stuck, leaving the cow stuck hanging half off the roof.

Now the wife had been cutting hay in the field all morning, and by this time she was quite hungry. She saw that the sun was overhead, but her husband hadn't rung the dinner bell yet, so she

continued

kept working for a while longer. Finally she set off for the house, thinking that lunch must be ready any time.

When she reached the house, she saw the cow hanging off the edge on the rope, so she cut the rope and set the creature free. At this she heard a loud cry from within the house. She hurried in and found her husband upside down in the fireplace, having fallen with his head in the porridge.

After all this, the husband returned to doing his own work and the wife to hers. Never again did the man grumble or complain about the way his wife did her work, and life was happier for both of them from this point on.

Notes on the Story
This is a Scandanavian tale. One published version of this tale with good readable text and well-done and humorous pictures that provide good support for the text is *The Man Who Kept House,* by P. C. Asbjørnsen and J. E. Moe, illustrated by Otto S. Svend (1991).

Intermediate

Jack and the Beanstalk

Once upon a time, a widow lived with her only son. They were so poor that they barely had enough to eat, and each day there seemed to be less in their cupboard than the day before. At last there was nothing to eat at all, so the mother decided that they must sell their dear, old cow.

"Son," said the mother, "we have not a single bite of food left, so take the cow to the market and sell her for the best price you can. That will give us something to buy food with, though after that money is gone, I do not know what we will do."

So Jack, her son, took the cow and began to lead her to the market. He had not gotten more than halfway there before he met a peddler on the road.

"Where are you off to, my boy?" asked the peddler.

"I'm taking our cow to the market to sell her, for we have no food and no money to buy more."

"Well," said the man. "I have a deal for you. I have here a handful of beans . . . not just ordinary beans . . . but magic beans. I will trade them for your cow, for my heart tells me your troubles will be over if you have these beans."

Well, Jack wanted their troubles to be over, so he traded the cow for the beans and headed off for home.

"Mother," he cried as he ran through the door, "You'll never guess what happened. I met a man who gave me some magic beans for our cow, so now our troubles are over."

"You fool!" she shouted. "You traded our cow for one handful of beans? What now shall we eat?" Then she seized the beans and threw them out the window and sent Jack to bed without supper.

In the morning, when Jack woke, he looked out his window and saw an enormous beanstalk reaching up into the clouds. Quickly he climbed out the window and began to climb the beanstalk. When he reached the top, he saw a great castle, so he went to it and knocked on the door.

An old woman opened the door and looked out.

"Please, ma'am," said Jack, "could you spare a bit of food to eat?"

"Oh, you shouldn't be here," said the woman. "A great giant lives here, and he likes nothing better than little boys for his supper. Still, he's out right now, so perhaps you can come in for a quick bite to eat."

But Jack had scarcely finished eating before the whole castle began to shake, and soon he could hear the pounding of the giant's feet as he came.

"Quick," said the old woman, "hide here in the oven."

So Jack slipped into the oven, and not a moment too soon, for in came the giant. Jack could hear him sniffing. Then the giant thundered,

> *Fee, Fie, Fo, Fum*
> *I smell the blood of an Englishman*
> *Be he alive or be he dead*
> *I'll grind his bones to make my bread*

"I'm afraid you're mistaken, my Lord," said the old woman. "You're just smelling the mutton that I've cooked for your dinner. So sit down now, and I'll bring it to you."

So the giant sat at his great table. He ate and ate, till at last Jack heard him cry, "Now bring me my gold so I can count it."

continued

Soon Jack heard the chink of coins being dropped and the giant's counting. But at last it grew still and then Jack heard the sound of the giant beginning to snore. So he slipped out of the oven and began heading for the door. Then he thought, "That gold would be handy. I'd better take some." So he climbed up one leg of the table and snatched a bag of gold from under the nose of the sleeping giant and ran for the door and slipped out. Then he climbed down the beanstalk and was soon home with his mother. He showed her the gold. She was overjoyed, both to find him safe and to find that they now had plenty to live on.

Well, not many days had passed before Jack decided to climb the beanstalk again. He headed for the castle. This time, he slipped in without anyone seeing him. The giant was out, and so Jack hid himself in a spot where he could see the room but not be seen.

It was not long before the giant came home. Jack could feel the castle shake as he approached. When the giant came, he again sniffed the air. Then he thundered,

> Fee, Fie, Fo, Fum
> I smell the blood of an Englishman
> Be he alive or be he dead
> I'll grind his bones to make my bread

"You must be mistaken, my Lord," said the old woman. "You're just smelling the mutton that I've prepared for your dinner. So sit down now, and I'll bring it to you."

So the giant sat down to eat, and when he was done, he cried, "Bring me my goose that lays the golden eggs."

So the woman brought the goose and placed it before the giant. "Lay, goose, lay!" cried the giant, and soon the goose had laid a large golden egg. Then the giant cried again, "Lay, goose, lay!" and before long the goose had laid another. This went on until at last the giant feel asleep again at the table.

Then Jack slipped from his hiding place and climbed up on the table and slipped the goose into a sack and then hurried for the door. Soon he was home showing his mother the new treasure he had found.

Well, not many days had passed before Jack began to feel adventurous, so he decided to climb the beanstalk again. He headed straight for the castle. Again, he slipped in without anyone seeing him. The giant was out, and so Jack hid himself again in a spot where he could see the room but not be seen.

It was not long before the giant came home. Jack could feel the castle shake as he approached. When the giant came, he again sniffed the air. Then he thundered,

Fee, Fie, Fo, Fum
I smell the blood of an Englishman
Be he alive or be he dead
I'll grind his bones to make my bread

"You must be mistaken, my Lord," said the old woman. "You're just smelling the mutton that I've prepared for your dinner. So sit down now, and I'll bring it to you."

So the giant sat down to eat, and when he was done, he cried, "Bring me my harp that plays itself."

So the woman brought a lovely, golden harp and placed it before the giant. "Play, Harp, play!" cried the giant, and a merry tune began to come from the harp, though no one was there to play it. Once again, the giant fell asleep at the table.

Jack slipped from his hiding place and grabbed the harp and started for the door. But he had not gotten far before the harp began to cry out with a loud voice, "Help, Master, help!"

By the time Jack was at the door the giant was awake and had seen him. "Stop, thief, stop!" cried the giant. Jack ran faster. He soon reached the beanstalk, but he could hear the giant coming after him, still bellowing, "Stop, thief, stop!" Before he was halfway down, he felt the beanstalk begin to shake as the giant started down after him.

"Mother," cried Jack, "get the axe!" When he reached the bottom, his mother was waiting with the axe. They could see the giant coming down above them. Jack snatched the axe and began to hack at the beanstalk. Before the giant reached the ground, Jack had cut through the beanstalk and it fell to the ground. The giant fell to the earth with a crash and was killed at once by the fall. Where he fell, there was a great hole in the earth, and it is still there today if you care to see it.

Notes on the Story
This is a traditional English folktale.

12 Developing analytical skills

We often think of analytical skills as being most suitable for advanced students with academic goals, and indeed these activities can be used to develop academic skills with advanced students, but with the right stories, these activities can be used with high-beginner/low-intermediate students. They are also very suitable for children as well as adults.

Evaluating and summarizing a story

Class level: Low-intermediate to advanced
Group size(s): Individuals, pairs, or small groups (3 or 4)
Objective(s): To provide general language practice while developing an awareness of considerations that affect summarizing and evaluating
Approximate class time: 20 to 30 minutes

The activity

PREPARATION

1. **Choose a story and write about 15 or 20 summary statements.**
2. **If you are going to give the story to students as a strip story, scramble the sentences** so students can cut them apart without getting the correct order.
3. **Make copies of the sentences for each student or group.** In contexts where it is not feasible to make copies, write them on the board, put them on an overhead, or dictate them to the students.
4. **Rank the importance of the strips yourself** (most important, moderately important, relatively unimportant), so that you are prepared to discuss the rankings with the students. Think about how to explain why you ranked each strip as you did.

IN THE CLASSROOM

1. **Have students read or listen to the story.**
2. *(Optional)* **If you scrambled the strips, have students cut apart the sentences and order them as a strip story.** See page 102.
3. **Individually or in small groups, have students rank the importance of each strip:** 1 = most important (key element of story; couldn't have the story without it); 2 = moderately important, 3 = relatively unimportant (could change this and it wouldn't really alter the gist of the story). For a long story, you might add another level or two. You can choose to tell students how many items should be in each group. (Sometimes this makes the task easier since it gives them something to shoot for, but it can make it harder since if they rank one strip differently, they may struggle to figure out which one.)
4. **Discuss the students' conclusions about how they ranked the strips.** If you have the strips written on the board or on an overhead, write down the ranks that students gave to each. Talk about factors that contributed to the rankings, paying particular attention to strips where you think students missed something important or where different students ranked them differently. Acknowledge places where

there are legitimate differences of opinion. In teaching students to do this type of evaluation, it is important for you to think aloud: Show students how you got to your conclusion rather than just telling them your conclusion. (For example, "I decided that Salem's buying a new shop was not one of the most important sentences because if we took it out, we would still have a story about his tricking Abraham into buying a house he couldn't live in and then making money out of the deal. But it still is somewhat important since it tells us why Salem did what he did. For example, if Salem had done this trick because he needed money to save his dying mother, it would still be a story about a trick but it would leave us with a very different feeling. The fact that many people came to look at the house and weren't interested didn't seem that important because even if we leave it out completely, we still have the same story . . . it doesn't affect our perception of either Salem or Abraham's character. . . .")

5. **Show how including or excluding different ranks creates different-level summaries.** Only including the level 1 strips gives a very short summary, including level 1 and 2 gives a medium-length summary, and including all of the strips gives a longer one. Write each on the board, show them on the overhead, or just read the different versions. Talk about contexts where each would be useful.

Variation

For more advanced students, don't provide the summary statements. After telling the story, have them write as many single sentence statements about the story as they can remember. (This can be done individually or in groups of up to three.) Then have them rank their own sentences and produce summaries with different degrees of detail. Compare the summaries produced by different groups to see how similar or different they are.

Ranked sentences for *Salem and the Nail*
(see page 104)

2	Salem's shop burned in a fire.
1	He decided to sell his house, except for one nail.
3	Many people came to look.
3	People went away shaking their heads.
3	Abraham argued about the price.
1	Abraham bought Salem's house.
3	Salem hung an empty bag on the nail.
3	Salem hung an old coat on the nail.
1	Salem hung a dead donkey on the nail.
2	Abraham complained that the donkey smelled bad.
2	Abraham took Salem to the judge.
2	The judge said Salem was in the right.
1	Abraham could not live in the house.
1	Salem bought his old house at half price.
2	Salem bought a new shop.

Ranked sentences for *Salem and the Nail*

Summary based on level 1 strips only

Salem decided to sell his house, except for one nail. Abraham bought Salem's house. Salem hung a dead donkey on the nail. Abraham could not live in the house. Salem bought his old house at half price.

Summary based on level 1 and level 2 strips

Salem's shop burned in a fire. He decided to sell his house, except for one nail. Abraham bought Salem's house. Salem hung a dead donkey on the nail. Abraham complained that the donkey smelled bad. Abraham took Salem to the judge. The judge said Salem was in the right. Abraham could not live in the house. Salem bought his old house at half price. Salem bought a new shop.

Summary based on all of the strips

Salem's shop burned in a fire. He decided to sell his house, except for one nail. Many people came to look. People went away shaking their heads. Abraham argued about the price. Abraham bought Salem's house. Salem hung an empty bag on the nail. Salem hung an old coat on the nail. Salem hung a dead donkey on the nail. Abraham complained that the donkey smelled bad. Abraham took Salem to the judge. The judge said Salem was in the right. Abraham could not live in the house. Salem bought his old house at half price. Salem bought a new shop.

Comparing two or more variants of a tale

Class level: Low-intermediate to advanced
Group size(s): Small groups, pairs, individuals
Objective(s): To provide integrated language skill practice while at the same time developing skills for compare/contrast, note taking, drawing inferences, critical evaluation, and connecting literature and real life
Approximate class time: 25 to 60 minutes

The activity

PREPARATION

Find two or more different variants (i.e., versions from different countries or cultures) of a story and make copies so that, when students are grouped, each student will get a copy of one of the stories. (This activity is easiest to do with written texts, but you could also incorporate listening practice by making recordings of the stories for students to listen to in a language lab.) You may want to put each story or variant on a different color paper; this makes it easier to see who has what and to regroup students.

If needed, create blank and/or partially completed graphic organizers to provide support for students who need it. See pages 258–259 for examples.

IN THE CLASSROOM

1. **Give each student one story variant.** For example, with fifteen students and three variants, give five students variant A, five students variant B, and five students variant C.
2. **Have each student carefully read the story so he or she can retell the story without looking at the text.** Rotate through the class to help if students get stuck.

   If the story is near the edge of the students' abilities, let students work together in small groups to understand their stories. (Using the example above, let all five students with variant A work together, etc.) Students can help each other with unknown vocabulary and with difficult parts of the story. If your assistance is needed to understand parts of the story, it also makes it easier for you to address difficult points with several students at once instead of having to do so with many students individually.

   If you are working on note taking, you could let students take notes while reading their stories.

   You can have students read their stories for homework so they come to class familiar with them (though you can get stuck if a few students don't do their homework or if a few students are absent and you end up with five people who have read one story and only two who have read another).

3. *(Optional)* **If you wish, have students complete a timeline (see page 72), a sentence ordering activity (see page 107) or some other similar activity to help them understand their stories.**

4. **Group students so that each person in the group has read a different story.** For example, if you selected *Cinderella* (commonly known and available; text not included in this book), *Strong Wind* (see page 108), and *Benizara and Kakezara* (see page 265) – three Cinderella variants – form groups of three with one student who has read *Cinderella,* one who has read *Strong Wind,* and one who has read *Benizara and Kakezara.* (It does not matter how many groups you have; this works well even with very large classes.)

5. **Each group member should tell the story he or she read to the other members of the group.** They may not read their story aloud; I usually require students to put the stories away to make sure this doesn't happen. They also may not show their stories to the other members of their groups; this forces oral participation of all members.

6. **Using some form of graphic organizer, have students write down similarities and differences between the stories.** Several examples of graphic organizers are shown on the following pages. These examples could have been filled in with much more detail, but the idea wasn't to analyze the story completely, just to illustrate the use of graphic organizers to help students understand the texts and relationships between them. You can either let students find as many points of similarity and difference as they can or specify a minimum number or similarities and differences for them to find. (For example, "Try to find at least seven ways the stories are the same and seven ways they are different.") The teacher can circulate among the groups to monitor discussion and take note of problems. You can provide questions that help draw attention to specific differences if this is needed based on the level of the students and how subtle the differences are.

7. **Once most groups are done, have one student tell each story to the class.** The student who tells the story must not have read it originally; he or she must only have heard it told by another member of the group. Other class members should listen for inaccuracies and important details that have been left out. At appropriate points you can let other students add or correct as needed. Allow for corrections first from those who heard the story told by a classmate rather than those who read the story originally. This provides review, listening practice, and focused listening practice all at the same time.

A GRAPHIC ORGANIZER COMPARING/CONTRASTING THREE *CINDERELLA* VARIANTS

	Cinderella	*Benizara and Kakezara*	*Strong Wind*
Antagonists	Two stepsisters	One stepsister	Two sisters
Place to meet prince	Ball	Theater	Lake shore
Characteristic that won the prince's heart	Beauty	Ability to compose elegant classical poem	Honesty
Fate of antagonists	Blinded	Falls over precipice	Turned into aspen trees

I sometimes outline the story on the board as it is told to model outlining or note taking.

8. **After retelling the stories, have students identify the similarities and differences that they found.** Briefly record the answers in some kind of chart on the board. I normally ask for one item at a time from each group in turn, so that all groups contribute to the total picture.

9. **To develop critical evaluation skills, have students identify which differences are most important.** For example, in *The Turtle and the Rabbit* and *The Whale and the Sea Slug*, the turtle won by perseverance while the snail won by an ingenious trick; this difference is more important than the fact that one race took place on land and the other took place in the sea.

10. **With more advanced students, talk about or get students to talk about what they can infer from the differences.** For example, in the *Cinderella* variants used here, one tale has beauty as the key characteristic; in another it is honesty (from a girl who has been physically disfigured); and in another the ability to compose a classical poem is central. In *Mother Holly* (see page 149), diligence and hard work are the key distinguishing factors; in *The Talking Eggs* (San Souci, 1989) not laughing at an elder is the key command (though diligence is also a key factor). Get students to discuss the values and perspectives reflected in the different tales. Many differences of this sort – some more subtle, some less – occur in folktale variants, and these differences can often lead to some interesting inferences.

Note: This activity takes a fairly formal and detailed approach to comparing and contrasting, but you can and should also do this more informally. For example, after reading a story, you might ask, "Now how is this story similar to _____" or "We read another story that talked about money . . . what was it? How is this story similar? How is it different?" Regularly asking students to think along these lines develops a habit of relating readings to other readings – seeing that readings are not isolated exercises but pieces that relate to a bigger picture is an important step in developing skill as a reader.

Providing different levels of support

In using graphic organizers, you can provide extra support ("scaffolding" is another term used for this) to help and guide students as they approach the text. The following samples (based on three *Cinderella* variants) illustrate three degrees of assistance. The second and third charts would each include more categories but have been shortened for the sake of space.

	Cinderella	*Benizara and Kakezara*	*Strong Wind*
Antagonists	Two stepsisters	One stepsister	Two sisters

This version provides minimal help: it gives a visual way to organize the findings, and it gives one example, but students have to identify both key points of comparison and specific differences.

	Cinderella	*Benizara and Kakezara*	*Strong Wind*
Antagonists	Two stepsisters	One stepsister	Two sisters
Situation of main character at beginning			
Where prince/lord is met			
Key characteristics that win the prince's heart			
Fate of main character			
Fate of antagonists			

This version provides more help by telling students where to look for differences in the text, but students still must find all of the information themselves. By showing students what to look for, you can help them focus their attention (a valuable cognitive strategy in its own right).

	Cinderella	*Benizara and Kakezara*	*Strong Wind*
"Bad" characters	Two stepsisters	One stepsister	Two sisters
Situation of main character at beginning			Cut hair, burnt by sisters, had to wear rags
Where prince/lord is met		Theater (place a play is acted out)	
What wins the prince's heart	Beauty		

This version provides even more help by identifying the categories in easier language, providing a definition, and giving an answer in one column for each category to help students anticipate what sort of answer they should expect to find in the text.

Variation

In the self-access classroom, provide variants for students to read or listen to on tape, and provide a blank chart or other graphic organizer for students to fill. Provide a completed version of the chart for students to check their work. See page 38 for more on self-access materials.

In the multilevel classroom

In the multilevel classroom, rewrite each of the variants at different levels as appropriate for your different levels of students. (For example, on page 262, *The Turtle and the Rabbit* is told at a high-beginner level, and *The Whale and the Sea Slug* is told at a low-intermediate level.) This way each student can have a story written at an appropriate level, while still keeping all students working together. (See page 38 for more details.)

Another option is to tell all the stories at roughly the same level but provide graphic organizers that give support to lower-level students while providing less or no support of this kind for higher-level students.

Adapting the activity for different levels

This activity can be made easier or harder in a number of ways: the difficulty of the individual stories, the degree of difference between the two variants (major differences are easier to identify than subtle ones), the number of points of similarity and difference that you expect students to find, and the amount of support you provide. Giving each student several stories and having students do the activity on their own makes it more difficult, and having several students work together to understand each story before doing the comparisons provides extra assistance and makes the task easier.

Doing this activity with unrelated stories

This same type of activity can be done with unrelated tales. For example, *King Midas* (commonly known; not in this book), *The Fisherman and His Wife* (see page 232), and *The Three Wishes* (Zemach, 1986) are, at least on the surface, dissimilar. One deals with a king whose touch turns everything to gold, one with a fisherman's wife who demands that her husband make requests from a magical fish for ever-increasing power, and one with a couple who are granted three wishes and end up wasting them when the husband idly wishes for a pan of sausages, and the wife then in anger wishes that they were attached to his nose. Yet while the tales are quite different, they address common themes: how getting what you wish for affects your life, contentment, and the relationship between money or power and happiness. Comparing outwardly dissimilar stories is usually more difficult than comparing stories with obvious parallels.

Stories to use with this activity

STORIES IN THIS BOOK

The Fisherman and His Wife (see page 232) vs. *The Stonecutter* (see page 5)

Gold in the Chimney (see page 269) vs. *Mother Holly* (see page 149)

The Riddle (see page 22) vs. the variant discussed in the note at the end of that story

Cinderella (available through many sources) vs. *Benizara and Kakezara* (see page 265) vs. *Strong Wind* (see page 108)

PUBLISHED STORIES

Most of the following stories have many other variants, and there are countless other tales for which interesting variants exist. Some books that can help locate variant versions are discussed in the *Bibliography* under *Books about folktales*.

Diamonds and Toads (Lang, Blue Fairy Book), *The Talking Eggs* (Sans Souci, 1989), *Mother Holly* (Lang, Red Fairy Book), *The Gold in the Chimley* (Clarkson and Gross, 1980), *Three Heads in a Well* (Opie, 1974), *The Three Dwarves* (Lang, Red Fairy Book), Busy Bride (Lang, Red Fairy Book).

Cinderella, The Indian Cinderella (Clarkson and Gross, 1980), *Benizara and Kakezara* (Seki, 1963), *Allerleireuh* (Lang, Green Fairy Book), *Cap O'Rushes* (Lurie, 1980). There are close to a thousand variants of the Cinderella story from different cultures.

Little Read Riding Hood, Lon Po Po (Young, 1989).

The Two Stonecutters, The Fisherman and His Wife (Grimm's; Lang, Green Fairy Book), *The Little Old Woman Who Lived in a Vinegar Bottle.*

Puss in Boots (Perrault), *Mighty Mikko* (Clarkson and Gross, 1980).

The Swineherd, Thrushbeard.

The Turtle and the Rabbit

Once the rabbit said that he was faster than any other animal. The rabbit was always asking other animals to race with him. One day, he asked the turtle to race. He was surprised when the turtle said, "Yes." They set a day for the race.

When the day of the race came, the rabbit and the turtle met. The other animals came to watch. The race began, and the rabbit was soon out of sight. The turtle, not discouraged by this, just slowly walked along.

Soon the rabbit could see the finish line. He wanted to wait for the rest of the animals to come so they could watch him win. So he sat under a tree to wait. With the warm sunshine, and the pleasant breeze, and the buzzing of the bees, the rabbit was soon asleep.

Several hours later the rabbit woke up. He heard cheering in the distance and saw the turtle close to the finish line. He jumped up and ran toward the finish line, still hoping to win, but the turtle crossed the finish line before the rabbit got there.

So people say, "Slow and steady wins the race."

The Whale and the Sea Slug

Long ago, the whale was very proud, and he was always bragging, "No animal is greater than I." The sea slug heard this and laughed. This made the whale very angry, so he challenged the sea slug to a race.

The sea slug agreed, saying, "Certainly, but not today. In three days we will meet at the beech at Yura, and then we will race."

After this the sea slug gathered up all of his friends. He told them, "I just agreed to race the whale. Now, of course, I cannot win, so here is what we must do: Each of us must go to a different beach around here. Since the whale can never tell us apart, each of you must pretend to be me. Then, when the whale arrives, you must call out, 'Are you just now getting here?' The whale will then think I have beaten him. If he wants to race to a different beach, the same thing will happen there." The other sea slugs all agreed, and so they went tumbling off through the sea to the different beaches.

After three days had passed, the whale and the sea slug met at the beach at Yura. "All right," said the slug, "let's race to the beach at Kohama." Then they both set off.

The whale swam swiftly and powerfully, but when he got to Kohama he was surprised to hear, "Whale, Whale, are you just now getting here? You did not swim very fast this time. But perhaps we should race again. Let us race to the beach at Shimoda." So they both set off again.

The whale swam even more swiftly than before, but again, when he arrived, he was surprised to hear, "Whale, Whale, are you just now getting here? You did not swim very fast this time. But perhaps we should race again. Let us race to the beach at Mori." So again they both set off.

And so it went. At each beach that they swam to, the slug was always there first, and so, in the end, the whale was forced to admit that he was defeated.

Analytical skills: Comparing two or more variants of a tale

A GRAPHIC ORGANIZER COMPARING/CONTRASTING *THE TURTLE AND THE RABBIT* AND *THE WHALE AND THE SEA SLUG*

	The Turtle and the Rabbit	The Whale and the Sea Slug
What was the story about?		
Where was the race?		
How were the animals different fom each other?		
Why did one animal ask the other to race?		
Describe the stronger animal's attitude.		
Who won?		
How did he win?		
What help did the winner have?		

Benizara and Kakezara

Long ago there were two sisters, Benizara and Kakezara. (Benizara means "Crimson Dish"; Kakezara means "Broken or Chipped Dish.") Benizara was the daughter of her father's first wife; Kakezara was the daughter of her father's second wife. Even though Benizara was always very honest and gentle, her stepmother was very cruel to her.

One day the stepmother sent the two girls out to gather chestnuts. She gave Benizara a bag with a hole in the bottom, but she gave Kakezara a good one. "Do not come back until you have filled your bag," she said to each of them.

The two set out for the mountains and began to pick up chestnuts. Before long Kakezara's bag was full, and she returned home, leaving Benizara alone. Benizara worked as hard as she could picking up chestnuts until it began to get dark. She heard a rustling sound, as though a wolf were coming toward her. She fled without looking where she was going, and she was soon completely lost in the darkness of the night. She was filled with despair but knew it would do no good to sit and cry, so she kept on walking, thinking that she might find a house. Suddenly she saw a light ahead. She went to where it was and found an old woman spinning. Benizara told what had happened to her, and asked if the woman could tell her how to get home.

The old woman carefully explained which roads to take. Then she filled Benizara's bag with chestnuts and gave her a little box. "Take the chestnuts to your mother. This little box is a magic box; if there is ever anything that you need, just say what it is and tap on the box three times and what you want will appear." Benizara thanked her for everything and started for home on the road she had been told to take.

Soon morning came. Her stepmother thought that during the night the wolves must surely have eaten Benizara. Just then, Benizara came home. The stepmother wanted to scold her, but since Benizara had a whole bag full of chestnuts, the stepmother could find nothing to scold her about.

It was not long after this that a play was to be given in the village theater. The stepmother took Kakezara to see it, but she gave Benizara a great deal of work that she insisted must be done

continued

before they returned home. Benizara was working as hard as she could when some of her friends came and asked her to go see the play with them.

"My stepmother has given me so much work to do," said Benizara, "that I cannot possibly finish in time to go."

But her friends answered, "We will help you, and then you can go." They all joined in at once, and so, all working together, they soon finished a whole day's work.

Her friends were all wearing beautiful kimonos, but Benizara had nothing but rags to wear. She was wondering what she should do when she remembered the little box that the old woman in the mountains had given her. She took the box out and said that she would like to have a kimono, and then she tapped the box three times. A beautiful kimono suddenly appeared. She quickly put it on, and then headed off to the theater with her friends.

While in the theater, Kakezara was begging her mother for some candy. Benizara saw this and threw her some. When she did this, a nobleman who had come to see the play saw what happened.

The next day the nobleman's colorful procession came to the village and stopped in front of Benizara's house. Kakezara's mother was overjoyed. She quickly dressed Kakezara in her very best to meet him. The lord got out of the palanquin and said, "There should be two girls here; bring the other one too."

The stepmother had hidden Benizara in the bathtub, but she had to obey the lord's command, so she brought her out. Dressed in rags once again, Benizara looked very shabby next to Kakezara. The lord said, "I would like to marry the girl that I saw at the play yesterday."

"It was this one – Kakezara," said the mother.

"No," answered the Lord, "It was the other one that I saw. It was not Kakezara."

"No," insisted the mother, "it wasn't that one. Kakezara was certainly the one you noticed." The mother kept insisting, so the lord said that he would like each of them to compose a song. He took a plate and put it on a tray. Then he piled some salt on the plate and stuck a pine needle in it. He commanded that they each compose a poem, with this plate as a subject.

In a loud voice Kakezara sang,

> *Put a plate on a tray,*
> *Put some salt on the plate,*
> *Stick a pine needle in the salt*
> *It will soon fall over.*

Then she hit the lord on the head and ran off in embarrassment.

Next Benizara sang,

> *A tray and plate, oh!*
> *A mountain rises from the plate,*
> *On it, snow has fallen.*
> *Rooted deeply into the snow*
> *A lonely pine tree grows.*

When the lord heard this song, he praised it highly. Wedding preparations were soon made, and Benizara rode off to the lord's palace in a beautiful palanquin.

Kakezara's mother watched in angry silence. Then she put Kakezara in a huge empty basket, saying, "Now, Kakezara, you too will go to the lord's palace." She dragged the basket along but did it so violently that the basket tumbled over the edge of a cliff, and Kakezara tumbled to her death.

Notes on the Story

This is a Japanese story, though apparently not one that is especially well known; most of my Japanese students have not been familiar with it.

Benizara means "Crimson Dish" (the color red is associated with happiness), and Kakezara means "Chipped Dish." In addition to being more elegant, Benizara's poem follows the rigid metric rules of the *waka* or *tanka* poetic form; Kakezara's poem, aside from being very mundane, doesn't follow any of the metric rules for traditional poetic styles.

Being more of a storyteller than a folklorist, I took the liberty of leaving out part of the original story. In the original, the old woman who gives the magical box also has two sons who are human-eating *oni*. She also gives Benizara some rice with instructions about how to put it in her mouth to look like maggots and pretend she is dead when they come along. This will cause them to think she is already dead and pass her by, thus letting her escape and make it home safely. For a more complete version of this story, see *Folktales of Japan*, edited by Keigo Seki and translated by Robert Adams (1963).

Analytical skills: Comparing two or more variants of a tale

A GRAPHIC ORGANIZER COMPARING/CONTRASTING *MOTHER HOLLY*
(SEE PAGE 149) AND *THE TALKING EGGS* (SAN SOUCI, 1989)

	Similarities	Differences
Mother Holly	Two sisters: one lazy and ill-tempered (but favored by mother), one diligent and kind Woman appeared strange (large teeth) Lazy girl and evil mother meet tragic end (girl covered with pitch and dies)	Took place in another world, reached by falling through a well Commitment to work diligently Girls' reward or punishment given by Mother Holly
The Talking Eggs	Two sisters: one lazy and ill-tempered (but favored by mother), one diligent and kind Woman appeared strange (removable head) Lazy girl and evil mother meet tragic end (girl chased by snakes and toads, and dies)	Took place in wood near home Commitment to not laugh Girls' reward or punishment based on their own choice of the talking eggs

This same compare/contrast could be represented in various other ways. Here is a Venn diagram:

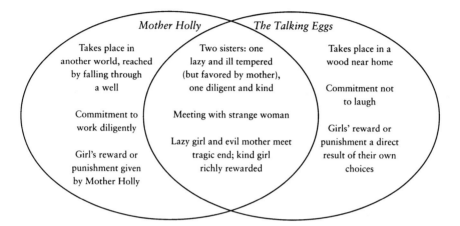

Mother Holly   *The Talking Eggs*

Takes place in another world, reached by falling through a well

Commitment to work diligently

Girl's reward or punishment given by Mother Holly

Two sisters: one lazy and ill tempered (but favored by mother), one diligent and kind

Meeting with strange woman

Lazy girl and evil mother meet tragic end; kind girl richly rewarded

Takes place in a wood near home

Commitment not to laugh

Girls' reward or punishment a direct result of their own choices

---

Low-intermediate

Gold in the Chimney

Once there were two sisters. One day, one sister went out. She came to a house that belonged to a witch. She asked, "Can I stay here?"

"Well," the witch said, "all right, you can stay. But I need to go out for a while. Whatever you do while I'm gone, you mustn't look up the chimney." As soon as the witch was out of sight, the girl looked up the chimney. There hung a bag of gold. So the girl grabbed the gold and set out from the house at once. As she went along, she came to a cow.

The cow said to her, "Please milk me, little girl. I haven't been milked for seven long years."

The girl answered, "I haven't got time." And she continued on her way.

Before long she came upon a sheep. The sheep said to her, "Please shear me, little girl. I haven't been sheared for seven long years."

continued

But the girl answered, "I haven't got time." And she continued on her way.

Before long she came upon a horse. The horse said, "Please ride me, little girl, I haven't been ridden for seven long years."

But the girl answered, "I haven't got time." And she continued on her way.

Before long she came upon a mill. The mill said, "Please turn me, little girl. I haven't been turned in seven long years."

The girl answered, "I haven't got time." Then she went and lay down behind the door and went to sleep.

Well, the old witch came back and saw that the girl was gone. She looked up her chimney and saw that her gold was gone too. So she set out after the girl at once. When she came to the cow she said,

> *Cow of mine, cow of mine,*
> *Have you ever seen that maid of mine,*
> *With a wig and a wag and a long leather bag,*
> *Who stole all the money I ever had?*

And the cow answered, "Indeed I have. She just passed."

The old witch went on, and when she came to the sheep she said,

> *Sheep of mine, sheep of mine,*
> *Have you ever seen that maid of mine,*
> *With a wig and a wag and a long leather bag,*
> *Who stole all the money I ever had?*

And the sheep answered, "Indeed I have. She just passed."

So the old witch went on until she came to the horse, and she said,

> *Horse of mine, horse of mine,*
> *Have you ever seen that maid of mine,*
> *With a wig and a wag and a long leather bag,*
> *Who stole all the money I ever had?*

And the horse answered, "Indeed I have. She just passed."

So the old witch went on until she came to the mill, and she said,

> *Mill of mine, mill of mine,*
> *Have you ever seen that maid of mine,*
> *With a wig and a wag and a long leather bag,*
> *Who stole all the money I ever had?*

And the mill answered, "Indeed I have. She is lying over there behind the door."

So the witch went over behind the door and turned the girl into a stone. Then she took her gold and went back home.

Well, before long the other sister came to the witch's house and said, "Can I stay here?"

The witch answered, "Yes, you can, but I need to go out for a while. Whatever you do while I'm gone, you mustn't look up the chimney."

As soon as the witch was out of sight, the girl looked up the chimney. There hung the bag of gold. So the girl grabbed the gold and set out from the house at once. As she went along, she came to a cow.

The cow said to her, "Please milk me, little girl. I haven't been milked for seven long years."

So the girl milked the cow, and then continued on her way.

Before long she came upon a sheep. The sheep said to her, "Please shear me, little girl, I haven't been sheared for seven long years."

So the girl sheared the sheep, and then continued on her way.

Before long she came upon a horse. The horse said, "Please ride me, little girl, I haven't been ridden for seven long years."

So the girl rode the horse, and then continued on her way.

Before long she came upon a mill. The mill said, "Please turn me, little girl. I haven't been turned in seven long years."

So the girl turned the mill, and then continued on her way.

Well, the old witch came back and saw that the girl was gone. She looked up her chimney and saw that her gold was gone too. So she set out after the girl at once. When she came to the cow she said,

> Cow of mine, cow of mine,
> Have you ever seen that maid of mine,
> With a wig and a wag and a long leather bag,
> Who stole all the money I ever had?

But the cow answered, "No, I have seen neither hide nor hair of her."

So the old witch went on until she came to the sheep, and she said,

> Sheep of mine, sheep of mine,
> Have you ever seen that maid of mine,
> With a wig and a wag and a long leather bag,
> Who stole all the money I ever had?

But the sheep answered, "No, I have seen neither hide nor hair of her."

So the old witch went on until she came to the horse, and she said,

continued

> *Horse of mine, horse of mine,*
> *Have you ever seen that maid of mine,*
> *With a wig and a wag and a long leather bag,*
> *Who stole all the money I ever had?*

But the horse answered, "No, I have seen neither hide nor hair of her."

So the old witch went on until she came to the mill, and she said,

> *Mill of mine, mill of mine,*
> *Have you ever seen that maid of mine,*
> *With a wig and a wag and a long leather bag,*
> *Who stole all the money I ever had?*

The mill answered, "I can't hear you well. Get up in my hopper so I can hear what you are saying."

So the witch got up into the hopper and said,

> *Mill of mine, mill of mine,*
> *Have you ever seen that maid of mine,*
> *With a wig and a wag and a long leather bag,*
> *Who stole all the money I ever had?*

The mill answered not a word, but began grinding at once and ground the old witch up. Then the girl came back, turned the stone back into her sister, and they lived happily ever after.

Notes on the Story

World Folktales, by Atelia Clarkson and Gilbert B. Cross (1980) contains an old African-American version entitled *Gold in the Chimley.*

Support and evaluation activity

Class level: Low-intermediate to advanced
Group size(s): Small groups of 3 or 4, pairs, individuals, whole class
Objective(s): To practice all language skills while having students identify similarities and differences in two or more stories, support their statements, and evaluate the importance of different points. This activity is also designed to provide an opportunity to review previous material.
Approximate class time: 20 to 30 minutes

The activity

Many college students (including native speakers) provide inadequate support for assertions they make. This activity provides practice in supporting conclusions. It also provides practice in evaluating the importance of different points and in noticing that different issues may be more or less important in different contexts.

Do this activity after students have read or listened to a number of different stories.

PREPARATION

If students need some support to do the activity, prepare a partially filled-in chart to get them started. Otherwise, no preparation is needed other than selecting the stories you want to use.

IN THE CLASSROOM

1. **List on the board the stories that students have read or listened to that you want them to work with for this activity.** If you prefer, you can also give students new stories to work with. (If you use new stories, you can do this activity like the *Comparing two or more variants of a tale* (see page 265), where each student in the group gets a different story to read and must tell his or her story to the group as part of the activity.)
2. **Have students identify the most important quality (or qualities) in each story.** These qualities can be either positive or negative. This and the following steps can be done individually, in pairs or small groups, or with the class as a whole.
3. **Have students identify something from the story that supports this.** Depending on the stories and the level of the students, you might ask for several pieces of support.

4. **In small groups, have students compare and discuss their answers.** Have them try to reach a consensus. You will usually get more interaction in this step by having students do the previous two steps individually so that everyone comes to the group with something to share.

5. **First individually, and then in small groups, have students evaluate the importance of the different ideas.** Students can be asked to evaluate the importance of the ideas for a single context, or they can be asked to evaluate them for several different contexts. For example, "How important are these qualities for you? For a potential spouse? For a politician? For an actress?" Students can also be asked to evaluate and represent the importance of the ideas in a number of ways. Three possibilities are illustrated on page 276.

6. **Have students write a phrase or sentence for each of the items explaining why they evaluated them as they did.** This provides an opportunity for students to support conclusions that are less objective than those that are supported directly by the text. For example: "I don't think beauty is that important for a spouse, since people get uglier as they get older anyway, and beauty doesn't really affect how nice the person is." "Sensitive skin would be bad for international tour guides, because they would be more like to get rashes and skin irritations in hot climates."

7. **Discuss conclusions and evaluations as a class (including why people thought certain elements were important or not important).**

Story	Key quality	Support
Benizara and Kakezara (Japanese Cinderella)	Ability to compose a traditional poem quickly	This was the test the prince used to decide whom to marry.
Cinderella (French)	Beauty, small feet	
Strong Wind (Native American Cinderella)	Honesty	The youngest sister's honesty is what made Strong Wind choose her for a wife even though she was initially disfigured.
The Princess and the Pea	Sensitive skin	Feeling a pea through many mattresses was the proof the parents wanted that the girl was a real princess.
The King's Fountain	Courage	The man needed courage to go and tell the king he was wrong, since the king might kill him.
The Turtle and the Rabbit	Perseverance	
The Whale and the Sea Slug	Craftiness	

Three ways to evaluate and prioritize

Ranking: Ranking items places them in their relative priority; it does not say how important or unimportant any item is independently – they might all be important or they might all be unimportant.

For me	*For my spouse*	*For a politician*
1. honesty 2. courage 3. perseverance 4. ability to write poetry 5. craftiness 6. beauty 7. sensitive skin 8. small feet	1. honesty 2. beauty 3. courage 4. perseverance 5. sensitive skin 6. ability to write poetry 7. craftiness 8. small feet	1. craftiness 2. beauty 3. courage 4. perseverance 5. ability to write poetry 6. honesty 7. sensitive skin 8. small feet

Continuum Line: Placing items on a continuum line shows how important different items are – independent of their relationship to each other.

Importance of different character qualities for a happy life

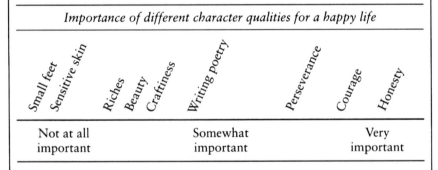

Not at all important	Somewhat important	Very important

Grouping: Placing items in a chart provides an opportunity to organize and group without making precise evaluations.

Qualities for an international tour guide			
Might be negative	*Doesn't matter*	*Somewhat important*	*Very important*
sensitive skin	writing poetry beauty small feet	honesty courage craftiness	perseverance

Bibliography

Illustrated picture books and folktales that are good for beginning students

Alexander, Lloyd. *The King's Fountain*. New York: Dutton, 1971.

Alexander, Lloyd. *The Fortune Teller*. New York: Dutton, 1992.

Allen, Pamela. *Hidden Treasure*. New York: Putnam, 1987.

Asbjørnsen, P. C., and J. E. Moe. *The Man Who Kept House*. New York: Macmillan, 1991.

Brown, Marcia. *Stone Soup*. New York: Scribners, 1947.

Demi. *The Empty Pot*. New York: Henry Holt, 1990.

Littledale, Freya. *Peter and the North Wind*. Chicago: Scholastic, 1988.

San Souci, Robert D. *The Talking Eggs*. New York: Dial Books for Young Readers, 1989.

Shulevitz, Uri. *The Treasure*. New York: Farrar, Straus & Giroux, 1978.

Titus, Eve. *The Two Stonecutters*. New York: Doubleday, 1967.

Vernon, Adele. *The Riddle*. New York: Dodd, 1987.

Walker, Barbara, and Ahmet E. Uysal. *New Patches for Old*. New York: Parents' Magazine Press, 1974.

Yeoman, John. *The Wild Washerwomen*. New York: Greenwillow, 1979; New York: Crown, 1986.

Young, Ed. *Lon Po Po*. New York: Philomel, 1989.

Zemach, Margot. *It Could Always Be Worse*. New York: Farrar, Straus & Giroux, 1976.

Zemach, Margot. *The Three Wishes*. New York: Farrar, Straus & Giroux, 1986.

Collections of stories

There are countless collections of folktales. Here are a few for those who need a place to begin. The collections by Lang, Grimm, and Cole are especially valuable because of the number and variety of tales.

Ashabranner, Brent, and Russel Davis. *The Lion's Whiskers and Other Ethiopian Tales*. New Haven, CT: Linnet, 1977.

Ausubel, Nathan. *A Treasury of Jewish Folklore*. New York: Crown, 1948. Contains hundreds of stories; 740 pages.

Bible. Not a collection of folktales, but it contains a number of useful stories. The gospels (Matthew–John) contain many parables and other striking stories; the Old Testament contains a variety of important stories. For a highly readable, modern English version, I recommend *Good News for Modern Man* (1971, New York: American Bible Society). For high-intermediate/advanced students, *The New International Version* (Zondervan, 1973) is also good.

Clarkson, Atelia, and Gilbert B. Cross. *World Folktales: A Scribner Resource Collection.* New York: Charles Scribner's, 1980. This book includes tales in a number of different categories and from various national backgrounds. It provides some scholarly notes on the tales, including some information on variant versions of the same tale or type of tale.

Cole, Joanna. *Best-Loved Folktales of the World.* New York: Doubleday, 1982. This collection includes over 600 tales. They are grouped by geographic origin, so it is easy to find tales from a particular background.

Courlander, Harold. *The King's Drum and Other African Stories.* New York: Harcourt, Brace & World, 1962. Thirty stories from various tribes and parts of Africa.

Grimms' Folktales (various translations and publishers). As with Lang's collections (see below), many translations of the Grimms' stories are now part of the public domain. Before copying, however, check the translation date: Even though the original tales are not copyrighted, more recent translations will be. A collection of over 200 Grimms' tales is available on the Internet (see below).

Lang, Andrew. *The Color Fairy Books* (various publishers, including Mackay, Dover, Viking, and Random House). Lang collected twelve volumes of folk and fairy tales. Each volume is named with a different color (*The Red Fairy Book, The Green Fairy Book,* etc.) This collection includes tales from Grimm and Perrault as well as tales from a variety of other sources. The *Red, Green,* and *Blue* books appear to contain the most commonly known Western tales. One advantage of these books, aside from their sheer volume of material, is that they are in the public domain: You can freely copy materials from them without violating copyright laws. In some cases the language is a little old-fashioned, but it is not hard to edit the tales to make them more contemporary. Several volumes of these books are available on the Internet (see below).

Lurie, Allison, *Clever Gretchen and Other Forgotten Folktales.* New York: Crowell, 1980.

Opie, Peter, and Iona Opie. *The Classic Fairy Tales.* London: Oxford University Press, 1974. Twenty-four tales emphasizing versions as they were first printed in English. Contains some interesting notes on the stories.

Seki, Keigo, ed., translated by Robert Adams. *Folktales of Japan.* Chicago: University of Chicago, 1963. Contains a large number of stories.

Folktale resources intended specifically for ESL students

With a growing interest in folktales, other new resources are becoming available; contact your publishers' representatives for additional suggestions.

Cameron, Penny. *Larger than Life: Folk Heroes of the United States*. Englewood Cliffs, NJ: Prentice Hall Regents, 1994. This book contains nine stories about American folk heroes (e.g., John Henry, Johnny Appleseed, Paul Bunyan, Calamity Jane) along with historical background, prereading and postreading activities, and related folk songs. Intermediate level.

Graham, Carolyn. *Jazz Chant Fairy Tales*. New York: Oxford, 1988.

Kasser, Carrol, and Ann Silverman. *Stories We Brought with Us*. Englewood Cliffs, NJ: Prentice Hall Regents, 1994. This book contains 21 stories, each told at two different levels, from different parts of the world. Each story is accompanied by prereading questions, activities to work on various aspects of grammar and language structure, comprehension questions, and discussion/writing ideas. High-beginning level.

Oxford Classic Tales. A number of individual folktales retold with limited vocabulary (200–400 words) for beginning to low-intermediate students. Especially appropriate for children, these illustrated tales include activities, puzzles, and an illustrated glossary.

Oxford Progressive Readers include several titles that include folktales. These books are graded in five levels ranging from 1,400- to 5,000-word vocabularies.

Books about storytelling

MacDonald, Margaret Read. *The Story Teller's Start-up Book*. Little Rock, AK: August House, 1993. This book includes a variety of useful suggestions for those who want help with the oral telling of tales.

Books about folktales

The following books can be used to find alternative versions of a particular tale, to find tales by nationality, and to find tales with particular themes or motifs. For example, if you have a class of Japanese students, you might start with Japanese tales so your material will be more familiar and hence easier to understand. Or you might want to focus on a particular type of tale – tales involving tricksters, or feasts, or wolves, or weddings – to give continuity, to reinforce particular themes, or to connect to other material that you want to use. These books include information that is more technical than the language teacher needs, but they still have useful information that can be gleaned without too much effort. The book by MacDonald is the easiest to use.

Bibliography

Aarne, Antti, and Stith Thompson. *The Types of the Folktale: A Classification of Biography*, 2d rev. ed. Helsinki: Folk Lore Fellows Communications, 1961. This is a fairly technical book but is fairly common in university libraries. It is useful for locating tales on particular themes and for locating variant versions of tales.

MacDonald, Margaret Read. *The Storyteller's Sourcebook: A Subject, Title, and Motif Index to Folklore Collections for Children.* Detroit, MI: Neal-Schuman, 1982. This book indexes a large number of tales by their titles, subjects, and motifs. It also includes an ethnic and geographic index, which is useful if you are looking for a collection of tales from a particular nation. The bibliography at the back of the book provides the information needed to locate any of the tales included in the index.

Thompson, Stith. *The Motif-Index of Folk-Literature*, rev. ed., 6 vols. Bloomington, IN: Indiana University Press, 1955–1958.) This is a fairly technical book but is common in university libraries. It is useful for locating tales on particular themes and for locating variant versions of tales.

Sources for folktales on the Internet

The Internet has a variety of sources for actual texts of folktales (and for a lot of other literature).

SEARCHING FOR INTERNET SITES

With the increasingly sophisticated tools for searching the Internet, you may want to try searching yourself to find stories. I have found that searching for "folktale" gets the most results, but searching for "fairy tale," "folk tale," and "folklore" will also yield some sites.

Searching for "folktale" can produce many thousands of listings, depending on how and where you search. Many of these are advertisements for books, some are just passing references, and others are bibliographies and other items that are not very useful for the language teacher. It takes some hunting to find the sites that actually have a collection of stories you can download (copy) to your computer, but they are out there if you keep looking.

You can limit your searches – for example, you might search for "folktale and Africa" or "folktale and trickster," but this does not necessarily eliminate listings you don't want. (Each search utility lets you limit your searches in slightly different ways; see the help for the search utility for details.)

SOME SPECIFIC INTERNET SITES

Internet sites and addresses change fairly often, so some of these addresses may change by the time this book is in your hands, but because it does take some hunting to find good sites, it seemed worth listing some of the best sites for stories:

Folktale, myth, and legend. This site contains links to Grimms' tales, several of the color fairy books by Andrew Lang, Aesop's fables, tales by Hans Christian Anderson, and a variety of others. It also includes links to the Cinderella and Red Riding Hood projects that compare a number of variants of these tales.
⟨http://www.acs.ucalgary.ca/~dkbrown/storfolk.html⟩

Folklore and mythology texts. This site contains links to a variety of tales. This site is sorted mostly by category and contains mostly different references from the previous site.
⟨http://www.pitt.edu/~dash/folktexts.html⟩

Other pages with links to a lot of stories. These sites contained many links to sites with good collections of stories.
⟨http://easyweb.easynet.co.uk/~cdaae/fairy/link.htm⟩
⟨http://www.nhptv.org/kn/vs/engla7.sht

Storytellers' sources. This site contains many useful links to stories and to other storytelling resources.
⟨http://users.aol.com/storypage/sources.htm⟩

Tales of wonder. Here you can find a number of good tales from around the world. Included are tales from Russia, Siberia, China, Japan, the Middle East, Scandinavia, Scotland, England, and Native Americans.
⟨http://itpubs.ucdavis.edu/richard/tales/⟩

Grimms' tales. This site contains 209 tales.
⟨http://www.ul.cs.cmu.edu/books/GrimmFairy/

Aesop's fables.
⟨gopher://spinaltap.micro.umn.edu/11/Ebooks/By Title/aesop⟩

Nesreddin Hodja stories (Turkish).
⟨http://w1.871.telia.com/~u87104365⟩

Native American stories
⟨http://www.indians.org/welker/stories.htm⟩

Many other sites contain tales of a particular nationality or smaller numbers of tales, but the sites above provide links to many of them so I won't list them here.

On-line discussion groups

At least two on-line (Internet/e-mail) discussion conferences may be able to provide some help – a folklore conference and a storytelling conference. If you subscribe, all of the messages sent to the group will be forwarded to you. Although many will be irrelevant to language teaching, you may find answers to specific questions.

FOLKLORE CONFERENCE

In this conference you might ask questions about variant versions of particular stories, or for sources for stories on a particular theme. To subscribe to this conference, send an e-mail message to:

⟨listserv@tamvm1.tamu.edu⟩

Your message should read:

⟨subscribe folklore [first name] [last name]⟩

The square brackets mean that your first and last names are optional. This message is read by a computer program, so it should be typed exactly as presented above. Do not send any questions to the e-mail address above; it is only for subscribing to the conference. Once you have subscribed, you will start to receive messages from the list and information on how to post messages on the list yourself.

STORYTELLING CONFERENCE

In this conference you might ask questions related to the oral presentation of stories. I posted a message saying that I was a beginning oral teller and wanted some advice and got a variety of responses.

Since the people who read and respond to messages in this conference are storytellers, they will probably also be willing to share stories on particular themes if you need a particular type of story and can't find what you needed. To subscribe to this conference, send an e-mail to:

⟨storytell-request@venus.twu.edu⟩

Your message should read:

⟨subscribe [first name] [last name]⟩

The square brackets mean that your first and last names are optional. This message is read by a computer program, so it should be typed exactly as presented above. Do not send any questions to the e-mail address above; it is only for subscription to the conference. Once you have subscribed, you will start to receive messages from the list and information on how to post messages on the list yourself.

Some longer children's books to consider

The books I have listed here are ones that have been consistently enjoyed by both children and adults. They also include many elements from the folk/fairy tale tradition.

C. S. Lewis. *The Chronicles of Narnia.* (New York: HarperCollins; New York: Macmillan). There are seven books in this series: *The Lion, the Witch and the Wardrobe; Prince Caspian; The Voyage of the Dawn Treader; The Silver Chair; The Horse and His Boy; The Magician's Nephew;* and *The Last Battle.* Many native speakers start reading these books in fourth or fifth grade. Lewis has a unique ability to use moderately difficult words in a way that their basic meaning can be inferred from context. The struggle between good and evil runs through the stories, just the way it does in folktales and fairy tales. Though these are children's stories, most adults seem to enjoy them as much or more than children.

There are also video versions of these stories. PBS aired a version with live actors, and there are also animated versions. These videos could be used to introduce the basic story to the students, providing visual, nonliterary clues to the meaning of the text, and they could also be used for listening practice in their own right.

Lloyd Alexander. *The Prydain Chronicles.* (New York: Holt). There are five books in this series: *The Book of Three, The Black Cauldron, The Castle of Llyr, Taran Wanderer,* and *The High King.* Aside from the place and character names being difficult (many of the names are drawn from Welsh mythology), the language is relatively easy. These tales, which embody the age-old struggle between good and evil, address many of the same types of themes that folktales touch on: a desire for greatness and what real greatness entails, romance, death and war, dealing with the discovery of evil in oneself, and so on.

These books are useful for introducing simile, metaphor, and analogy. The character Eilonwy in particular is continually uttering short analogies: "That's like putting caterpillars in someone's hair," or "It's like inviting someone to a feast and then making them do the dishes." The images are striking and easy to understand, yet they introduce the type of symbolic use of language that occurs in literature.

Disney has made an animated film version of *The Black Cauldron.*

Natalie Babbit. *The Search for Delicious.* (New York: Farrar, Strauss, and Giroux). This is a humorous tale about a kingdom where the prime minister sets out to write a dictionary using definitions like "affectionate is your dog" and "bulky is a big bag of boxes." The problem is that no one can agree on the definition for "delicious." Quarreling breaks out among the entire court, and war is only narrowly averted.

Aside from being a fun story, there are some potentially fun language-type activities, such as making a dictionary using such metaphorical definitions. Students could negotiate about the definitions in small groups, and then each group could produce one small dictionary – or the class could generate a combined one.

J. R. R. Tolkien. *The Hobbit* and *The Lord of the Rings.* (New York: Houghton-Mifflin; New York: Ballantine). These books might also be a place to continue with students who particularly like the mythic genre. These books are very long, and there are features that might be too much for someone learning English: strange names, strange places, and unusual people. Native speakers are able to learn about these places without difficulty as they go along, but they are not trying to figure out language at the same time. Still, the text itself (aside from being, in my mind at last, very interesting) is quite readable: Constructions tend to be coordinate, and vocabulary and ideas (especially in *The Hobbit*) are very concrete. Consider the opening lines from *The Hobbit*:

In a hole in the ground there lived a hobbit. Not a nasty, dirty, wet hole, filled with the ends of worms and an oozy smell, nor yet a dry, bare, sandy hole with nothing in it to sit down on or to eat: it was a hobbit-hole, and that means comfort.

It had a perfectly round door like a porthole, painted green, with a shiny yellow brass knob in the exact middle. . . .

I am impressed with the vividness and the concreteness of the language. It is potentially difficult, but I would be tempted to try it with students who like the genre and who have made it successfully through the more advanced types of folktales.

The BBC has produced a dramatized audio version of the *Lord of the Rings,* which is available on tape; this might be used either independently or in conjunction with the books.

Animated film versions of these stories have also been made. Although I disliked the animated versions (both because of deviations from the text and because they portray many points differently than my imagination did), many people enjoyed them. They might serve as a useful introduction to the stories, or, again, as a valid listening activity in their own right.

Research, studies, and other sources

Appelt, Jane E. "Not Just for Little Kids: The Picture Book in ESL Classes." *TESL Canada Journal* 2, (Mar 1985): 67–78.

Asher, James J. "The Total Physical Response Approach." In R. W. Blair (ed.), *Innovative Approaches to Language Teaching,* 54–66. New York: Newbury House, 1982.

Beard El-Dinary, P., Michael Pressley, and T. Schuder. "Teachers Learning Transactional Strategies Instruction. In C. Kinzer, and D. Ley (eds.), *Literacy Research, Theory, and Practice: Views from Many Perspectives. Forty-first Yearbook of the National Reading Conference,* 453–462. Chicago: National Reading Conference, 1992.

Bell, Anita Molly, and Som Dy. "Tales from the Homeland: Developing the Language Experience Approach." Tacoma, WA: Tacoma Community House, 1984.

Carrell, Patricia L. "Facilitation ESL Reading by Teaching Text Structure." *TESOL Quarterly* 19 (1985).

Cromwell-Hoffman, Carole, and Linda Sasser. "A Literature-Based Cooperative Lesson for ESL." Paper presented at the Annual Meeting of the California Association for Bilingual Education, Anaheim, CA, Feb. 17, 1989.

DeBarros, Judy, et al. "Family Story Curriculum Project. Refugee Women's Alliance." Seattle, WA: Refugee Women's Alliance, 1991.

Dickinson, Leslie. *Self-Instruction in Language Learning.* New York: Cambridge, 1987.

Dowhower, Sarah Lynn. "Effects of Repeated Reading on Second-Grade Transitional Readers' Fluency and Comprehension." *Reading Research Quarterly* 22 (1987): 389 ff.

Duffy, Gerald G. "Teachers' Progress toward Becoming Expert Strategies Teachers." *Elementary School Journal* 94 (1992): 109–120.

Dungey, Joan M. "Fairy Tales and Fantasy: Bridges to Literature – Using Fairy Tales and Fantasy to Motivate the Reluctant Reader." Paper presented at the Annual Meeting of the National Coucil of Teachers of English Spring Conference (6th), Louisville, KY, Mar. 26–28. 1987.

Elley, Warwick B. "Vocabulary Acquisition from Listening to Stories." *Reading Research Quarterly* (1989): 174 ff.

Elley, Warwick B. "Acquiring Literacy in a Second Language: The Effect of Book-Based Programs." *Language Learning* 41 (1991): 375–411.

Ellis, Rod, Yoshihiro Tanake, and Asako Yamazaki. "Classroom Interaction, Comprehension, and the Acquisition of L2 Word Meanings." *Language Learning* 44 (1994): 449–491.

Feitelson, Dina, Zahava Goldstein, Jihad Iraqi, and David L. Share. "Effects of Listening to Story Reading on Aspects of Literacy Acquisition in a Diglossic Situation." *Reading Research Quarterly* 28 (1993): 71 ff.

Gaskins, Irene W. "Classroom Applications of Cognitive Science: Teaching Poor Readers How to Learn, Think, and Problem Solve." In K. McGilly (ed.), *Classroom Lessons: Integrating Cognitive Theory and Classroom Practice,* 129–53. Cambridge, MA: MIT Press, 1994.

Gass, Susan, and Evangeline Varonis. "Input, Interaction and Second Language Production." *Studies in Second Language Acquisition* 16 (1994): 283–302.

Hague, S. A., and R. Scott. "Awareness of Text Structure: Is There a Match between Readers and Authors of Second Language Texts?" *Foreign Language Annals* 27 (1994): 343–360.

Jones, Beau Fly, Jean Pierce, and Barbara Hunter. "Teaching Students to Construct Graphic Representations." *Educational Leadership* (Dec. 88–Jan. 89): 20–25.

Lightbown, Patsy M. "Can They Do It Themselves? A Comprehension-Based ESL Course for Young Children." In R. Courchêne, J. I. Glidden, J. St. John, and C. Therien (eds.), *Comprehension-Based Second Language Teaching/L'Enseignement des langues secondes axé sur la compréhension,* 353–370. Ottawa: University of Ottawa Press, 1992.

Long, Michael H. "Input, Interaction, and Second Language Acquisition." In Harris Winitz (ed.), *Native Language and Foreign Language Acquisition. Annals of the New York Academy of Sciences* 379 (1981):250–278.

Long, Michael H. "Native Speaker/Non-Native Speaker Conversation in the Second Language Classroom. In Mark A. Clarke and Jean Handscombe (eds.), *On TESOL '82,* 207–225. Washington, DC: TESOL, 1983.

Long, Michael H., and Patricia A. Porter. "Group Work, Interlanguage Talk, and Second Language Acquisition." *TESOL Quarterly* 19 (1985): 207–228.

Martinez, Miriam, and Nancy Rosen. "Read It Again. The Value of Repeated Readings during Storytime." *Reading Teacher* 38 (1985): 782–786.

Mendonça, Cassia O., and Karen E. Johnson. "Peer Review Negotiations: Revision Activities in ESL Writing Instruction." *TESOL Quarterly* 28 (1994): 745–769.

Nelson, Gayle L., and John M. Murphy. "Peer Response Groups: Do L2 Writers Use Peer Comments in Revising Their Drafts?" *TESOL Quarterly,* 27 (1993): 135–141.

Nessel, Denise D. "Storytelling in the Reading Program." *The Reading Teacher* (Jan. 1985): 378–381.

Nist, S. L., and D. L. Mealey. "Teacher-Directed Comprehension Strategies." In R. F. Flippo and D. C. Caverly (eds.), *Teaching Reading and Study Strategies at the College Level,* 42–85. Newark, DE: International Reading Association, 1991.

Nuttall, Christine. *Teaching Reading Skills in a Foreign Language.* London: Heinemann, 1982.

O'Brien, Kathy. "Tricksters in Folktales." In Katharine Busch and Margaret Atwell (eds.), *Proceedings of the Annual California State University, San Bernardino, Reading Conference,* May 17, 1989.

Oscarsson, Kristen L. "Haitian Folktales as a Literary Strategy for Elementary Haitian ESOL Students." M.S. Practicum, Davie, Florida: Nova University, 1992.

Pica, Theresa, and Catherine Doughty. "Information-Gap Tasks: Do They Facilitate Second Language Acquisition? *TESOL Quarterly* 20 (1986): 305–325.

Pica, Theresa, Richard Young, and Catherine Doughty. "The Impact of Interaction on Comprehension." *TESOL Quarterly* 21 (1987): 737–758.

Pressley, Michael et al. "Transactional Instruction of Comprehension Strategies: The Montgomery County, Maryland, Sail Program. *Reading and Writing Quarterly* 10 (1994): 5–19.

Sheering, Susan. *Self-Access.* Oxford University Press (1989).

Stahl-Gemake, Josephine, and Guastello, Francine. "Using Story Grammar with Students of English as a Foreign Language to Compose Original Fairy and Folktales." *Reading Teacher 38* (November 1984): 213–216.

Tang, Gloria. "The Effect of Graphic Representations of Knowledge Structures on ESL Reading Comprehension." *SSLA 14* (1992): 177–195.

Valeri-Gold, Maria. "Uninterrupted Sustained Silent Reading Is an Effective Authentic Method for College Developmental Learners." *Journal of Reading 38* (1995): 385–386.

Index of stories by culture

This index contains stories that are clearly connected to a nationality or culture. Many stories (for example, those from Aesop) are so widely known that they are not associated with a specific culture; for those, see the *List of Folktales* on page viii or the *General Index*.

Index of story themes

Index of story themes

General index

Aarne, Antti, 279
abstract vocabulary, using folktales to make concrete, 14
abstractness of concepts, 14
academic goals, developing analytical skills, 250
acting, by audience during story presentation, 25
active listening, using questions to encourage, 99
activities, photocopying, 19
adjectives, 136
adolescent fantasy literature, making transitions to other types of literature with, 30–31
adult themes, addressed by folktales, 15
Aesop, 155
  Androcles and the Lion, 130
  Belling the Cat, 128
  Dog and the Meat, The, 57
  Donkey's Brains, The, 130
  Fox and the Crow, The, 128
  Fox and the Stork, The, 128, 158
  Frog and the Ox, The, 128
  Internet sources for tales by, 280
  Lion, the Fox, and the Beasts, The, 130
  Lion and the Mouse, The, 130
  Man and His Two Wives, The, 40
  Mercury and the Woodman, 40
  Turtle and the Rabbit, The, 262
Alexander, Lloyd, 283
ambiguous strip story, 110–114
Amin and the Eggs, 147–148
analogy, introducing students to, 283
analysis of story structure in multi-level classroom, 35

analytical skills, 250–276
Anansi (Spider), 77
Androcles and the Lion, 130
animal stories, *see* fables
animal vocabulary, 90
antonyms, working on with matching cards, 183
apprehension of students about folktales, addressing, 29–30
Asbjørnsen, P. C., 246, 277
assistance for students, examples of different degrees of, 258–259
atmosphere improved by group work, 101
attitudes, improving, through stories from students' culture, 22
audience involvement while telling stories, 25
Ax Soup (variant of *Stone Soup*), 85

Babbit, Natalie, 283
background knowledge, 16, 31
Belling the Cat, 128
Benizara and Kakezara, 265
Best-Loved Folktales of the World, 278
Biblical stories, 30
  Good Samaritan, The, 220
  King and the Baby, The, 113
  Prodigal Son, The, 62
  Unmerciful Man, The, 216
Black Cauldron, The, 283
book of student stories, creating, 178–180
Book of Three, The, 283
Boy Who Cried Wolf, The, 139
  drama based on, 208
  example of teaching grammar, 135

Lightning Source UK Ltd.
Milton Keynes UK
25 March 2010

151873UK00001B/136/A